Prejudice

T0347082

Prejudice

A Study in Non-Ideal Epistemology

ENDRE BEGBY

OXFORD
UNIVERSITY PRESS

OXFORD
UNIVERSITY PRESS

Great Clarendon Street, Oxford, OX2 6DP,
United Kingdom

Oxford University Press is a department of the University of Oxford.
It furthers the University's objective of excellence in research, scholarship,
and education by publishing worldwide. Oxford is a registered trade mark of
Oxford University Press in the UK and in certain other countries

© Endre Begby 2021

The moral rights of the author have been asserted

First published 2021
First published in paperback 2022

Published in the United States of America by Oxford University Press
198 Madison Avenue, New York, NY 10016, United States of America

British Library Cataloguing in Publication Data
Data available

Library of Congress Cataloging in Publication Data
Data available

ISBN 978–0–19–885283–4 (Hbk.)
ISBN 978–0–19–288525–8 (Pbk.)

Contents

Acknowledgments

I didn't set out to become an epistemologist, but stumbled into it as a result of teaching, eventually discovering that recent developments in social epistemology, in particular, could provide an excellent platform for bringing together my interests in language, communication, cognition, and social philosophy. So it seems appropriate to begin by thanking students and colleagues in the Department of Philosophy at Simon Fraser University for providing such a fun, stimulating, and hospitable work environment over the last eight years, encouraging junior faculty to follow their philosophical whims wherever they might lead. (The one question I've never heard at anyone ask at SFU is, "so how is this philosophy?")

From early days I have been fortunate to work with mentors who would not only provide gentle guidance to my first faltering steps in philosophy but would also provide models of the kind of scholar-person I might aspire to become. These include Bjørn T. Ramberg and Kristin Gjesdal at the University of Oslo, Henrik Syse and Gregory Reichberg at the Peace Research Institute, Oslo (PRIO), and finally, John McDowell, Ted McGuire, and Jim Bogen at the University of Pittsburgh.

In developing this project, Holly K. Andersen has been there every step of the way: discussions with her have led to improvements in virtually every paragraph of the book. Nic Fillion, likewise, has patiently endured countless attempts at developing the ideas and getting the arguments right.

For further discussion and/or written feedback, I am indebted to Kathleen Akins, Brian Ball, Rima Basu, Erin Beeghly, Sam Black, Elisabeth Camp, Yan Chen, Chris Copan, Katie Creel, Josh DiPaolo, Catarina Dutilh Novaes, Mahan Esmaeilzadeh, Arianna Falbo, Will Fleisher, Danny Forman, Sanford Goldberg, Martin Hahn, Michael Hannon, Emily Hodges, Jonathan Jenkins Ichikawa, Ian Kahn, Thomas Kelly, Gabriel Lariviere, Maria Lasonen-Aarnio, Clayton Littlejohn, Matt Maxwell, Matt McGrath, Robin McKenna, Richard Moore, Sarah Moss, Dana Nelkin, Thi Nguyen, Varsha Pai, Katherine Puddifoot, Susanna Siegel, Julia Staffel, Evan Tiffany, Kelsey Vicars, Caroline von Klemperer, Jeremy Wanderer, various contributors to the Social Epistemology Network and Board Certified Epistemologists Facebook discussion groups, audiences at VU Amsterdam

(May 2015), the Western Canadian Philosophical Association (Edmonton October 2016), the Pacific APA (Seattle April 2017, San Diego April 2018, Vancouver April 2019), UMass Boston (May 2017), the Berlin School of Mind and Brain (July 2017), the University of Oslo (May 2018), King's College London (May 2018), and the Central APA (Denver 2019), as well as Peter Momtchiloff, for expressing early enthusiasm for the project and for seeing it through to completion, and two external referees at OUP, whose detailed comments helped set the final revisions on the right track. I would also like to extend my sincere gratitude to the always friendly staff at Club Ilia (Burnaby) and Tamburen Pub (Fredrikstad), where large portions of this book were first drafted.

Some of the arguments in this book have appeared in different form elsewhere. I am grateful to Wiley-Blackwell for permission to reuse material from "The Epistemology of Prejudice" (*Thought* 2013) in chapters 4–5 and "Evidential Preemption" (*Philosophy and Phenomenological Research* 2020) in chapter 6, and to the University of Arkansas Press for permission to reuse material from "Doxastic Morality: A Moderately Skeptical Perspective" (*Philosophical Topics* 2018) in chapters 9–10.

In writing the book, I have benefited from the financial support of the Social Sciences and Humanities Research Council of Canada (Insight Development Grant 430 2016 0460, "The Epistemology of Prejudice").

On a more personal note, I would like to thank my parents—Kari Håheim and Olav Begby—who have always supported my academic endeavors (a first in my family) and have never complained about the fact that as a result of those endeavors, I have now spent almost half my life living abroad. Finally, thanks to my many friends back home, who have never failed to provide me with an anchoring point and a sense of belonging, even after all these years.

This book is for Holly, Annika, and Erik, for making it all worthwhile.

Endre Begby

Burnaby, September 2020

Introduction

Prejudice is endemic to human life. It is a contributing cause to many of the persistent ills that beset our societies: war and conflict, repression and marginalization, harassment and bullying.[1] We can speculate that its origins may lay deep in the recesses of the human mind, maybe in some primitive urge to mark a distinction between self and others—or, in collective terms, between us and them, in-group and out-group—and to imbue such distinctions with significance. Most often, these demarcations come to settle on contingently salient markers, such as skin color, gender, religion, or ethnicity. But it is quite possible that these serve as common anchoring points of prejudice only *because* they happen to be salient. In principle, it seems, prejudice could come to focus on any odd property: after all, when it comes to determining a person's value as a human being, what could be more arbitrary than their gender or skin color?

If prejudice were merely a foible of individual minds, we might not be so concerned about it. But it is not: instead, it tends to spread outwards, permeating large features of society, consolidating itself in institutional and para-institutional structures, regulating access to social opportunities connected to work, leisure, education, health care, and more.[2] It must fall to sociologists, economists, and others to document these consequences of prejudice. What can philosophers contribute to our understanding of this phenomenon? As moral philosophers, our first instinct is no doubt to condemn it. After all, it predictably leads to a host of unwarranted harms. But prejudiced belief also falls within the purview of another normative vocabulary, namely that of epistemology. Epistemologists routinely classify beliefs (and the epistemic processes by which we form our beliefs) as good or bad, justified or unjustified, warranted or unwarranted. And when philosophers attempt to view prejudice through the normative lens of epistemology, their conclusion is typically swift, clear, and likewise

---

[1] For an overview of a wide range of "consequences of prejudice," see Hanes, Hanes, and Rudd (2007: chapter 11).

[2] Cf. the notion of "institutional racism" developed in Carmichael and Hamilton 1967.

negative: no one can be epistemically justified in holding a prejudiced belief; prejudiced belief, whenever it occurs, is a symptom of some kind of breakdown of epistemic rationality.

This book argues that this conclusion is overhasty and in an important sense unduly optimistic: as we move toward a "non-ideal" form of epistemological theorizing—emphasizing the intrinsic capacity limitations of the human mind, as well as the particular and highly contingent informational constraints that ordinary agents are forced to operate under—we might find that there is no good grounds for saying that prejudiced belief, simply in virtue of being prejudiced, lacks epistemic warrant, and that prejudiced believers are always manifesting some form or other of epistemic irrationality. In brief, we rely on others for information in forming our beliefs, and could not do otherwise, given the kinds of minds that we have. Our socio-epistemic contexts thereby limit (for better or for worse) the epistemic opportunities that are open to us. In sufficiently warped socio-epistemic contexts, there may just be no rational path to true belief: even when our cognitive capacities are operating at their critical best, even when we are doing everything we should (epistemically speaking), there may be no guarantee that the result is not prejudiced.[3]

Epistemology is simply too slender a reed from which to weave a comprehensive account of the wrongs of prejudice. It is important to understand that there may be many routes to prejudiced belief: while prejudice may certainly arise from individual epistemic pathology, it can also arise in rational response to socially sanctioned and institutionally supported information-structures. As I will argue, this insight is important not only in improving our conceptual grasp of *what prejudice is*; it can also guide us in developing new inroads on remedial action, ultimately providing a new platform on which to vindicate the moral and legal standing of those who are victimized by prejudice.

0.1 Chapter-by-Chapter Overview

In the opening chapter, I begin by providing a working definition of prejudice in terms of a negatively charged stereotype targeting some group

---

[3] Note also that, although the book focuses on prejudiced belief, this is essentially a case study only, a "proof of concept" of the viability and importance of the broader framework of non-ideal epistemology. This framework can also be modified to apply to a range of other problematic socio-epistemic phenomena, such as conspiracy theories and the recent "fake news" phenomenon.

of people, and derivatively, the individuals who comprise this group. I then turn to situating my approach in the larger landscape of contemporary epistemological theory. In chapter 2, I draw on developments in social and cognitive psychology for insight into the structure and function of stereotypes, the central component of our definition of prejudice. In particular, I argue that stereotypes are a fundamental feature of human social cognition. In chapter 3, I make my case for a "non-ideal" approach to epistemology. We need to consider constraints arising from distinctive capacity limitations of the human mind (what I call "endogenous non-ideality") as well as those arising from specific limitations on the information environments that epistemic agents are forced to operate within ("exogenous non-ideality"). Taking a non-ideal approach to epistemology does not, however, mean giving up on epistemic normativity altogether: to the contrary, I argue that non-ideal epistemology provides the only way for such norms to provide a genuine critical grip on human cognition at all.

Chapters 4 and 5 jointly develop the core of the book's argument that prejudiced belief can very well be the result of human cognitive faculties operating at their best in their information environment. If this argument is successful, it shows that no good case can be made that prejudiced belief is always symptomatic of some kind of breakdown of epistemic rationality. Chapter 4 considers the problem in light of the *acquisition* of prejudiced belief. I argue that canons of inductive inference as well as considerations from the epistemology of testimony strongly support the view that individuals can come to acquire prejudiced belief without compromising their epistemic rationality. In fact, given the information environments they find themselves in, these might well be the beliefs that they *should* form, epistemically speaking, in the simple sense that they are the beliefs that are best supported by their evidence. This insight naturally leads us to consider the question of prejudice *maintenance*: how could anyone be epistemically rational in retaining their prejudiced beliefs in the face of the significant amounts of contrary evidence confronting them in their everyday lives? In chapter 5, I argue that much of this evidence can be easily absorbed by prejudiced believers, in keeping with our best canons of epistemic rationality. Drawing on recent work on generic generalizations, I argue that prejudiced beliefs are in no sense falsified by single contrary instances, or even larger swaths of them. Even when subjects are rationally required to recognize these as providing contrary evidence, the correct response may simply be to reduce one's credence in the relevant proposition. The result may be that they are somewhat less prejudiced than before. But they are still prejudiced, even as, by hypothesis, they have responded correctly to their evidence. (It would be too simplistic, then, to dismiss prejudice simply as an instance of "affected ignorance" (Moody-Adams 1994) or "active ignorance" (Medina 2013).[4] Sometimes, to be sure, people hold prejudiced beliefs despite their evidence or take active measures to shield themselves from relevant evidence not yet in their possession. But in other cases, it may just be that their evidential situation is set up in such a way that even flawless epistemic rationality will lead to prejudiced belief.)

Chapters 6–8 add significantly more detail to this basic account of the epistemology of prejudice. So far we have worked on the assumption that the confrontation with contrary evidence always requires rational believers to reduce their credence in the relevant propositions. In chapter 6, I introduce the notion of "evidential preemption," which occurs when a testifier, in addition to offering testimony that p, also warns the hearer that others will try to persuade them of contrary views. I argue that whenever it is rational for someone to accept the "ground-level" testimony on offer, it is also rational for them to accept the warning about what others will tell them. Now, when they subsequently are confronted with this contrary testimony, its evidential force has effectively been neutralized. It is, essentially, information the subject has already conditionalized on, and which will therefore not require significant revision of belief. In this way, evidential preemption can serve as a tool for "epistemic inoculation," all but ensuring that subjects cannot make rational use of the contrary evidence to correct their beliefs.

Chapter 7 introduces a different perspective, outlining a way to study the social dynamics of prejudice even in the absence of "prejudiced believers." I start by pointing out how stereotypes—including prejudicial stereotypes— can govern our social interactions by way of providing us with "social scripts." I argue that we often have incentives to comply with these social scripts even in situations where we don't endorse their content. This is because we have reason to believe that others endorse these scripts, and because there are typically sanctions associated with raising questions about their validity. But of course, these others may be in exactly the same situation. So we could find ourselves in a position where *no one* endorses the stereotypes encoded in our social scripts, even as these scripts continue to govern our mutual interactions to much the same effect as though everyone believed them. Reverting to notions of "collective" or "shared"

---

[4] Or "white ignorance" (Mills 2007) if we were concerned specifically with racial prejudice.

epistemic responsibility provides no real traction with these kinds of situations, nor does it provide any novel perspectives on remedial action. As a case study, I offer the paradox of "perceived electability," where I—and presumably many others—refrain from casting my vote for a preferred minority candidate, just because I believe others will not vote for her.

In chapter 8, I address recent concerns about "algorithmic bias," specifically in the context of the criminal justice process. The threat of algorithmic bias is insidious in the sense that prejudiced reasoning now comes to take on the sheen of objectivity and impartiality. Starting from a recent controversy about the use of "automated risk assessment tools" in criminal sentencing and parole hearings, where evidence suggests that such tools effectively discriminate against minority defendants, I argue that the problem here has nothing in particular to do with algorithm-assisted reasoning; nor, more surprisingly, is it in any clear sense a case of epistemic bias. Instead, given the dataset that we have to work with, there is reason to think that no improvement to our epistemic routines would deliver significantly better results. Instead, the bias is effectively encoded into the dataset itself, via a long history of institutionalized racism. This points toward a different diagnosis of the problem, which I dub "Gendler's Dilemma" (with a nod to Gendler 2011): in deeply divided societies, there may just be no way to simultaneously satisfy our moral ideals and our epistemic ideals.

This diagnosis finally brings to the fore the moral (and socio-political) dimension of prejudice, which occupies us in the last two chapters of the book. Until this point, the argument has operated on the assumption that moral normativity and epistemic normativity run on separate tracks, steadfastly focusing on the latter. This assumption has recently come under pressure from developments such as "moral encroachment" and "doxastic morality." At stake here is the idea that in certain morally charged scenarios—for instance where we stand to impart unwarranted harms on others by forming certain beliefs about them—our epistemic requirements change: beliefs that would be justified by the evidence in a morally inert scenario may no longer be justified once the "moral stakes" are taken into account. In this sense, morality can act as a constraint on rational belief formation. After arguing that none of these approaches can quite carry out the task set for them, I turn in chapter 10 to considering the possibility that the relation between morality and epistemology in fact runs in the opposite direction: that the range of our epistemic responsibility constrains the range of our moral responsibility. This may initially seem like an unwelcome and in many ways defeatist resolution to our inquiry. To the contrary, I argue that this insight may in fact put victims of prejudice in a better position to seek redress. To see how, consider that moral responsibility is a multi-dimensional concept: while it is plausible that ascriptions of moral *blame* track ascriptions of epistemic responsibility, it may yet be that other forms of moral liability do not. Drawing on insights from tort law and discrimination law, I argue that there are important forms of moral responsibility which can attach even to epistemically blameless agents. I argue that this is a potentially liberating insight: victims' claims to have been wronged should in no way depend on their ability to demonstrate that their victimizers were in a position to know that their actions were wrong. This frees victims of prejudice from the substantial burden of having to show that prejudiced believers are—universally, or in any specific case—epistemically irrational in believing as they do. Quite simply, the presumptive link between prejudice and epistemic wrongdoing is an extraneous conceptual association placing additional obstacles in the path of remedial action.

1

Prejudice from an Epistemological Point of View

As we have noted, prejudiced belief raises both moral and epistemic concerns. There is a clear tendency in the philosophical literature to associate the two: somehow the moral wrong of discriminatory treatment (for example) is grounded in the epistemic wrong of holding prejudiced beliefs against people in the first place. They could know better and they should know better. It is in virtue of committing such blameworthy epistemic errors that prejudiced believers make themselves morally accountable for the harms that their beliefs cause. I believe this is a mistake: minimally, we want to be in a position to claim that victims of discrimination have been *wronged* long before we are in a position to assess the epistemic situation of those who perpetrated the discrimination. Accordingly, we will begin by firmly dissociating these two strands of thought—the epistemic and the moral—so as first to investigate on its own terms the widespread supposition that prejudiced belief must involve some manner of epistemic wrongdoing or cognitive pathology. However, we will return to the moral problem of prejudice in the book's closing chapters.

This book is primarily intended as a contribution to situated (or "applied") social epistemology. What I call "situated" epistemology is not to be confused with the "standpoint epistemology" familiar from contemporary feminist epistemology and philosophy of science. As Elizabeth Anderson explains (2015: section 2), standpoint epistemology involves claims to "represent the world from a particular socially situated perspective that can lay a claim to epistemic privilege or authority." Along these lines, the oppressed working class (following Marx), women, disabled persons, and other relatively marginalized subjects, are positioned to *know* certain things that others, who lack the same standpoint, cannot. While these subjects are socially marginalized in various ways, they may nonetheless thereby possess a certain kind of *epistemic* privilege, which gives them the authority to speak, specifically, about the nature and consequences of their marginalization.[1] Virtually the opposite will be the case for what I call "situated epistemology." First, and most obviously, I make no supposition that the subjects whose epistemic situation we are considering are generally socially marginalized. Second, and more importantly, there is no way in which their situation should give rise to any special kind of epistemic privilege, specifically that of being in a special position to *know* (and therefore to speak to) a certain range of truths.[2] I have no problem accepting the claim that prejudiced people are generally ignorant (i.e., there are certain truths that elude them). My point is not about knowledge: instead, I argue that they can very well be *justified in believing* the things that they don't know.

As a contribution to situated social epistemology, it is part of the book's design that it be comparatively thin on theory but rich in application. That said, a number of theoretical choices and suppositions must go into shaping the argument nonetheless. Many of these choices will be controversial, if only because the theoretical foundations of epistemology are controversial. I think all these choices can be defended as independently motivated and as jointly providing a natural and productive starting point for the sort of integrative perspective on situated social epistemology that this book seeks to develop. In this opening chapter, I will clarify the central theoretical commitments that shape this perspective, in order (hopefully) to avert confusions and objections at later stages. I do not intend any of these clarifications as "knockdown arguments" against alternative theoretical approaches. In other contexts of inquiry, other choices may well be appropriate. My contention is simply that these are good choices to make for the particular orientation of this book. (Readers who are not particularly interested in recent theoretical discussions in epistemology should feel free to skip from section 1.2 to section 1.6.)

1.1 Defining Prejudice

We will find it useful to define a prejudice, at least for working purposes, as a *negatively charged stereotype, targeting some group of people, and,*

---

[1] For further perspectives, see, e.g., Medina 2013; Toole 2019.
[2] As Mills argues (2007: 15), "[the] idea of group-based cognitive handicap is [...] a straightforward corollary of standpoint theory: if one group is privileged, after all, it must be by comparison with another group that is handicapped."

derivatively, the individuals who comprise this group. It is worth noting from the outset that we will thereby be approaching the concept of prejudice in a rather different manner than, say, Kate Manne has recently approached the concept of misogyny. Manne writes (2017: 66):

> when it comes to calling an *agent* a misogynist on the whole, there are reasons to be cautious about the risk of overplaying our hand and engaging in some of the very moralism that attending to misogyny teaches us to be wary of. And, of course, there are also relevant considerations of fairness. One generally does not want to attach a shaming label to someone in virtue of a near-universal trait of character, attitude, or behavioral disposition. I hence suggest that the term 'misogynist' is best treated as a *threshold* concept, and also a *comparative* one, functioning as a kind of 'warning label,' which should be sparingly applied to people whose attitudes and actions are *particularly* and *consistently* misogynistic across myriad social contexts.

Precisely because I am proposing to divest the concept of prejudice of its moralistic and "shaming" tone, I have no qualms about treating prejudice as a "low-threshold concept," on which most of us, most of the time, will be prejudiced to some degree or other. This is not in any way a criticism of Manne's approach, of course, but rather an illustration of the fact that different approaches are warranted in different kinds of inquiry.

Additional clarifications are required. First, this working definition identifies prejudice in terms of an underlying psychological generalization, viz. a stereotype.[3] I will defend this choice more fully in the next chapter, with reference to developments in psychological research. But for now, we can note that this entails that I cannot really be said to be prejudiced against you *qua* individual. I can, however, be prejudiced against you *qua* tall person, slovenly shaver, Steely Dan fan, etc. I think this is the right result: it is important to distinguish between prejudice in the sense that worries

---

[3] One might wonder: if prejudiced beliefs just are stereotypes and we routinely talk about positive as well as negative stereotypes, why do we so rarely hear talk about "positive prejudices"? The answer, presumably, is that we surely *could* talk about positive prejudices, even if we usually don't: the restrictions here are entirely terminological rather than metaphysical. But as a matter of fact, the extant literature (whether in philosophy, psychology, or sociology) is primarily concerned with negative stereotypes, to the extent of grouping them together under a distinct lexeme (i.e., "prejudice"). My approach inherits this focus (as well as the associated terminology). But as the arguments themselves will hopefully serve to make clear (see, in particular, sections 4.1.2–4.1.3), while there may be moral reasons to focus on the negative cases in particular, there is nonetheless a clear sense in which the positive and negative cases are entirely symmetrical from an epistemological point of view.

psychologists and philosophers, which is always filtered through some sort of group-level generalization, and the negative attitudes one might come to harbor against particular individuals as a result of having had repeated, irksome interactions with them ("oh, no, not him again!").

Another issue concerns the supposition that the stereotypes that underlie prejudiced beliefs must be negatively charged. This is arguably an over-simplification, but one that I think can be defended on grounds of expediency. The over-simplification comes to this: it is possible that there is no comprehensive classification of ascribable properties such that all of them will be universally either positive, negative, or neutral. Of course, some properties probably are universally considered as negative (e.g., duplicity). But others are more difficult to classify. There are a host of properties frequently ascribed in social cognition which, broadly speaking, we would want to classify as positive or even admirable traits, but when they are deployed in particular contexts they may turn out to be negative and "prejudicial." One example would be the property of "being caring," stereo-typically ascribed to women. This is generally presumed to be a positive property. But it can clearly be prejudicial in certain contexts, such as a search for a CEO, where a certain kind of ruthlessness might be taken to be a job qualification. (Conversely, of course, we can imagine that the stereotypical image of men as "competitive" or "ruthless"—apparently desirable traits in a CEO—can likewise prejudice one's chances of being invited to coach one's daughter's soccer team.) So, when I define a prejudice as a "negatively charged" stereotype, I am not supposing that all properties one might ascribe in social cognition are either positive, negative, or neutral when considered in their own right. Rather, what I have in mind is that the property would be generally seen as negative in the relevant context of deployment.

Finally, a vexed question is whether our working definition should also include the supposition that prejudiced beliefs are false. Many philosophers who have written on prejudice and associated phenomena have taken this route.[4] See, for instance, Lawrence Blum (2004: 256): "The falseness of a stereotype is part of, and is a necessary condition of, what is objectionable about stereotypes in general."[5] But as Miranda Fricker points out (2007: 32–3), even if it should turn out that prejudiced beliefs are false (simply in virtue of being prejudiced), it is not clear what bearing this should have on

---

[4] Including myself: see Begby 2013.
[5] For important criticism, see Beeghly 2015, forthcoming, MS.

their epistemology. Quite simply, whether a belief is true or false tells us nothing about its epistemic standing.[6] So while it may be correct to say that prejudiced beliefs are false, this additional specification carries no real weight in an epistemological inquiry.[7] We might nonetheless want to know whether it *is* correct. If it is, it can hardly, I think, be *true by definition*. (For instance, we may note that there is currently an emerging body of research claiming to support the idea of "stereotype accuracy"—i.e., the notion that truth predominates over falsity in stereotype reasoning.[8] This notion will play no crucial role in my own argument, and I continue to harbor concerns about the underlying research. (See section 2.1 for a brief discussion.))

My reason for not including falsity in a working definition of prejudice is different. It stems from the realization that stereotypes come in different degrees of abstractness: at some level of abstraction, a stereotype might well be true, even as it is contextually deployed in a way that solicits incorrect inferences. As a case in point, consider the claim that immigrant populations are overrepresented in crime statistics. In many jurisdictions, this is factually correct. The problem, however, is that it contextually elicits the inference that immigrants therefore have less respect for the law. This inference seems to follow naturally. But in many cases, it is actually deeply misguided: immigrant populations tend, for instance, to be significantly younger than overall populations; when the statistics are normalized with respect to age and other relevant demographic factors, the crime rate discrepancies will tend to dwindle, often falling below the threshold of statistical significance.[9]

---

[6] This is, of course, one of the many controversial choices that inform the background theory of this book. For more on this particular point, see section 1.2 below.

[7] Perhaps one might think that the classification of prejudiced belief as false belief could matter to our assessment of the *moral* consequences of prejudice, on the assumption that no one could be wronged (and thereby suffer unwarranted harm) by a true belief. But this would, I think, be an extremely naïve view. In particular, even if a prejudiced stereotype were true, in the sense of tracking the demographic distribution of a certain property, it doesn't follow that it would be correctly applied to a particular individual. This is central to the line of argument considered in chapter 9.

[8] See, in particular, Jussim et al. 2009; Jussim 2012.

[9] This example is inspired by a discussion in Norway after a number of politicians and media organizations attempted to frame the policy debate on immigration in terms of non-adjusted numbers on crime rate disparities supplied by the Norwegian Statistics Bureau. On this see, https://www.faktisk.no/artikler/By/innvandrere-langt-mer-kriminelle-skrev-listhaug-og-viste-til-ujusterte-tall. This discussion brings to mind the "reference class problem," often relevant in statistical research. (See Hajek 2007 for an overview of its philosophical consequences.) Essentially, the reference class problem arises because every individual simultaneously belongs to a number of different "reference classes": e.g., young/urban/male/immigrant/Muslim. Significantly different statistical projections will be made if we identify a subject as belonging

But it can still be true to say that immigrant populations are overrepresented in crime statistics.

Finally, what is perhaps most conspicuously absent from our working definition is the supposition that the prejudiced belief be irrational, held contrary to evidence, or in some other way lacking in relevant epistemic credentials. This is regularly taken to be part of what constitutes a belief as prejudicial, and it is the burden of this book to argue that this is not correct. Certainly, some—possibly many—prejudiced beliefs will be irrational. This can hardly be a surprise: beliefs of virtually any stripe can be irrational in this sense, even where there is ample evidence to support them.[10] Meanwhile, it will be shown that recognizably prejudiced beliefs can constitute a perfectly rational response to one's evidence in many socio-epistemic contexts (on any notion of epistemic rationality that can usefully serve in an inquiry such as this).

1.2 Epistemic Normativity

Epistemology adopts a normative approach to belief. We do right or wrong in forming our beliefs. What constitutes beliefs as right or wrong in the

---

to one category rather than another. Awareness of these questions is key to responsible policy-making. But this does not change the fact that it may nonetheless be *true* to say things that aren't, ultimately, particularly explanatory or particularly predictive.

[10] Cf. the familiar distinction between propositional and doxastic justification: subjects can hold a variety of beliefs (e.g., scientific beliefs) for which ample justification is *available*; but they might still not be justified if they failed to *avail* themselves of it, or otherwise processed the evidence incorrectly. Concerned readers might want to know whether I do in fact hold that most (or many) prejudiced beliefs are epistemically justified in this sense. If the question were meant simply to elicit an empirically informed hunch as to whether most people's beliefs in this particular domain were justified, I would probably say "no." But to fasten on this answer would be to miss the larger point of the book, which is to discourage philosophers (and psychologists, etc.) from making such broad-swathe claims about what particular people would be justified (or not) in believing based simply on *our* assessment of the evidence that bears on the question, and without considering *their* evidential situation, and how they process the evidence at their disposal. If the thesis under consideration is that there is something intrinsically epistemically irrational about prejudiced belief, a rebuttal shouldn't have to do more than point out that, given plausible socio-epistemic contexts, there would be plenty of possible routes to justified prejudiced belief. Modality is crucial here: the question is whether they *could* be justified, not whether they are. Quite generally, and with regard to *any* type of belief, philosophers should simply refrain from answering the question, "are people (generally) justified in holding these beliefs?" With respect to the question, "could this particular person be justified in holding a belief of this sort?", they should commit to an answer only after a careful examination of that person's epistemic situation.

relevant sense is not, for instance, whether they are conducive to amicable social relationships or increase our biological fitness. Rather, the idea is that as epistemic agents, we are beholden to a distinctive epistemic norm— roughly, and to be elaborated further below, that one should believe in accordance with one's evidence.[11] When we violate that norm, that is, when we believe *without evidence* or *contrary to our evidence*, we open ourselves up to a distinctive sort of sanction: epistemic blame.[12] As in the case of moral responsibility, one might be in a position to claim an *excuse* even in cases where one violates the norm. But one could never be "in the right"—morally or epistemically—when violating the relevant norm.

While there are interesting analogies between epistemic and moral normativity, the two domains of normative assessment are clearly separate. Nonetheless, they can come together in a variety of ways, giving rise to puzzles about what one *ought to believe*, all things considered. In such cases, moral and epistemic considerations appear to pull in contrary directions. For instance, forming a certain belief might cause one to act in a way that risks violating someone's moral rights. Accordingly, questions arise as to whether there are special epistemic duties of circumspection that apply in cases where one's beliefs might affect other people in morally important ways. More radically still, we might wonder whether there are certain things one should just resolve—on moral grounds—never to believe, whatever one's evidence says. We will have occasion to explore such issues in more detail in chapter 9.

The assumption that epistemic norms attach to the relation between one's beliefs and one's evidence suggests that epistemic normativity is best understood as a "process-notion" and not a "product-notion."[13] That is, the norms apply primarily to the process by which one forms one's belief, and only derivatively to the beliefs that constitute the product of this process. This supposition leads naturally to the recognition that people can have false beliefs which are nonetheless in perfectly good epistemic standing. By contrast, some philosophers insist that the epistemic norm dictates that one should only have true beliefs. But this would put, for instance, our ancient ancestors (though not *only* our ancient ancestors) in an impossible position. Presumably, in many cases, they just didn't have access to evidence

---

[11] For a classic statement, see Clifford 1877.
[12] For discussion, see, for instance, Lackey 2007, Peels 2016, Brown 2018, and Boult (forthcoming).
[13] As such, my approach has certain affinities with the "process reliabilism" associated, for instance, with Goldman 1979. I will return to this point shortly.

that would support true beliefs. Should they, then, just refrain from forming any beliefs altogether?[14] To my mind, this is unacceptable. First, beliefs have an intimate connection with rational agency. And as rational agents, we often find ourselves in situations where we are required to act even on scarce and highly uncertain evidence.[15] But more importantly, they *have* evidence, even if that evidence is ultimately "misleading evidence," i.e., evidence that doesn't support true beliefs. And from the point of view of epistemic normativity, one should form the beliefs that are best supported by one's total evidence, including evidence that would—with more knowledge—turn out to be misleading evidence. Simply refraining from forming any belief is not an option.[16]

In a nutshell, then, my view is that we can criticize a person's epistemic standing to believe a certain proposition only if we can make the case that the proposition is not supported by their evidence, or evidence that they should have taken into consideration. This helps refocus our discussion of the epistemology of prejudice, away from some presumptive morbidity in the belief itself—for instance, its being false, or simply its being prejudiced— and over toward the sense that prejudiced believers must be *doing something wrong with their evidence* in order to end up believing as they do.

Finally, one might intuitively feel that pursuing a "non-ideal" epistemology of the sort that I aim to do here must risk seriously compromising the

---

[14] Note, then, that this is not a question of whether they could be *excused* (after the fact) for forming false beliefs. The question is rather, given their evidence such as it was, which belief(s) *should* they have formed, according to our best conception of epistemic rationality?

[15] Of course, some philosophers (e.g., Feldman and Conee 1985; Dougherty 2014; Maguire and Woods 2020) might object to the idea there is any interface between our normative conception of epistemic rationality and the norms of rational agency more broadly. Needless to say, this is not the conception that I have in mind: in any form of situated epistemology, we want our conception of epistemic rationality to interface in productive ways with norms of rational agency and reflection.

[16] Differently put, epistemic normativity is not in the business of granting *permissions to believe*, only *obligations to believe*: once an epistemic subject has determined that their evidence supports *p* to *n* degree, they face no further question about what they should believe, or even if they should believe anything at all. (Note that this does not entail any particular stance on the question of "permissivism" v. "uniqueness" in epistemology (cf. White 2005). The question at stake in that debate is whether, for any body of evidence, there is a unique credence which is *the* rational credence to adopt, or whether a variety of credences are rationally permissible, so long as they fall within a certain range. The arguments in this book do not depend in any way on assuming a permissive stance on epistemic rationality in this sense (see, e.g., Schoenfield 2012). Even assuming uniqueness, there will typically be enough variation in people's background beliefs (etc.) to explain why it can be rational for them, even as they update on the same evidence, to end up with very different credences. In an important sense, this is just what is meant by taking a "situated" approach to epistemology and epistemic rationality. (We will look at a specific example of this in chapter 5.))

very idea of a normative stance on epistemology. But it need not be so. In chapter 3, I will describe two distinct dimensions of non-ideality in epistemology, which I will call endogenous and exogenous non-ideality. My point is that *relative* to these dimensions of non-ideality, we both can and should retain a normative perspective on subjects' epistemic performance. On this view, there need be nothing intrinsically wrong about the norms discussed in traditional "idealizing" epistemology. It's just that these norms are extremely abstract. For these norms to be of any real, critical use to us, they must be contextualized. But when they have been appropriately contextualized, they can serve as benchmarks—and quite exacting ones at that—for evaluating individual subjects' epistemic performance. I think of non-ideal epistemology precisely as a template for supplying that kind of contextualization.

1.3 Justified Belief and Epistemic Rationality

A belief is justified only if it is one that is rationally held in light of one's evidence. We'll talk in more detail about evidence in the next section. But even pending a clarification of what one might mean by "evidence," it will seem that we are already courting controversy here, by adopting an "evidentialist" stance on epistemology. Some of these controversies, I believe, can be mollified if we adopt a suitably irenic conception of evidence. We can allow, in particular, that evidence comes in a variety of heterogeneous forms, for instance, direct observation, reflection, testimony, and perhaps most perplexingly, evidence about other (sources of) evidence. When all of these forms of evidence are gathered together, I think the real concern here should be not whether evidentialism is true, at some level of abstraction, but rather whether all these various sources of evidence can be brought together and calibrated in a way that would uniquely single out one hypothesis over its many competitors.[17] But that is a challenge that any approach to epistemology must contend with.

According to some philosophers, an epistemically rational belief is simply an epistemically blameless belief.[18] Others object to this view by

---

[17] Note the connection with debates about uniqueness and conciliationism in the epistemology of disagreement (cf. Elga 2007; Christensen 2010; Kelly 2010).
[18] See, for instance, Steup 1999, as well as Booth and Peels 2010, responding to Weatherson 2008.

emphasizing, as I did above, the notion of an epistemic excuse. Epistemic excuses attach to unjustified beliefs which are nonetheless blameless. I agree that justifications and excuses are importantly different categories. But I disagree with the motivation some have offered for taking this view. Consider Stewart Cohen's "New Evil Demon" scenario.[19] A subject which is duped by an evil demon into thinking that the world is as it appears to be may have done everything right by their evidence, says Cohen. Insofar as we view justification as a normative notion, we ought also hold that the duped subject is epistemically justified in believing as she does (cf. Cohen 1984: 282). So-called "epistemic externalists" (e.g., Williamson 2000; Littlejohn 2012, forthcoming) reject this intuition but offer in its stead the recognition that the duped subject is of course in possession of a "cast-iron excuse" for believing as she does (Williamson forthcoming: 18). Nonetheless, being blameless in believing that p does not entail being epistemically justified in believing that p.

We will look more closely at associated externalist ideas in the next section. But briefly, I see no compelling grounds for holding that the subject in this scenario is not justified in believing as she does. In particular, if she isn't so justified, we owe an explanation of what, then, she *should* do with the evidence (or apparent evidence, pending clarification in the next section) that she is in possession of. According to our best conception of epistemic normativity, she can't simply disregard it. We need to make a distinction between the person who forms her beliefs in accordance with what she has reason to believe is good evidence (even if it isn't), and the person who doesn't. Presumably, that distinction should center on the idea that the person who takes the (apparent) evidence into account in forming her beliefs is *doing something right*, epistemically speaking, that the other person is not.[20] And that notion of "doing something right" is clearly a

---

[19] Consideration of the New Evil Demon might seem out of place for a book like this, and I agree. But note that we will be forced to consider a rebooted and recharged version of the New Evil Demon, much more relevant to our present concerns, in chapter 3.

[20] One way to meet this objection would be to revert to a distinction between "prescriptive norms" and "evaluative norms" (cf. Simion et al. 2016). This view essentially cedes the point about what the subject should do with their evidence, while insisting that the resulting beliefs should *also* be evaluated according to a separate norm, which no false belief could satisfy. Essentially, then, we would have distinct norms for process and product. I have no objection to this view per se, but find no use for the putative evaluative norm. (I might also add that if the evaluative norm is genuinely not prescriptive, then it presumably cannot give rise to any kind of "epistemic dilemma" for a subject who is facing evidence strongly supporting a false proposition. What she *should do* is simply to form her beliefs in accordance with her evidence. If the

process-notion, and cannot therefore be dependent on the product of the process conforming to some external standard, e.g., being true.

Importantly, though, this is not to say that the notion of justified belief collapses into that of blameless belief. I take a different approach here. The norms bearing on epistemic agency are potentially very exacting; they can be draining both in their own right, and especially so when combined with other circumstantial pressures. In brief, I think we can make good sense of the idea of excusable performance errors as marking a distinction between justified and blameless belief. If someone is facing serious fatigue or is running up against the limits of computational complexity, we routinely forgive them certain epistemic lapses. This is in no way to say, however, that they are justified in believing as they do. (I will return to this point in chapter 2.)

1.4 Evidence, Truth, and Knowledge

If evidence is what justifies belief, what then is evidence? This turns out to be a surprisingly difficult question to answer in any illuminating way. Nonetheless, here's an attempt that I favor: evidence is any bit of information that increases or decreases the probability of a hypothesis under consideration.[21] On such an approach, it should be clear that there will be *a lot* of evidence in the world, and that the relationship between evidence and hypothesis can be very complex indeed.

A first thing to note is that evidence provides different degrees of support for a hypothesis. For instance, hearing your neighbors shouting with joy is evidence that the local team just scored a goal. However, it is weaker evidence than watching the goal happen via live transmission.

Evidential support can also be surprising and indirect. For instance, suppose we have a deck of ten randomly drawn cards. We turn one over— the ace of spades. This is evidence for the hypothesis that none of the cards in the deck is a jack. But, of course, it is evidence only in the circumstantial sense that the hypothesis *none of the cards is a jack* is "left standing" even

---

evaluative norm is not prescriptive, then there is no "should" according to which she should only form true beliefs.)

[21] This mirrors the standard Bayesian definition of evidence, on which E is evidence for H iff the probability of H given E is greater than the probability of H alone ($P(H \mid E) > P(H)$), and conversely for E's being evidence against H. On this, see for instance, Kelly (2006/2014).

after the disclosure of the evidence. One piece of evidence which *could* have fully undermined the hypothesis turned out not to. Now we only have nine bits of potentially disconfirming evidence left. So we should readjust our assessment of the probability that the hypothesis is true, from .449 to .487 (i.e., from $(12/13)^{10}$ to $(12/13)^9$).

Finally, one bit of evidence can provide support at one and the same time for multiple, incompatible hypotheses. Seeing that an object appears to be red is evidence that it is red. But it is also evidence for the incompatible hypothesis that the object is white but flooded in red light. Learning that the object *is* flooded in red light strengthens the hypothesis that it is white, but is still compatible with its actually being red.

Some further oft-made assumptions about evidence also require brief discussion. For instance, Bayesian epistemology works on the idealizing assumption that one's evidence consists only of propositions of which one is subjectively certain, i.e., propositions to which one ascribes probability 1.[22] This is not an assumption that I will take over, as I don't think it is an assumption that fares well in serious consideration of social epistemology. Quite simply, much of the evidence that we have to go on in social epistemology is highly uncertain, and our theoretical approach will have to accommodate this fact.

Another proposed restriction on evidence, this time from externalism, has it that one's evidence consists only of propositions that one knows (Williamson 1997, 2000). Since knowledge is factive, this means that only true propositions are eligible to serve as evidence. It is worthwhile noting that whereas the Bayesian restriction that one's evidence be certain is defended mostly as an idealization, the externalist restriction that "E = K" is defended as a substantive insight. I don't agree with this framework. Nonetheless, I think that most of what I say in the following is ultimately compatible with it. One might think not, simply because much of the evidence in question will consist of false testimony, e.g., testimony that women are less adept at math than men. The reason my argument can nonetheless accommodate E = K is that the correct specification of the evidence in such cases is not *that women are less adept at math than men* but rather *that such-and-such told me that women are less adept at math than men*. And this, obviously, is something that we can know, even in cases where the proposition attested to is false.[23]

---

[22] For an overview, see Titelbaum (forthcoming: 4.2).
[23] Cf. Williamson (2000: 201–2).

I fully accept that knowledge is factive: one can only know what is true. But at the same time, knowledge plays no crucial role in my account: note, for instance, how my arguments do not attempt to solicit intuitions about what epistemic agents are "in a position to know" in various circumstances; rather, they explore different dimensions of the question of what these subjects are in a position to *justifiably believe*. Of course, in saying this, I presume that there are states of justified believing which do not amount to knowledge. I think this is a good presumption. Otherwise, we would have to make the implausible claim, for instance, that scientists who once believed that Pluto is the cause of the perturbations of the orbits Neptune and Uranus couldn't possibly have been justified in believing as they did. Moreover, we would be in a position to claim that they were not justified without even having to look at their evidence, but only by looking at their conclusion. Again, this seems to me a wrong result. More generally, I contend that a knowledge-centered epistemology is the wrong starting point for an inquiry into prejudiced belief.[24] If we assume that most (possibly all) prejudiced beliefs are false, that would pretty much be the end of the story, so far as externalism is concerned. If they're false, they're not knowledge; if they're not knowledge, then we're not justified in believing them. But as I will argue, there *is* more to be said about the epistemology of prejudice, none of which is any deep way shaped by the question of whether these beliefs are ultimately true or false.[25]

---

[24] Or conspiracy-theories, susceptibility to fake news, etc.

[25] And just to be very clear about this, I don't think there is any relevant sense in which my resistance to "externalist" accounts of evidence and of epistemic norms more broadly should be taken as signalling a commitment to a competing "internalist" account. (Indeed, the presumption that this distinction somehow exhausts our possibility-space seems to me a significant barrier to progress in contemporary epistemology.) There are different ways to characterize the externalism-internalism distinction. For instance, Williamson argues that non-externalist theories of evidence "distort the concept in the attempt to make evidence something that we can infallibly identify. Characteristically, they interiorize evidence: it becomes one's present experience, one's present degrees of belief, or the like. Those attempts are quaint relics of Cartesian epistemology" (2000: 193). Less abusively, one might state the point in terms of a supervenience-thesis (e.g., Wedgwood 2002; Srinivasan 2020): justification supervenes on the believer's "internal" (non-factive) mental states, such that two "internal duplicates" cannot differ in terms of epistemic standing. Pending further argument in chapter 3, let me just note for now that I believe epistemic agents are often answerable to more evidence than is currently in their possession. Therefore, my account does not interiorize evidence, nor does it leave one's epistemic standing to supervene on one's non-factive mental states. This is not because *factive* mental states are of crucial epistemic relevance; rather, it is because I don't conceive of evidence as supervening on mental states at all. (In fact, I believe—although this is not the place to develop the point in full—that this provides an opportunity to turn the tables on externalism. E = K does commit exernalists to the view that only mental states constitute evidence (since knowledge is a mental state). It seems fair to ask, however, how this account could ever permit

But even while false beliefs can be in good epistemic standing, many philosophers nonetheless find it natural to assume that there must be a deep link between epistemic rationality and truth. Epistemic rationality consists in forming one's beliefs in accordance with one's evidence. The reason why it is rational to take evidence into consideration in forming one's beliefs is that it increases the probability that one's beliefs will be true. (The value of having true beliefs, let's assume, is not in question at this point.) My own approach has certain affinities with "process-reliabilism," which likewise generally defines a "reliable process" as one that reliably takes us closer to the truth. This approach is not unreasonable on the face of it. But "processes" are individuated and assessed for "reliability" at some level of abstraction. We must guard against the assumption—surely too strong— that any *application* of a generally reliable process of belief formation must necessarily take us closer to the truth.[26] In certain kinds of evidential contexts, specifically many of the contexts that we will be looking at in this book, it is quite plausible that taking the evidence into account will in some important sense bring us further away from the truth. Nonetheless, from the standpoint of epistemic rationality, this is the evidence that subjects will be required to take into account in forming their beliefs.[27]

1.5 Belief, Credence, and Acceptance

Evidence is complex. Most propositions have significant bodies of evidence counting both for and against. To model epistemic rationality under such conditions, we must adopt a credence-based framework. "Credence" is a

---

us to hold that a lazy inquirer's persistent habit of "neglecting evidence" could ever jeopardize their epistemic justification. Quite simply, since what is neglected is not known, it can't be evidence. But if evidence is what justifies belief, epistemic agents should then be fine to only consider what they already know. Their lackadaisical investigative dispositions would have no bearing on the question of whether they are justified in believing as they do.)

[26] Again, this is not something that we can dodge by reverting to an externalist position. Even known, and therefore true, propositions can lend compelling support to a false hypothesis.

[27] Maybe there is something pathological about such cases. But the pathology, one would want to say, lies in the epistemic community as a whole, not in the individual who responds to his evidence as he should. Nonetheless, I am cautiously skeptical of attempts to fashion an account of "collective epistemic responsibility" by simply transposing our concept of individual epistemic responsibility on to a collective agent. On such analyses, we would remain, in a crucial sense, committed individualists, even if the individual we are scrutinizing is now a collective agent. As I will argue in more detail in chapter 7, it is not clear that we stand to gain anything from such a perspective-switch.

measure (from 0–1) of one's confidence that a proposition is true, given one's evidence. This framework is crucial for making headway in complex evidential situations, such as social epistemology will inevitably involve. It is simply not the case that upon discovering evidence that *not-p*, one should right away abandon one's belief in *p*. Instead, and depending on how things stand with one's total body of evidence, one should respond in the more measured way of reducing one's confidence in *p*. In many cases, however, one can still be said to *believe that p*, even after adjusting one's credence.

On this sort of credence-based approach, "belief" is often understood simply as a shorthand for having one's credence fall somewhere in a relevant range of the scale, perhaps above a certain threshold. This makes intuitive sense: you and I can both believe that NN is the best candidate for president, even though you are apparently a lot more confident than I am.

That said, many hold that in addition to credences, we also need a qualitatively different concept, sometimes glossed as "outright belief," sometimes simply as "belief" (as opposed to credence). This is not a concept that I will find use for in the present book. Accordingly, when I speak of simply of "belief," I will mean a doxastic state where the exact credence doesn't matter for the purposes at hand, so long as it falls within a certain range. Even when we ascribe the same "belief" to two persons, we must always be prepared take into account the relative confidence that each has in the proposition, in order to explain, for instance, how they would reason and act under various counterfactual (and perhaps soon to be actual) circumstances.[28] For instance, to explain why one will and another won't give up that belief when confronted with contrary evidence, we will have to say something about the relative strength of their beliefs, their rational resilience in light of new evidence. And this just *is* to speak in terms of credences. Perhaps the easiest way to see this is the following. Lots of things that we are said to "believe outright" are things that we are fully aware is less than certain on our evidence. As such, we remain open to the possibility that new evidence may emerge forcing us to reduce our confidence. So let's say we run into some such evidence, and make the appropriate adjustments. Is it possible that we are still in a situation of outright belief? If the answer is yes, which it seems it must be, then an argument can be made that reference to

---

[28] That ascriptions of belief should have this sort of explanatory, rationalizing connection with agency more broadly, is something I take for granted, though other philosophers might not. Nonetheless, we might agree that *if* the concept of belief is to have these kinds of connections, then it had better be relativized to credences.

"outright belief" is really just vague talk for having a credence somewhere in a certain range.

"Outright belief" obviously cannot mean anything like having absolute certainty (i.e., "Credence 1") in a proposition. To have absolute certainty in a proposition means, essentially, that there not only isn't but also couldn't be any evidence against it. If anything were to be presented as evidence against it, I would be rationally required to dismiss it.[29] By contrast, in the sorts of cases that philosophers have been tempted to describe as involving "outright belief," I will not only concede that there *may be* evidence against it; I will actually concede that there *is* evidence against it, even if it is evidence that is swamped by my evidence in favor. Under any sensible concept of belief, it cannot be that I am entitled to believe that *p* only if I have satisfied myself that there is no evidence of any sort, weak or strong, against *p*. So belief—even "outright belief"—must be able to coexist with significant divergence in assessment of just how strongly supported *p* is by its evidence. And in certain cases, that, once again, must surely play a significant role in how *p* figures in the subject's cognitive economy. And with that, it is unclear how "outright belief" is supposed to play a distinct and irreducible role from credence after all.

Nonetheless, the intuitions that push philosophers toward thinking that we need a distinct notion of (outright) belief, separate from and irreducible to the notion of credence, should not simply be dismissed.[30] I will try to accommodate these intuitions by proposing that these issues are ultimately not best understood in terms of belief at all, but in terms of a distinct psychological state that we may call "acceptance" (drawing on Cohen 1989). Acceptance, as I think of it, is an executive decision to treat something as "actionable," i.e., as sufficiently evidenced to act on in context, to draw further inferences from, and so on. Moreover, once a proposition is accepted, it typically also means that we put on hold any active pursuit of further evidence, including active pursuit of evidence for alternative hypotheses.[31] This is not to say, however, that we rationally accept a proposition only once we have determined that there is no further relevant evidence.

---

[29] Cf. the "dogmatism paradox" discussed, for instance, in Kripke 2011, Harman 1973, and Kelly 2008.

[30] See, for instance, Easwaran 2015, Jackson 2019, and Weisberg 2020. For critical discussion, see Staffel 2019a, 2019b.

[31] See, for instance, van Fraassen 1980, Cohen 1989, and, for illuminating discussion to which I am much indebted, Fleisher 2018.

Quite the contrary, we can accept a proposition (in context) even in the knowledge that there (probably) is further evidence out there, evidence which could well overturn the accepted proposition. The point of acceptance is simply to say that *in this context*, one's belief in *p* is sufficiently evidenced, such that one can forego further inquiry without jeopardizing one's justification for believing that *p*.[32] (Outright) belief is simply the wrong notion here. Even when one accepts a proposition, suspends active inquiry, and so forth, one does so with the understanding that the proposition in question might well be false, that propositions can be more or less supported by evidence, and so forth.

Nonetheless, acceptance and belief are obviously related in important ways. As L.J. Cohen puts it (1989: 369), "[a] person who accepts everything that he believes is dangerously credulous, but a person who accepts nothing that he believes is irrationally sceptical." But crucially, the two notions can also come apart in both directions. For instance, we might find ourselves in situations where our evidence is sufficiently poor that it doesn't warrant us in accepting any particular proposition. Of course, we can still rank candidate propositions in terms of their probability given what little evidence we have. But even though I have higher credence in H1 than in H2, I might not be inclined to accept either. Now, it might be protested that marking this distinction is precisely what the concept of outright belief was supposed to do for us: in such cases, we should say that though I might have different credences in different propositions, I don't, strictly speaking, *believe* any of them, as can be seen precisely from the fact that I don't act on them, don't draw further inferences from them, and so on. Effectively, then, acceptance is just what converts mere credence into outright belief. So to more fully differentiate acceptance from outright belief, it is important to note that I can also accept propositions which I take to be *less* well supported on my evidence than some of its competitors.[33] Our current situation with

---

[32] And needless to say, perhaps: I take it that *whether* one was justified in believing that *p* in that context does not depend on whether, ultimately, *p* turned out to be true or not.

[33] Effectively, then, one can "accept against the evidence," but not "believe against the evidence." Note, by contrast, how Bolinger (2020), in an otherwise wonderfully illuminating paper, seems to argue that the candidate for rational acceptance should always be the proposition most highly ranked in terms of evidential probability. In other words, it is fine, in a particular context, to accept none of the propositions on offer. But if you *do* accept one, it should be the candidate in which you invest the highest credence. For this reason, Bolinger also remains open to the possibility that "acceptance" may in fact be just another word for "belief."

the highly uncertain evidence regarding Covid-19 provides a rich source of illustrations: for instance, whether I believe that surface contamination is a significant factor in spreading the virus has little bearing on the question of whether I should accept that it does and modify my behavior accordingly. Given the relatively low cost of the behavioral modifications, the high expected utility of adopting these measures if it were true, and the relatively low expected utility of seeking to improve one's evidential situation on the matter, what I should accept is in no clear way determined by what I should believe. I can *believe* that surfaces are highly unlikely to be a factor in virus spread, even as I *accept* the proposition that it is, and modify my behaviors accordingly.[34]

Because acceptance involves an executive decision, we get essentially for free the connection with moral evaluation that has long plagued any talk of the "ethics of belief."[35] That is to say, we will no longer have to be committed to doxastic voluntarism (or have to develop some theory on which moral responsibility does not require voluntary control) in order to say how it is that "belief" can be a fit subject matter for moral assessment, not just epistemic assessment.[36] Moreover, given its connections with overt agency and rational reflection (i.e., accepting a proposition means that it's action-able in context, and suitable to serve as a premise in further inference), there is no longer a question of how our faculty of belief interacts with agency: its interface is acceptance. Finally, taking this route will also allow us to clarify precisely what is at stake in perplexing contemporary discussions of issues such as moral encroachment and certain cases of apparent "believing against the evidence."[37] Precisely because it is an executive decision, we can embrace the idea that acceptance should be responsive to a wider range of consider-ations than merely evidential ones.

---

[34] Similarly, we can criticize authorities who refused to issue public health recommendations regarding mask-wearing until they felt they were in possession of sufficient scientific evidence of their effectiveness. See https://hscif.org/mask-or-no-mask-a-look-at-uks-policy-over-time/ for a startling account of how the UK government and bureaucracy claimed to peg its policy recommendations on "hard evidence," which evidence was found to be lacking as late as early April 2020, but then determined to be "marginal but positive" by early May. Only after their credence crossed some threshold, then, did they see it fit to issue a recommendation to wear face masks in public places.

[35] For an overview, see Chignell 2010/2018. For the classic statement, see Clifford 1877 with the rejoinder by James (1896). To my mind, the sorts of considerations levied by James are best seen as bearing on the rationality not of belief, strictly speaking, but rather of acceptance.

[36] Cf. Cohen (1989: 368–70).   [37] See chapter 9 for a full development of these ideas.

1.6 Conclusion

On the sort of approach that I favor, whatever the epistemic norm is, it is a norm that provides guidelines for decision making under uncertainty.[38] Inference from evidence is inherently a risky strategy, even if it is the best strategy we have. No matter how scrupulous one is, the possibility that we can end up with a false belief can never be fully eliminated. This is part of the human predicament.

In particular, it is naïve to think that our evidence is always "good" evidence, i.e., evidence which, if we take it into proper account, will bring us closer to the truth. Similarly, it is naïve to think that by reflection alone, we can generally put ourselves in a position to tell what is good (i.e., truth-conducive) evidence, and what is not.

One thing that I hope will emerge from the arguments to follow is the sense in which access to information is a privilege. There are severe limitations to what we can do on our own, epistemically speaking, to supply ourselves with information. It is the peculiar fate of human cognizers that their epistemic situations depend so much on others. In some cases, it may be that despite our best, coordinated efforts to find out how things are, we still fall short: we lack the technical or intellectual wherewithal to gather or process the information that is nonetheless "out there" in some important sense. (Obviously, many eventually discarded theories from the history of science will fall in this category.) But in other cases, we are subjected to significant disinformation. And just like access to information is a privilege, so being subjected to disinformation can amount to a form of victimization. I think this is an important reason to distinguish the question of whether someone is right to believe as they do (given their evidence) from whether what they believe is "right." It should also, I believe, be reflected in how we treat these people as moral and epistemic agents. However, and as I will argue in the book's final chapter, this rethinking of the normative contours of epistemology and reflective agency has no bearing on the question of whether the harms that might result from my mistaken (but justified) beliefs can violate others' moral (and legal) rights, and if so, whether they can rightly seek compensation for those harms.

---

[38] Primarily, of course, these "decisions" are to be construed in narrowly epistemic terms— i.e., what should we believe given our evidence? Answers to these questions then provide inputs to more familiar, practically oriented decision-making.

2

The Psychology of Stereotypes

We have provisionally defined a prejudice as a negatively charged stereotype, targeting some group of people, and, derivatively, the individuals who comprise this group. In defining prejudice in terms of stereotypes in this way, we are taking our cues from developments in twentieth-century cognitive and social psychology. To get our inquiry off on the right track, it will be helpful to have a brief look at some of the more relevant strands of this research. This can be beneficial not simply in the sense that it is often good to attempt to illuminate a problem from multiple angles at once. As we shall see in chapter 3, reflection on psychological research can also provide us with important information about where to set our normative ideals. Specifically, I will argue, we should set our epistemic ideals in a way that reflects the distinctive and inherent capacity limitations of the human mind. This is a crucial part of what I call "non-ideal epistemology."

2.1 Prejudices as Stereotypes

Psychologists commonly define prejudice as an attitude that has at once a doxastic, an affective, and a conative component (cf. Jackson 2011: 10ff; Dovidio et al. 2010: 5). Since this is an epistemological inquiry, much of our focus will naturally be with the doxastic component, i.e., the component that most closely resembles the notion of "belief" that is so familiar from philosophical discussion. Nonetheless, it behooves us, if only in passing, to also acknowledge the other dimensions. If prejudice were simply an entirely detached intellectual attitude, the pressure to write a book like this, not to mention the pressure to frame new policy initiatives and legal resources to combat discrimination, would be significantly decreased. Quite simply, the power of prejudice to motivate action through affective responses—so-called "hot cognition"—is central to defining it as the kind of problem that it is.[1]

---

[1] We can also mention the very real possibility that the affective and conative aspects of prejudice can linger in subjects even after the doxastic component has been defeated. This,

Psychologists of many stripes are broadly agreed that the doxastic component of prejudice can be specified in terms of a *stereotype* (cf. Ehrlich 1973; Brown 2010: chapter 4; Stangor 2009: 2–4; Jackson 2011). Stereotypes are broad ascriptions of salient or in some contextually relevant sense noteworthy properties to particular social groups, and derivatively, to the individuals who compose the group. Stereotypes can apparently take any valence—positive, negative, or neutral—corresponding to whether the property ascribed is taken to be positive, negative, or neutral. Theoretically, the social groups to which the properties are attributed could be individuated in any odd way. But it is hardly surprising that they quite often come to center on contextually salient social categories, such as gender, skin color, nationality, religion, etc. Familiar examples will include the stereotypes that Asians are good at math, Scandinavians are tall, Americans are crass, and so on. But there is nothing to stop us from also stereotyping more esoteric social categories, for instance in holding that Bostonians are bad drivers, golfers are snobs, or that Steely Dan fans lead impoverished social lives.

As noted in the previous chapter, we will leave open the question of whether prejudices—conceived in terms of stereotypes—must also be false. The primary motivation for leaving this question open is simply that, from the epistemological point of view that this book develops, nothing much hangs on the answer. While the "falseness-hypothesis" may seem intuitive, it is a matter of continued dispute among philosophers and psychologists whether it is correct.[2] Some psychologists, in particular Lee Jussim (see, e.g., Jussim et al. 2009; Jussim 2012), have argued that stereotypes often contain a "kernel of truth," and hold that this is key to explaining their persistence and social prevalence.[3] This research on "stereotype accuracy" remains controversial, and nothing in what follows will depend on it. In brief, though, I will point out that some of the examples that Jussim works with—e.g., "on average, women earn about 70% of what men earn" (Jussim et al., 2009: 202)—aren't particularly representative stereotypes, if indeed they are stereotypes at all. The problem has to do with the presence of statistical operators such as "on average" (or "most of," etc.) in the content of the attitude. On the view that I take, it is characteristic of stereotypes that

---

I surmise, is central to much of the research that goes on under the heading of "implicit bias," more about which in section 2.3 of this chapter.

[2] See, in particular, Beeghly 2015, forthcoming, MS.

[3] That is to say, they also serve a *cognitive* role beyond their presumptive role in consolidating our identity around some perception of "us" and "them" (or "in-group" and "out-group").

they involve a distinctive kind of qualitative, so-called "generic" ascription of properties, such as "women earn less than men." What Jussim's research may show is that a surprising number of people are reasonably up-to-date on basic social statistics. But these findings have no direct bearing on the psychology of stereotypes.[4]

We might, though, expect to find a surprising degree of accuracy along another dimension, namely in people's estimates of which stereotypes are prevalent in their society. That is, stereotypes tend to be broadly familiar—they are often part of "common ground" if not in the culture at large, then in some relevant sub-portion of it—even to people who plausibly claim not to endorse them. This is an important impetus for research on implicit bias, which we will look at in section 2.3. I will delve further into this aspect of stereotypes in chapter 7. We should also note that, even among people who do endorse a stereotype, there can be varying degrees of confidence in that stereotype. This will be an important point in chapters 4 and 5.

In defining prejudice as a negative stereotype, we are, then, following in the tracks of important research in twentieth-century cognitive and social psychology. As we go on, we will remain mindful of the slight complication noted in the previous chapter (1.2), namely that the question of which properties are negative in the relevant sense can be a highly context-sensitive affair. Moreover, we will note that the degree of negativity can of course vary, as will the degree to which being subjected to the prejudice is likely to affect people in their daily lives.[5]

2.2 The Cognitive Fundamentality of Stereotypes

With this minimum bit of theoretical scaffolding in place, it will be helpful to take a somewhat deeper dive into the underlying cognitive picture. One natural question is, if stereotype reasoning is what gives rise to prejudice, why is there stereotyping at all? Stereotyping seems like a "risky" form of cognition: not just epistemically risky, but morally risky as well.[6] Given these

---

[4] For a recent criticism of Jussim's work along these lines, see Bian and Cimpian 2016. I first defended the view that stereotypes are to be understood on the model of generics in Begby 2013, and develop it in more detail in chapter 5.

[5] Conceivably, we can have prejudiced beliefs about, say, some group's dietary habits which evoke very strong affective responses, but which wouldn't be very likely to seriously affect their targets in their professional or personal lives.

[6] For discussion, see Beeghly 2015, 2018, MS; Puddifoot 2017a, 2019.

risks, there's a reasonable question why we would use it. The answer points toward underlying structural features of human cognition: we use it because we must.

The human mind, let us agree, is an information processing system operating in real time. It is virtually trivial that any physically implemented information processing system will have certain inherent capacity limitations. There is only so much information it can store. There are only so many independent variables it can compute at a time. Given these limitations, and given the complexity of the environments that we find ourselves in, our minds face a constant threat of information overload. To deal effectively with this problem, we have evolved a number of specialized cognitive sub-systems, such as perception in its various modalities, several sorts of memory, mechanisms for allocating limited attentional resources, and so on. Additionally, we have developed a variety of algorithms for compressing or "chunking" this information for swift processing, storage, and retrieval. These evolved coping strategies, we might add, are not simply there to subserve a detached intellectual interest in how the world is. They are key to our coping and survival in our natural and social environments.[7]

Perception provides a richness of examples along these lines. Philosophers have long tended toward a view of perception as serving the functional role of providing us with maximally high-fidelity representations of what's going on in the world around us. We measure its success in terms of how closely it approximates this ideal. But as modern perceptual psychology convincingly shows, this suggests a hugely distorted picture of how perception actually works: perception involves an enormous amount of information filtering and compression at early stages, so as to facilitate efficient (and relevant) processing at later stages. From a highly detached ("idealizing") point of view, we can certainly ask whether it would not, in some sense, have been "better" if our perceptual systems engaged in less filtering and compression than they do, thereby providing us with less "biased" representations of the world. The right answer to this question must surely be that, well, if we had very different kinds of minds with significantly higher real-time processing capacities, then, yes; but given that we have the kinds of minds that we do, this is probably as good as (or sufficiently close to as good as) we can expect to do. The upshot of this reasoning, then, is that even forms of cognitive processing that involve

---

[7] See also Antony 2016 for a similar perspective, couched in terms of innate "biases."

significant filtering and compression and thereby an appreciable loss of "fidelity," can nonetheless be cognitively optimal, relative to our highly contingent, "non-ideal" cognitive starting points.

A central concept in these developments is that of *categorization*. Our distinctive mode of object cognition involves swiftly assigning stimuli to categories, and then drawing inferences from category membership. Color perception provides a good example. As is well-known, color stimuli occur along a continuous spectrum. Nonetheless, our color experiences swiftly assign particular stimuli to particular categories, e.g., "blue" or "green." Even when we look at continuously spaced color tiles (as in the Munsell color charts employed in the famous Berlin and Kay experiments)[8] the partition of the color spectrum into categories with relatively sharp boundaries is phenomenologically massively salient. Now, if it were simply the case that we *perceive* the spectrum as continuous and merely abide by a convention to name a certain portion of that spectrum "blue," another "green" and so on, there might not be much relevance to it. But things are not so simple. Specifically, we perceive two stimuli categorized as blue as being "more similar" (i.e., closer together on the color spectrum) than a stimulus categorized as blue and a stimulus categorized as green, despite the fact that the blue and green stimuli may actually be closer in shading than the two blue stimuli. This phenomenon is generally known as "intra-category assimilation" and "inter-category differentiation." It is a categorical bias deeply embedded in our information processing software. Again, we should feel free to ask questions here: inasmuch as it is a bias, it seems to involve misrepresentation or distortion of the phenomenon; so doesn't that mean that it is epistemically suboptimal? And in a way, surely it is; but again, only in the sense that we can imagine an information processing system with a different evolutionary history, greater computational powers, etc. Given *our* particular history, on the other hand, and the kinds of minds we have as a result, we can be reasonably certain that categorization is part of an optimal (or near enough) strategy for coping with complex information in real-time. The point is not simply that we are incapable of controlling the operations of these low-level evolved systems (i.e., they are automatic and "mandatory," in something like the sense of Fodor (1983)). Rather, the point is that despite the bias, despite the information loss, they are plausibly part of an overall cognitive optimization strategy, a strategy that we can imagine significantly

[8] Berlin and Kay 1969.

improved on only if we can imagine a significantly different, more high-powered cognitive system.[9]

The prevailing understanding of stereotyping in the psychological literature is that it is essentially just another manifestation of this cognitively fundamental operation of categorization, only localized to the domain of social cognition (cf. Fiske and Taylor 1991; Kunda 1999: 314; Hamilton and Sherman 1994; Brown 1995; Gaertner et al. 2010; Banaji and Greenwald 2013). That is to say, categorization is a fundamental cognitive process, operative in a wide variety of domains. Some of these operations fall within the remit of social cognition, i.e., cognition about other human beings, social relations, institutions, etc. Similar tendencies apply here: our basic socio-cognitive processes tend to overplay intra-group homogeneity and exaggerate inter-group contrast. So, in an important sense, our basic cognitive operations entail compression of complexity, and a resulting loss of fidelity and information. But that doesn't make stereotype reasoning a second-rate form of cognition, one that we could do without if, for instance, we made a concerted cognitive effort, paying closer attention to individual uniqueness.

2.2.1 The Role of Stereotypes in Social Cognition

To see better how this works, it is worthwhile taking a moment to consider just how rich and complex much of our social cognition is, and how lost we would be if we couldn't rely on the assumption that group membership could at least potentially provide valuable information about individuals. Quite simply, an enormous amount of bona fide knowledge is embedded in our classifications of people according to demographic traits, such as gender,

---

[9] Here's one perspective on this. Psychologists like Kahneman and Tversky (see Kahneman 2011 for a widely read popular account) have built careers out of demonstrating how our reliance on certain kinds of "heuristics" (i.e., shortcuts in cognitive processing) show that we are, much of the time, hopelessly irrational in our decision-making. Without disputing particular experimental findings, however, a good case can be made that many of these results are no more telling of irrationality than, say, the demonstrations of persistent perceptual illusions that are the currency of modern perceptual psychology. Demonstrations of perceptual illusions are scientifically useful in allowing us to reverse engineer the underlying computational principles of the relevant perceptual system (vision, audition, olfaction, etc.). The fact that they sometimes lead to distinctive kinds of error is not a strike against them: any compression algorithm will generate some such errors. The situation is similar in social and cognitive psychology: the characteristic errors on display in these experiments is no indication of widespread irrationality, but rather a matter of reasonable ("ecologically rational") heuristics being "caught out." (For perspectives on this, see Gigerenzer 2008; Gigerenzer and Brighton 2009; Lieder and Griffiths 2020. For philosophical reflection, see Dallmann 2017).

age, nationality, ethnicity, religion, and much else besides. More precise knowledge comes from stacking these categories on top of each other. Banaji and Greewald (2013: 81–2) provide a nice example of a "Six-Dimensional Person Category Generator" that randomly generates categories of people according to race, religion, age, nationality, gender, and occupation. The point is, you might never have met a white/Jewish/middle-aged/French/Female/professor, but you would certainly not start from epistemic scratch if you were introduced to one. These categorizations can provide genuine knowledge about the probability-space that this person moves within. We spontaneously use these stereotypes to draw further inferences, guide our social interactions, and so on.[10] Construed in such terms, these stereotype categories are not mere crutches of convenience, but "indispensable cognitive devices for understanding, negotiating and constructing our social world" (Brown 2010: 98). If we were consigned to respond to each individual anew we wouldn't be engaging in anything resembling social cognition as we know it.

It is worth noting that even philosophers who are strongly inclined to say that prejudice is intrinsically epistemically irrational will essentially agree on this point. For instance, Miranda Fricker emphasizes how such stereotype reasoning is crucial to normal human epistemic interactions. For instance, in deciding whether to trust another person's testimony, we must form on-the-fly "credibility judgements." She writes (2007: 32):

> barring a wealth of personal knowledge of the speaker as an individual, such a judgement of credibility must reflect some kind of social generalization about the epistemic trustworthiness—the competence and sincerity—of people of the speaker's social type, so that it is inevitable (and desirable) that the hearer should spontaneously avail himself of the relevant generalizations in the shorthand form of (reliable) stereotypes. Without such a heuristic aid he will not be able to achieve the normal spontaneity of credibility judgement that is characteristic of everyday testimonial exchange.

(As an example of such a reliable socio-epistemic generalization, she offers the stereotype of the "dependable family doctor.") In this sense, it is not just expedient to avail oneself of these generalizations in filtering and assigning

---

[10] As I will argue in chapter 7, the fact that they are so useful and so widespread, also provides people with a minimal incentive to comply with the stereotype expectations.

weight to incoming information. It is *necessary*, in the sense that we are faced with a variety of obligatory cognitive tasks whose timely execution fully depends on it.

Likewise, we may presume that packaging information in categorical terms—i.e., in the form of stereotypes—is a crucial way to effect social learning. In fact, it is very hard to imagine what social learning might consist in if it did not at least in significant part make reference to social categories and their salient properties. One way to put this point is to ask ourselves how, in many cases, one could even acquire the "wealth of personal know-ledge" that Fricker speaks about, except by using stereotype knowledge as a starting point. (It is, of course, important to teach *that* they are stereotypes, and that one should always remain mindful of the possibility that particular individuals may be "non-representative" in important respects. But that's fully consistent with the notion that stereotypes can encode socially signifi-cant knowledge, and may well, in many cases, be the only format in which to package and disseminate that knowledge.)

That said, there certainly are complications to consider here. For one, social cognition involves distinctively high-level forms of cognitive process-ing as compared with the more basic forms of processing involved, say, in perception. Many of the categories involved in perception (e.g., shape, color, texture) are plausibly innate, whereas the salient categories in social cogni-tion are largely learned. (For example, the notion of "nationality" as a distinctive and important social category is clearly a historically contingent product.) This is a learning process over which we can be expected to exercise some degree of cognitive control. Which is to say that the categories typically deployed in social cognition are precisely not mandatory in the way that the categories of perception are. As it happens, I think this is an important point, one that we would do well to fold into our further inquiries. But two brief points can be made in response. First, it may turn out that some of the categories involved in perception are also learned and not innate.[11] Second, the point can remain that even though the specific categories—and, relatedly, the specific content of the stereotype judgments we rely on—are highly contingent, the cognitive requirement of processing one's social experiences in categorical terms at all may still be innate. The

---

[11] For instance, I have argued at length (Begby 2017) that categories involved in the perceptual exercise of reading are the product of culture-specific learning. For another example, consider the claim (due to Winawer et al. 2007) that differences in conventional naming of parts of the color spectrum (e.g., the Russian language lexically encodes darker and lighter shades of blue under different names) yields differences in perception.

only question is which categories these are going to be. And here, contingent facts about one's social context—its institutional structure, cultural history, and so on—will play a crucial role in shaping one's learning environment. An argument could be made that no one could successfully navigate *this* particular social space—shaped as it is precisely around the widespread assumption, often institutionally encoded, that these are relevant social categorizations—without relying on these particular categories. (As we shall see in chapter 8, we can find ourselves in situations where we can genuinely bemoan the fact that these are relevant categories at all—for instance, categories of race in the contemporary United States—at the same time as we are effectively forced to carry out epistemic tasks using those very categories.)

In sum: prejudices are best understood as negative stereotypes. Stereotypes are rooted in the cognitively fundamental process of categorization; indeed, in an important sense, stereotyping just is the manifestation in the domain of social cognition of that cognitively fundamental process. So the first answer to the question, why should we rely on stereotypes at all, must surely be that we cannot but. Given the kinds of minds that we have, there is no other way that we could carry out a myriad of the obligatory epistemic tasks that confront us. After a brief detour via the concept of implicit bias, we will set about in chapter 3 drawing some important philosophical consequences of these insights.

2.3 Excursion: Why Not Implicit Bias?

At this point, a small excursion will be helpful in situating our inquiries in the larger landscape of contemporary philosophical discussion. Current discussion of issues related to prejudice, discrimination, and cognate phenomena are often cast in terms of the theoretical construct of "implicit bias," which purportedly reveals the "unconscious roots of prejudice."[12] Nonetheless, this concept plays no crucial role in my exposition, and I owe an explanation as to why.[13]

---

[12] See "Roots of Unconscious Prejudice Affect 90–95 Percent of People" https://www.wash ington.edu/news/1998/09/29/roots-of-unconscious-prejudice-affect-90-to-95-percent-of-people-psychologists-demonstrate-at-press-conference/.

[13] For recent expressions of philosophical interest in the concept, see Brownstein and Saul 2016; Beeghly and Madva, eds. 2020, and, for a bigger picture, Brownstein 2018.

As a scientific concept, the idea of implicit bias is of relatively recent vintage. It finds its natural home in a larger theory of the mind often referred to as "dual process theory." Dual process theory distinguishes between two levels of the mind, one "implicit," the other "explicit." "System 1" (the "implicit mind") is fast, approximative, largely automatic and operating below the threshold of conscious awareness. By contrast, "System 2" (the "explicit mind") is essentially the process of conscious reasoning: it is slow and effortful, but also promises to yield more precise computations. Whereas System 1 is highly economical, System 2 is a significant drag on resources, both cognitive and metabolic. Implicit biases exist at this automatic, largely inaccessible level of the mind. When they manifest in behavior, it can represent a conflict between System 1 and System 2.

In light of this, it is not uncommon to hear philosophers speak about implicit biases as though they were essentially "unconscious beliefs," or at least can be operationally defined, as beliefs often are, in terms of their impact on behavior. See, for instance, Keith Frankish (2016: 24): "a biased person is one who is disposed to judge others according to a stereotyped conception of their social group (ethnic, gender, class, and so on), rather than by their individual talents [...] A person is *implicitly* biased if their behaviour manifests a stereotyped conception of this kind, even if they do not explicitly endorse the conception and perhaps explicitly reject it."

These kinds of definitions are tendentious at best. It seems that we would want to know what an implicit bias is, while leaving open the question whether, to what extent, or in what contexts, it would have an appreciable impact on behavior.[14] More immediately, it seems like our best account of what implicit bias *is* makes no assumption that these biases are particularly belief-like. Instead, they are better understood as automatically activated conceptual associations.[15] Such associations play a crucial, functional cognitive role. The concepts that stock our minds are not organized listwise, but form an integrated structure of nodes with differential connectivity. Cognitive processing occurs at a furious pace: to ready ourselves for incoming stimuli, an activation of one concept will also activate (to a greater or lesser extent) a whole host of other concepts, which one is then ready to deploy in further processing. So, for instance, many of us presumably have

---

[14] In fact, I think it is a mistake to define even the more traditional concept of belief in terms of its impact on behavior (cf. my reflections on the belief-acceptance distinction in sections 1.5 and 9.1.3).

[15] See, for instance, del Pinal and Spaulding 2018.

fairly strong conceptual associations between "Italian" and "pasta." This sort of automatic co-activation strongly reduces processing time and effort. This pattern of automatic co-activation, then, is what an implicit bias is.

It is a fine question how these patterns of conceptual co-activation come to be tuned in the way that they do. It is certainly not a requirement that one endorses the notion, for instance, that all Italians love pasta. (Such endorsement would be a System 2 attitude: part of what is exciting about implicit bias research is precisely the wedge that it promises to drive between our consciously held attitudes and our underlying biases in cognitive processing.) Instead, they are tuned by exposure, either directly (by observing correlations) or indirectly (absorbing the stereotype that Italians eat a lot of pasta).[16] One particularly interesting strand of recent research into this suggests that even people who explicitly do *not* endorse the relevant stereotypes are nonetheless likely to encode the same implicit biases as the rest of us. In other words, mere exposure to a widespread stereotype will lead you to form the relevant implicit biases. In short, the implicit mind cares not one whit about what you *believe*, or which political or moral ideals you espouse. It cares only about efficient processing of information.

Precisely because implicit biases are so different from the epistemologist's standard notion of belief, it is very hard to know how to apply traditional normative epistemic categories to them. They are not, in any straightforward way, right or wrong (since they don't have propositional content). Nor do questions of epistemic justification arise, since they aren't beliefs formed in the light of evidence. Finally, since they take place at deep levels of cognition, below the threshold of awareness, and outside the remit of cognitive control, taking a normative stance becomes very challenging.[17] As the research suggests, even young Black males often encode an automatically triggered conceptual association between "young Black male" and "violence." Being socialized into a culture where this is a widespread stereotype is sufficient to generate the bias.

Considered simply in these cognitive terms, implicit bias might not seem like much. Nonetheless, it can have startling and sometimes tragic

---

[16] See Munton 2019a, for an account of how even the perceptual system can come to encode bias by way of its sensitivity to contingent demographic regularities in the social environment.

[17] See, e.g., Kelly and Roeddert 2008; Saul 2013; Fricker 2016; Levy 2016, 2017; Washington and Kelly 2016; Zheng 2016; Faucher 2016; Puddifoot 2017b; Lassiter and Ballantyne 2017; McHugh and Davidson 2020, for attempts to align our intuitions about moral responsibility for discrimination and harm with the reigning cognitive picture of implicit bias as operating below the threshold of awareness, being non-responsive to rational correction, etc.

real-world effects. For instance, in Keith Payne's famous "weapons bias" studies (Payne 2006), subjects are found to be significantly more prone to misidentify an everyday object (e.g., a tool) as a gun if primed with the face of a Black male. This phenomenon is plausibly explained by the assumption that our minds encode fairly strong conceptual connections between Black males and violence, whether or not we explicitly endorse this connection. Once our concept of Black male is activated, it automatically co-activates a host of other concepts, many relating to violent behavior. This then leads us to bias our visual search toward objects which fall within the remit of that concept-cluster, such as guns or knives. Shapes that without the prime would be readily seen as everyday objects are now interpreted by the visual system as weapons. In real-life situations such as law enforcement, or even ordinary citizens presuming to exercise their right to "stand their ground," the outcome can be as predictable as it is tragic.

Much of the present discussion centers on the "Implicit Association Test" ("IAT"),[18] a publicly available online test which purports to measure the degree to which particular individuals encode relevant biases. The Implicit Association Test works in the following way: subjects are presented with two tasks in succession; in the first task, they are asked to determine whether a certain stimulus (a word or a picture) belongs in this or that disjunctive category (e.g., "flower or pleasant," "insect or unpleasant"). The second task is the same, except the disjunctive categories have been mixed up: "flower or unpleasant"; "insect or pleasant." Your "score" on the test is the measure of the difference between the speed and accuracy with which you completed the second portion of the test and the speed and accuracy with which you completed the first portion of the test. The higher your score, the stronger your "automatic preference" for flowers over insects.

Now, presumably, no one really cares about our implicit attitudes with regard to flowers and insects. Moreover, it is hardly a surprise to learn that we encode such biases, insofar as they comport well with introspectable facts about ourselves. What is surprising, then, is the discovery that we get essentially the same range of results on these tests when we substitute categories of gender, race, sexuality, body type, etc. Moreover, individual people's scores on these tests do *not* seem to correlate with their explicit beliefs, espoused ideals, etc. It seems even non-racists can (and often do) encode "automatic preference" for White people over Black people.

---

[18] https://implicit.harvard.edu/implicit/takeatest.html.

After an initial period of fervor and excitement, during which the concept of implicit bias has taken hold of the public imagination in a way that few other psychological constructs have,[19] it is perhaps inevitable that the Implicit Association Test has more recently come in for heavy weather. One strand of critique concerns the IAT's "test-retest reliability." As it turns out, among the things that one's IAT score does not do very well is predicting how one will score the next time one takes the IAT.[20] To some, this strongly suggests that the IAT, despite the reassurances of Banaji and Greenwald, does not measure stable features of our cognitive outlooks. Instead, our results seem to fluctuate by arbitrary situational factors.[21]

A more immediately philosophically relevant concern has to do with "predictive validity." We want to know what we can infer from learning that a person receives a relatively high score on the IAT. Does it mean, for instance, that this person is more likely to engage in discriminatory behavior than someone with a lower score? Banaji and Greenwald (2013: 47–9) certainly argue that it does: they claim that IAT scores have been shown in individual studies to predict certain kinds of non-verbal behaviors (like coolness or apparent discomfort in speaking to a person of different race), as well as readiness to rate Black faces as more hostile or angry than White faces. Importantly, they claim that it also manifests in "real-world" behaviors like judging male candidates more favorably than female candidates with the same qualifications, or recommending different courses of treatment for Black and White patients in a medical setting.[22] Accordingly, they conclude (Banaji and Greenwald (2013: 47)) that the Race IAT "predicts discriminatory behavior even among research participants who earnestly (and, we believe, honestly) espouse egalitarian beliefs."[23]

Now, it is one thing to say that the IAT has some degree of predictive power (after all, we shouldn't in general be surprised to learn that our patterns of reflective reasoning are also mirrored in low-level cognitive

---

[19] See, for instance, high-profile public statements in 2016 from Hillary Clinton and James Comey, as well countless pamphlets, training programs, sponsored awareness campaigns, etc.

[20] See, for instance, Blanton and Jaccard 2008 for an early overview.

[21] Some researchers seem to have taken this problem to heart. For instance, a recent paper by Payne, Vuletich, and Lundberg (2017a: 233) argues that we should think of implicit bias tests "as measures of situations more than persons." For responses and further reflection, see, e.g., Kurdi and Banaji 2017; Rae and Greenwald 2017; Mitchell 2017; Payne, Vuletich, and Lundberg (2017b). (Thanks to Erin Beeghly for bringing this discussion to my attention.)

[22] Note, though, that they say very little about the size of this effect, i.e., just *how much* more favorably these subjects tended to judge the male candidates, etc.

[23] As we have seen, some philosophers go even further, essentially defining implicit bias in terms of its effects on behavior.

biases with more direct ties to our behavioral systems). Instead, what's exciting about this program is the suggestion that in cases where our explicit attitudes and our implicit biases appear to diverge, our best explanations will be lodged at the implicit level. This view is echoed also in a number of philosophical discussions. For a prominent example, consider Elizabeth Anderson (2010: 52):

> Several lines of evidence—notably, laboratory studies of implicit bias in cognition and covert discrimination, and public opinion surveys—support the view that racial stigmatization has gone underground in the face of laws and social norms that discourage racism—that is, explicit expressions of racial antipathy and overt discrimination. In form, racially stigmatizing ideas are now more likely to be embodied in subtle cognitive biases than in strongly felt emotions, more likely to be implicit, unconscious, or deniable than explicit and consciously avowed.

In brief: recent changes to laws and social norms haven't eradicated racism and other forms of prejudice so much as they have forced them "underground." They are now encoded in "unconscious" implicit biases which continue to exert a significant degree of control over our behavior, even as most of us, at a conscious, reflective level, continue to espouse egalitarian ideals. Presumably, then, the claim is that implicit bias fares significantly better at predicting (and explaining) racial discrimination in our current environment than do traditional "explicit" measures of belief (such as one might obtain from questionnaires based on the Modern Racism Scale).[24]

In the meantime, however, several meta-studies have emerged claiming to show the opposite: the IAT is in fact a rather poor predictor of discriminatory behavior, and indeed fares significantly worse in terms of predictive validity than the explicit measures.[25] Banaji and Greenwald have disputed these findings, and offered their own meta-analysis which paints a somewhat more hopeful picture. Luckily, we don't have to settle here the question of who is right on the precise details. The point is that even on Banaji and Greenwald's more hopeful picture, the predictive validity of the IAT is significantly weaker than what many philosophers seem to assume.

---

[24] On the motivations behind the Modern Racism Scale, see McConahey 1986.
[25] See, for instance, Oswald et al. 2013, 2015. For a response, see Greenwald, Banaji, and Nosek 2015. For a recent perspective, see Schimmach 2019.

Banaji and Greenwald claim to find that IAT scores show a "moderate" correlation with "discriminatory judgments and behavior" (Banaji and Greenwald (2013: 50). They write as follows: "Among researchers, there is a conventional understanding that a correlation of .10 is small, one of .30 is medium, and one of .50 or greater is large." Their reported correlation coefficient for the Race IAT and discriminatory behavior is .24, "close to the conventional 'medium' value of 0.30." Let's say we accept this claim;[26] what follows now? Banaji and Greenwald provide a helpful unpacking: "The correlation value of .24 means that, in a situation in which discrimination might be shown by 50 percent of those for whom we have Race IAT scores, we can expect that discrimination to be shown by 62 percent of those having automatic White preference scores in the top half of the overall distribution of scores, compared to the 38 percent of those in the bottom half" (2013: 51).

Let us take a moment to consider what this means. Let's say we have twenty people, ten of whom will have been found independently to display some kind of discriminatory behavior. Now we take their IAT scores and sort them into two piles, one containing the highest 50 percent of the scores, the other containing the lowest 50 percent of the scores. (Note that we do no further ranking of the scores in each group, nor do we ask what the variance in score is between the high group and the low group.) Now, the claim is just that, of these ten people, six will come from the high group, four will come from the low group. Even in the best of circumstances, then, we should expect that the IAT only slightly outperforms a random choice in terms of predicting discriminatory behavior.

In other words, even if we accept Banaji and Greenwald's own account of the predictive validity of the IAT, it seems like the results are still some way off from providing support for the sweeping claims that are sometimes made in its name, for instance, that "we" (presumably meant to be a maximally inclusive "we") are "very likely to make inaccurate judgments" about who is the best candidate for a job, about which paper is better than another, and so forth (Saul 2013: 246). Maybe we are. But the IAT provides very little evidence to this effect.

Now, of course, there is more to the notion of implicit bias than the IAT, a point that often goes missing among critics. The IAT is merely a proposed

---

[26] We might still have substantial concerns about publication bias in the meta-study: if the meta-study only includes published works, then there is good reason to believe it will be significantly biased in favor of positive results, simply because inconclusive results are less likely to be published.

tool for detecting and measuring implicit bias, and should not be confused with the phenomenon itself.[27] So I want to be very clear about one thing: I do believe that implicit bias exists; in fact, I take its existence to be predicted by pretty much any viable theory of the mind. We can presumably agree to this, even if we disagree about the extent to which popular tests like the IAT are scientifically reputable means of detecting and measuring such bias. What is in question is what we can assume about its effect on discriminatory behaviors. Payne's weapons-bias cases are among the best supported of these studies. But note that, as Payne reports (Payne 2006: 287–8), the observed effect only obtains under severe time pressure (at time intervals shorter than half a second). It all but goes away in a "self-paced" condition, when subjects are given more time to consider the situation.

Of course, this is hardly a trivial result. Since this is precisely the time scale on which life-and-death decisions are regularly made by law enforcement officers, it is indeed quite plausible that weapons bias can serve as a causal, explanatory factor with respect to the apparently racially motivated discrepancies in police violence records. Moreover, it is plausible that it can have this effect regardless of whether the officers in question would also be found to hold "explicit" racial prejudice. But this just highlights the fact that most of us are not called on to make our cognitive decisions under such time restrictions (or similar pressure factors), and so, there is very little empirical grounds for extending the claim to discrimination, say, in hiring decisions. To be very clear: I am obviously not disputing that such discrimination exists and merits an explanation, quite the contrary. What is in question, instead, is the extent to which appealing to implicit bias, as opposed to the more familiar phenomenon of ("explicit") prejudice, will be a helpful part of that explanation.

I want to note that it fundamentally doesn't matter to my argument that prejudiced belief be construed as "explicit" *as opposed to* "implicit." For instance, it is perfectly consistent with my position that "belief" can come in varying degrees of reflexive awareness. Moreover (and as we shall see in more detail in chapter 10), it is no part of my view that agents can only be held morally accountable for their actions if they prescind from reflectively avowed values and ideals. Finally, I believe that implicit bias is a genuine phenomenon (i.e., not an artifact of a particular measurement tool or a misguided theory of the mind), and I am fully open to the possibility that

---

[27] See, e.g., Payne, Niemi, and Doris 2018.

there can be situations in which our explicitly held beliefs and our implicit biases pull in different directions. But none of this entails that we generally do better to seek accounts of prejudice which bypass the level of belief and focus instead on implicit bias. Importantly, it seems that research on implicit bias is also coming around to de-emphasizing the implicit-explicit contrast (cf. Brownstein, Madva, and Gawronski 2019, Beeghly and Madva 2020). As such, I am perfectly happy to allow that these may be complementary rather than competing forms of explanation.[28]

2.4 Summary and Look Ahead

In sum, psychological inquiry over the past half century helps sheds philosophical light on the question not just of what prejudiced belief is—viz. a form of stereotype judgment—but also reveals stereotyping as being a deep-rooted, arguably unavoidable feature of our cognitive architecture. Reliance on stereotypes is essential to our ability to function in complex social settings.

In the next chapter, we will begin to probe the epistemological consequences of these insights. As a brief preview: I will argue that no epistemological aspersions can be cast on prejudice as such, simply in virtue of the fact that it instantiates a particular kind of cognition, namely stereotyping. So a direct argument to the effect that prejudice is always a manifestation of epistemic irrationality will have to take the more circuitous route of probing specific cases. This will be my focus in chapters 4 and 5. Meanwhile, please note that to say that stereotyping is cognitively fundamental, and therefore not intrinsically epistemically irrational, does not mean that we never commit epistemic wrongs in stereotype reasoning. Of course we do: we can, for instance, *overrely* on stereotypes, failing to absorb relevant new information, in particular, failing to track stereotype-discordant information about particular individuals. It will turn out to be a complex question, however, just how our epistemic norms will require us to update our prejudiced beliefs in light of new information. (This is our topic in chapter 5.)

---

[28] Thanks for Erin Beeghly for discussion.

3

From Psychology to Philosophy

The Case for a Non-Ideal Epistemology

In chapter 1, we introduced some theoretical choices which jointly make for a relatively familiar form of epistemic fallibilism. The problem of epistemology, as I conceive of it, is essentially a matter of decision-making under uncertainty. Epistemic norms are guides to such decision-making. But these norms are not fool-proof: they can only ameliorate the risk, not eliminate it altogether. The world being what it is, even perfect epistemic rationality is no guarantee of true belief.

After surveying some relevant psychological work on stereotyping and prejudice in chapter 2, we are now in a position to transform this so-far rather non-assuming form of epistemic fallibilism into a more radical program which we can call "non-ideal epistemology." "Non-ideal epistemology" is a term that has gained some currency in recent years. Still, it remains a neologism of sorts, and it is not obvious what one should mean by it. In one way, the term can serve as a powerful reminder that knowledge—as well as claims to know, social routines for settling who gets to make such claims, and so forth—is often entangled with questions of power and ideology. The critical impetus behind non-ideal epistemology in this guise is the notion that epistemologists should devote more time to considering how practices of knowledge are situated in non-ideal social contexts.[1] As such, "non-ideal epistemology" could be seen primarily as a complement to the call for a non-ideal approach to questions of social and political justice, echoing recent criticisms of Rawlsian "ideal theory" approaches.[2]

I certainly share this interest. Even so, my own attempt to give content to the notion of non-ideal epistemology proceeds, at least initially, in a

---

[1] See Begby 2020b for a parallel development in philosophy of language.
[2] See, in particular, Mills 2005, but also Anderson (2010: section 1.2); Medina (2013: 11–13). Though notice how Mills already includes assumptions about "idealized capacities" and "idealized cognitive sphere" as part of his criticism of ideal theory.

somewhat different direction. It is certainly my hope that it may end up contributing crucially also to a critical analysis of the social structures that underlie information production, dissemination, and consumption. By going the more indirect route, however, we may be able to connect our inquiry in a more decisive way with traditional conceptions of epistemic normativity, thereby giving more force to the call for an applied, situated social epistemology.

3.1 Dimensions of Non-Ideal Epistemology (i): Endogenous Non-Ideality

A first concern one might have about the epistemological standing of prejudiced belief is simply that it is rooted in a particular *form* of cognition, viz. stereotyping. Ideally, one might think, our reasoning about other people should exclusively track individuals and their (relevant) properties. By contrast, reliance on stereotypes is lazy reasoning, "the (mental) sluggard's best friend" (Gilbert and Hixon 1991: 509).

One interesting upshot of this way of thinking is that it would seem to entail that prejudiced belief could be identified and corrected by intro-spective reflection alone. That is, subjects can recognize that their mental representations instantiate a certain *form*, namely that of stereotyping. Without having to consider further the merits of the belief-content itself, they could thereby know that any belief of that form is epistemically sub-par. If they are suitably motivated by epistemic virtue, they can then foreswear its use altogether, either replacing it with more circumspect representations (where these are available) or simply giving up on having thoughts in this area at all. So if one cannot think in more precise terms, say, about women's mathematical abilities, then one just shouldn't have any thoughts about it at all.

But this is a *very* naïve view. The naivety, though, would not lie in the thought that we can introspectively ascertain when we are engaging in stereotyping. Rather, the naivety would lie in the twin assumptions that (i) we are capable of refraining from stereotyping at will,[3] and (ii) that anything good, epistemically speaking, would come out of our doing so. As we saw in chapter 2, contemporary psychology teaches that stereotyping is cognitively

---

[3] We might be capable of so refraining in particular instances, but presumably not across the board.

fundamental for human beings: it is the basic shape of our social cognition, just like categorization is the basic shape of our object cognition more broadly. To refrain from deploying stereotypes is just to stop engaging in certain kinds of cognition. This is not something we can do, and it wouldn't be to anyone's epistemic benefit if we did.

This reasoning provides crucial input to non-ideal epistemology under the guise of what I will call "endogenous non-ideality," a form of non-ideality that arises from intrinsic capacity limitations of the cognitive system itself.[4] Non-ideal epistemology, as I propose to think of it, is first and foremost a systematic attempt to render epistemological norms relevant and applicable to the human situation. The claim at stake here is not whether idealization can ever have any role to play in epistemology, or that we couldn't learn anything from explanations that invoke idealized models. What is at stake, rather, is the nature of the concessions that epistemological theory must make to contingent facts about human beings and the settings in which they typically exercise their epistemic agency. It is often assumed that our epistemic "ideals"—i.e., our epistemic norms in the fullest sense—should make no such concessions. Human cognitive frailties and imperfections of various kinds can only be considered as excusing conditions at best. Studying them provides no insight into the nature of justified belief.

While familiar and commonplace, I don't think such a view can be sustained. Any sensible approach to epistemic normativity must begin by taking account of the kind of cognitive system to which the norms are supposed to apply. We can think about it this way: whatever the epistemic norms are, they are norms that are meant to govern the transition from evidence to belief. So right away, we must consider what range of evidence the system is capable of responding to. For a simple example, consider the fact that normal human hearing tapers off quite dramatically around 20 kHz. From one perspective, this is surely non-ideal: after all, dogs can hear frequencies up to 45 kHz. If we had that ability, we would be able to respond to a greater range of evidence than we in fact are. But being non-receptive to ultrasonic frequencies is hardly an imperfection in human information processing. Rather, it is a systemic constraint: our perceptual

---

[4] See Dallmann 2017 for a particularly illuminating illustration of the importance of taking distinctively human capacity limitations into account. For a broader motivation from philosophy of science, see Wimsatt 2007.

system is just not built that way.[5] Our applications of epistemic norms must reflect this systemic constraint: we cannot routinely be held responsible to evidence outside the range of our perceptual sensitivity.

Similar systemic constraints exist also for information processing that occurs fully "inside the mind": we have limited memory, limited attentional capacities, etc. When human beings taking part in the famous experiment of Simons and Chabris on inattentional blindness fail to register the presence of a gorilla moving around in the middle of their visual field, they aren't simply being stupid. Rather, they are taking part in a psychological demonstration carefully crafted to showcase the specific resource limitations of human visual attention.[6]

As philosophers, we can certainly transport ourselves into a frame of mind where we can think that these system limitations are in some important sense "non-ideal." This is just to say that we can imagine cognitive systems with more capacious memory, greater attentional capacities, etc. But we can't plausibly let such flights of fancy set our epistemic norms, since at the limit, we would essentially just be imagining a cognitive system with no such constraints. Leibniz's God might serve as an example. Here's our problem: we said that the epistemic norm, whatever it is, is a norm that governs inference from evidence (and typically incomplete evidence at that). Precisely in virtue of being omniscient, however, Leibniz's God is not in the business of drawing inferences from evidence at all. Therefore, no such norms would apply. Alternatively, consider Laplace's Demon, which could in some sense be said to engage in inference from evidence (i.e., strict computation). But Laplace's Demon is provided from the start with complete evidence, and moreover evidence that is known to be complete (i.e., the laws of nature, plus a complete state description of the physical universe at a given time). This is precisely what we couldn't have, given the kinds of minds we are supplied with. Accordingly, Laplace's Demon is licensed to deploy epistemic procedures that are unavailable to us. (Even if, impossibly, we did have the complete evidence, we couldn't know that we did, and so we wouldn't be in a position to validate the computational processes in question. No such concerns arise for Laplace's Demon.)[7]

---

[5] Similar, of course, for vision: while human eyes have three photoreceptors, those of the mantis shrimp have up to sixteen, enabling them, among other things, to detect polarized light. I admit, this would be *way cool*. But sadly, our eyes are not built that way.

[6] Simons and Chabris 1999.

[7] A similar theme is sounded in David Christensen's critique of "ideal credibility" conceptions of evidence. On this, see Christensen 2010.

Inference from incomplete evidence is inherently uncertain, and so is only a viable epistemic strategy for finite minds such as ours. Accordingly, the epistemic norms we seek must be ones that provide guidance for decision-making under uncertainty. As such, they don't even apply in the limiting case of an infinite intellect. They apply only to recognizably finite minds. Now, all finite minds are essentially "non-ideal" along some parameter or other. Our epistemic norms must make *some* concession to cognitive finitude. So why not just relativize them right away to a realistic picture of human cognitive limitations? After all, it would be quite arbitrary to relativize them to some other hypothetical cognitive system, perhaps less constrained than ours, but nonetheless decidedly non-ideal.

The first lesson for non-ideal epistemology, then, is that we must take care to articulate our epistemic norms in a manner that takes into account the intrinsic limitations of the cognitive system whose performance we are trying to assess. As epistemologists, we tend not to consider the fact that it is *human* epistemology—not Chimpanzee epistemology, or Universal Turing Machine epistemology—that we are interested in studying.[8] But surely it is: the familiar teachings of traditional epistemology would not even apply to cognitive systems with hugely different sensory systems or conceptual resources than ours.

To return to our topic: it is undeniably true that stereotyping involves compression of information and therefore an appreciable loss of fidelity in processing. But this compression algorithm is arguably written into the cognitive architecture of human beings. Even algorithms that involve systematic information loss in this sense can be cognitively optimal (or near enough) *given* our non-ideal cognitive starting points. In general, cognitive systems are tasked with devising strategies that offer a beneficial trade-off between processing cost and information gain. It is assumed that a strategy that involves an appreciable loss of fidelity can nonetheless be cognitively optimal (i.e., possess the highest expected utility overall).

Therefore, no epistemological aspersions can be cast on prejudiced belief just in virtue of its instantiating a certain form of cognition. These reflections on the epistemic significance of cognitive finitude speak to a form of

---

[8] It is remarkable how different, in this regard, much of our contemporary discourse is from the tradition of philosophers like Hobbes, Locke, Hume, Berkeley, Reid, Condillac, and Mill, all of whom were intensely preoccupied with developing our understanding of the *human* epistemic predicament in particular.

endogenous non-ideality, i.e., a form of non-ideality which arises from intrinsic capacity limitations of the cognitive system itself.

3.1.1 Objections to Non-Idealized Epistemic Normativity

Nonetheless, the idea that an acknowledgement of such capacity limitations should be built into the epistemic norm itself may seem to run counter to a number of philosophical intuitions, some older, some more recent. For instance, one long-standing objection to the kind of approach I offer would point to the fact that psychology is engaged in a "descriptive" enterprise whereas epistemology is engaged in a "normative" enterprise: since we can't derive an "ought" from an "is" we should resist the idea that our epistemology of prejudice could take its cues from empirical psychology in this way. That is, the psychological account of prejudice as rooted in a non-optional form of cognitive processing may well be correct, but is still of dubious relevance to the agenda of a normative epistemology. I hope we can put this sort of worry to rest at this point: far from abdicating the task of giving content to epistemic norms by drawing lessons from empirical psychology, non-ideal epistemology sets us on the path to uncovering the correct (relevant) norms. As I have argued, an account of epistemic normativity which presumed to make no such concessions would hardly even be cogent.

A much more sophisticated objection comes from contemporary externalists, who argue that the fact that a certain norm is impossible to fulfill does not mean that the norm does not hold, or is not binding.[9] Specifically, it does not mean that the norm is really something else, for instance an obligation to *approximate the ideal* or to *do one's best to fulfill the norm*, to the extent that our limited abilities permit.[10] Certainly, we can acknowledge the force of this objection in certain cases: say I have promised to pick you up at the airport at 5.15. I set out from home at 4, but then halfway there my car breaks down, leaving me with no actual way to get to the airport on time. I can't claim at that point to have fulfilled my obligation to you simply in virtue of having *done my best* to pick you up at the airport. All I can do is ask

---

[9] On analogy, perhaps, with Kant's view of virtue as an objectively unattainable ideal which it is nonetheless our duty to seek "constant approximation to" (Kant 1797: 167). For contemporary discussion of the binding force of unfulfillable norms, see Zynda 1996 and DiPaolo 2019.

[10] Cf. Williamson forthcoming.

to be excused for my failure to fulfill my obligation, because circumstances beyond my control prevented me from doing so.

But it is doubtful whether this strategy could apply in full generality, making no concessions to capacity limitations. Take an epistemological analogy: π figures in many important calculations. Let's say someone proposed that we are epistemically obligated to make our calculations maximally transparent and precise, and so, that we should ideally know all the decimals of π. The reason this couldn't be an epistemic obligation is not that it would be pointless, and that we have better things to do in our epistemic lives (though these are also relevant concerns). Rather, the reason is precisely that π has infinitely many decimals, and we have only finite minds. (By contrast, Leibniz's God could—and does—know all the decimals of π. But as Leibniz might say, this is not because he has calculated the sequence to its end—there is no such end—but rather because he grasps the whole sequence in a single instance.[11] That's not the kind of mind that we have.)

Importantly, though, even if we do relativize our epistemic ideals in concession to capacity limitations in this way, we can honor the externalist intuition that even unfulfillable norms can be genuinely binding. For instance, our account of epistemic normativity takes no heed of the fact that human beings, plausibly, also have a number of other non-epistemic obligations weighing on them, which limit the extent to which they can fulfill their epistemic obligations. So it is not, in general, as if by drawing the epistemological consequences of cognitive finitude, we are deflating all epistemic obligations to "do the best that you can."[12] On the view that I am proposing, epistemic norms should be relativized to *intrinsic capacity limitations* on information processing, not to *extrinsic constraints on performance* which limit our ability to maximize our epistemic potential in

---

[11] Cf. *Theodicy* § 360.

[12] Compare Alston (1988: 145), who argues for a distinction between "counsels of perfection" and "what it is reasonable to expect of a person." Similarly, José Medina warns against conceptions of epistemic normativity that would be "*overly demanding*" (2013: 156): instead we must seek to establish "reasonable normative expectations, without demanding heroic behavior" (2013: 120). My approach to non-ideal epistemology is perfectly compatible with the idea that the requirements of epistemic normativity may far exceed "what it is reasonable to expect of a person" in this sense. Similarly, I hope it will be clear that my account is not simply an instance of "ought-implies-can." Admittedly, there is no univocal sense of "can" which is assumed throughout discussions of "ought-implies-can" (cf. King 2019). But with respect to developing an account of endogenous non-ideality, the driving concern is not so much that we couldn't—because of our cognitive limitations—be able to fulfill the more exacting norms; rather, the idea is that any creature exhibiting *no* such limitations wouldn't be engaging in the kind of activity to which such norms would apply in the first place.

context. For instance, our information processing mechanisms have fairly high metabolic demands: quite simply, we have to eat well to perform well, in cognition no less than in athletics. There is no need, however, to bring these limitations into our account of epistemic normativity. If someone performs poorly because of low blood sugar, they may be excused, but will not have satisfied the epistemic norms.

This, then, shows how non-ideal epistemology can accommodate the distinction between justified belief and blameless belief, which is so important to externalists. A belief is justified if and only if it is the output of a cognitive process working optimally given its endogenous constraints. For the system to work optimally, certain peripheral conditions also must be in place, such as sufficient caloric intake to support the metabolic demands: an unjustified belief can be blameless if it is the result of one of the peripheral conditions failing. For instance, someone who is facing serious cognitive depletion and miscalculates a quadratic equation under time pressure may well be excused. He might have done as well as he could; but he has not done something right, epistemically speaking.[13]

Finally, we can also note how the terminology itself can be apt to get us confused here. Some might think that "ideal" here just means "norm" (i.e., in the sense of "something to strive for"), so that "non-ideal epistemology" could only ever signal a form of epistemology which entirely jettisons the normative perspective. But this is a mistake: "non-ideal" means a lifting of idealizations, not an abandonment of goal-setting. An idealization would be, for instance, the assumption that human beings have infinite working memory.[14] By jettisoning that idealization, we are not abandoning the normative perspective, but rather working toward setting a relevant norm.

---

[13] Further questions lurk down this path, of course. For instance, if our epistemic performance depends on our metabolic system, should we also recognize a norm of maintaining a good diet before engaging in difficult epistemic tasks? Moreover, are these "sandwich reasons" (as discussed in Fleisher 2018 and Horowitz 2019) themselves epistemic reasons or simply practical reasons? While certainly interesting, there is no need to address these questions in full here. The present point is simply that epistemic norms should (minimally) be relativized to our intrinsic capacity limitations. I have argued that one may be epistemically blameless but never justified in a case where one's error is the result, say, of cognitive depletion from forgetting to eat. The debate about "sandwich reasons" is best understood as the question of the extent to which one is even blameless in these situations. This has no bearing on my claim that a belief is justified if and only if it is the output of a cognitive process working optimally given its endogenous constraints. (Thanks to Arianna Falbo for calling my attention to these discussions.)

[14] Cf. Chomsky (1965: 3), who thinks that factors such as limitations on memory, attention, etc., should not be reflected in our scientific account of linguistic competence. So far as our linguistic competence is concerned, Chomsky argues, there is no barrier, for instance, to producing and processing infinitely long strings. The fact that we can't do so is entirely down

Even within non-ideal epistemology, we can clearly do better or worse as epistemic agents. In particular, while I have argued that the non-ideal perspective shows that there is nothing intrinsically wrong with deploying stereotypes in one's social cognition, one can still violate one's epistemic obligations by *overrelying* on stereotypes—for instance, by entirely failing to open mental files tracking stereotype-discordant information about individuals. So non-ideal epistemology is fully consistent with the notion that epistemology sets cognitive "ideals" that we can fall significantly short of. It is just a question of where those ideals should be set, and, in particular, to what extent they should reflect the intrinsic capacity limitations of the human mind.[15]

3.2 Dimensions of Non-Ideal Epistemology (ii): Exogenous Non-Ideality

The argument so far has sought to establish the claim that we cannot cast serious epistemological aspersions on prejudice simply in virtue of its instantiating a certain form. Nothing further will be added to this claim in the following. But this marks only one dimension of non-ideality; it is now time to introduce a second dimension, whose full consequences we will in effect be charting over the next several chapters.

Epistemology is about norms of information processing, specifically about inference from evidence. To articulate these norms, we must not

---

producing and processing infinitely long strings. The fact that we can't do so is entirely down to performance limitations, which shouldn't be reflected in our account of competence. My point here is not to endorse or criticize the utility of such idealizations in the context of linguistic theory. But notice, crucially, that Chomsky's "ideal speaker-listener" is in no way a "normative ideal," i.e., something that ordinary speakers should aspire to. The sort of normative perspective that epistemologists routinely adopt is completely foreign to Chomsky's approach.

[15] This terminological confusion can show up in surprising ways. For instance, in an otherwise wonderfully perceptive article, Robert Pasnau (2014) quite clearly equates "epistemic idealization" with the setting of epistemic norms (e.g., "ideals"). On this basis, he contrasts such a normative project with the more metaphysically tinged project of setting minimum boundary conditions for something to count as knowledge. But then, when it comes to saying where these "ideals" should be set, Pasnau assumes that "no one will dispute" that the account should "not involve abstracting away from all human cognitive limitations" but should instead focus on "what would count as perfection for beings such as us, in a world such as ours" (Pasnau 2014: 1006–7). It is clear, then, that what Pasnau calls "epistemology idealized" is essentially just what

only look at the internal workings of the information processing system, but must also consider how that system is supplied with information, i.e., the "input" to the whole process. As we attempt to reflect systematically on this, we must eventually reckon with a second dimension of non-ideality—perhaps more familiar to philosophers than the first—namely *exogenous* non-ideality. This is a form of non-ideality which stems from limitations on the informational context that the subject is forced to operate within.

In thinking about epistemological normativity, we must distinguish between perfect rationality and perfect information. Even an agent who evinces perfect rationality in information processing is hostage to the quality of information she has access to.[16] Mainstream epistemological approaches sometimes underplay this distinction. For instance, Bayesianism is often taken to proceed from the assumption that it doesn't matter where your priors are set, since it will all wash out with enough evidence. Differently put, two perfectly rational agents with arbitrarily set priors (short of 0 or 1) will converge on posteriors with enough evidence, simply in virtue of being rational, i.e., by following the canons of Bayesian conditionalization.[17] This is plausibly correct on certain idealizations. But it is extremely doubtful that these idealizations have much application to human epistemology. Most obviously, Bayesian convergence requires a fullness of time which is simply not realizable in the life span of human agents.

Much of the pathway toward considering exogenous non-ideality is broadly familiar to contemporary epistemologists, albeit in a fragmented and unsystematic way. And ultimately, we might well have to concede that these issues—which get extremely complicated very soon—cannot be finally resolved. Nonetheless, even some rather quick reflections should be sufficient to provide us with a workable sense of what is at stake, enough to put us on track for the argument of the following chapters.

To get us started, let us assume, as noted in chapter 1, that evidence is what justifies belief. Right away, we have a problem: *how much* evidence is required to justify a belief? Considerations from endogenous non-ideality

---

[16] By contrast, recall from above how a cognitive system like Laplace's Demon can be presumed to simply have all the relevant information already, and, moreover, to know that its information is complete.

[17] This is generally known as "Bayesian-convergence-to-the-truth." See, for instance, Joyce (2010: 446), who argues that convergence is to be expected "because the data is so incredibly informative in the limit that the subject's prior beliefs are irrelevant to her final view as a matter of logic."

dictate that the answer cannot be *all* of the evidence. No cognitively finite agent could ever possess all the evidence, and would not be able to process it even if they did.

But at the same time, it seems rather too permissive to say that beliefs are justified (or not) simply in light of the evidence that the agent actually has in her possession. In familiar ways, an agent might have neglected to gather evidence which would, for all she is entitled to believe, have defeated her justification.[18] So, for instance, if you are an Internal Reviews officer investigating an alleged case of police brutality, you are not justified in exonerating your fellow police officer if you simply fail to interview witnesses or seek out CCTV footage.

A familiar way of articulating this point is to say that our epistemic responsibilities encompass not only how you process the evidence that you have, but also what you do to provide yourself with evidence. You could be culpably violating your epistemic responsibilities in both these dimensions. That is, you have a secondary epistemic obligation to supply yourself with evidence. Specifically, you cannot retain your justification by neglecting or shielding yourself against new evidence.[19]

So, what justifies belief cannot be all the evidence, nor can it simply be the evidence that the agent actually has in her possession. What, then? It seems quite common now to seek a compromise of sorts: beliefs are justified (or not) in light of the *evidence available to the agent*, whether or not she has actually availed herself of this evidence. As Thomas Kelly puts it (Kelly 2006/ 2014): "Given the thesis that evidence is that which justifies belief, one's intuitions about the evidence that is available to an individual in a hypothetical scenario will shape one's views about what the individual would be justified in believing in that scenario."

The available evidence thesis has the air of a truism: something that just has to be right. Even so, there are concerns. One concern that is sometimes voiced is that the thesis is dubiously helpful, even if it is true. We can point to particular cases where an agent's neglect of available evidence undermined her justification. (Aristotle's belief that women have fewer teeth than men

---

[18] Cf. Harman 1973: 151–2. See also Clarke 2014 and Goldberg 2017 on "should have known."

[19] For a particularly clear example, see Hall and Johnson (1998: 133): "For any proposition that is less than certain on one's present evidence, one has an epistemic duty to seek more evidence about that proposition." See also Buchak 2010 and Horowitz 2019 for more critical discussion of the assumption of a generalized epistemic obligation to seek more evidence.

seems like a good candidate.)[20] But it's difficult to say in general terms what it takes for a particular piece of evidence to be available.[21] Michael Zimmerman captures this frustration nicely: "We must distinguish between evidence that is *available* to someone and evidence of which that person in fact *avails* himself. Available evidence is evidence of which someone *can*, in some sense, and *ought*, in some sense, to avail himself. I confess that the exact sense of this "can" and "ought" still elude me" (Zimmerman 2008: 35–6).

We cannot hope here to settle precisely what it means for some piece of evidence to be available, such that epistemic agents should be held responsible to it. But even the vague, "intuitive" sense of availability is arguably sufficient to ground the meta-epistemological lessons we need to draw here.

The unavailability of potentially important pieces of evidence is a feature of the human condition. It is reflected in our best epistemic methods. It is why we opt for a fallibilist epistemology, and why we counsel rational believers never to assign credence 1 to inductively acquired beliefs.

Some of the ways in which evidence can be unavailable are familiar and easy to ascertain. It can be buried deep on the ocean floor, where we have no technological means of gathering it. It can be evidence that will only unfold in a fullness of time that may lay well beyond the reach of human existence. The epistemic norm governing inference from evidence *has* to be a norm which permits us to form beliefs on limited evidence. No epistemologist should hold that we are never justified in forming any beliefs, simply because our evidence base is incomplete. Exogenous non-ideality, then, is simply the idea that which beliefs you are justified in forming must presumably reflect the particular, contingent subset of the total evidence that is available to you. Other subjects, with access to different subsets of the total evidence, would be justified in forming a different set of beliefs.[22]

---

[20] HA 2.3.501b19–21.   [21] Cf. Lycan 1977 for an early catalogue of such difficulties.

[22] Again, it is worth noting that this is not simply an instance of ought-implies-can transposed to the domain of epistemic normativity. For the claim at stake is not that someone would be *incapable* of forming true beliefs in this context, but that it wouldn't be *epistemically rational* for them to do so. A quick dip into the history of philosophy provides a valuable lesson here. Aquinas (*ST* I-II, q. 76, art. 2) terms "invincible ignorance" any form of ignorance that cannot be "overcome by study." In apparent keeping with ought-implies-can, he then argues that since subjects operating under invincible ignorance are "unable to know," they cannot be committing a sin. Vitoria (1532, relevant selections reprinted with commentary in Reichberg, Syse, and Begby 2006: 295–6) provides a crucial amendment to this argument. Vitoria's context is the question of whether the native peoples of America were committing a sin in failing to accept the word of Christ as presented to them by the Spanish *Conquistadores*. Vitoria's rebuttal does not claim, per se, that they would be incapable of entertaining the Christian faith: after all,

But there's a particular way in which evidence can be unavailable which can cause greater concern. Quite often, our access to evidence will be modulated by *human interference*. This certainly sounds ominous, calling to mind ideas about censorship, information suppression, and manipulation. But it can't *always* be bad: as epistemologists have become accustomed to recognize, our epistemic dependence on others is really a feature of the human condition. No one can expect to live anything remotely recognizable as a human life—probably no life at all—if they weren't set up to consume information from others.

So, what information is available to us will depend in part on our socio-epistemic context. In any complex society, what information is available, boosted, given the stamp of authority, and so on, will carry this imprint of human interference. In many cases, this is an immense epistemic boon. But in other cases, it will be bad. It could be bad simply because there is widespread ignorance in the society in question. But it could be even worse if the society is in the grips of a pernicious ideology, such as sexism or racism.

In general, we cannot expect individuals who find themselves in such contexts to be able to tell whether what they are provided with is genuine information or misinformation. There may well be no decisive higher-order evidence that individual subjects can call upon to tell whether they are being subjected to manipulation, whether their society is in the grips of ideology. As a consequence, there may not be any way to distinguish, simply in terms of a subject's belief-forming policies, the "good," enabling cases from the "bad," necrotic cases. In such a situation, there is no plausible way of charging the individual cognitive subject with the epistemic responsibility of carrying out a conclusive higher-order investigation of the quality of the information environment they find themselves in. In this sense, we must recognize that people can *blamelessly* find themselves in socio-epistemic contexts where their access to information is severely restricted, perhaps along ideological lines.

---

as he powerfully argues elsewhere, they have the power of reason; in this sense, their ignorance could be "overcome by study." Instead, Vitoria takes a different approach: the reason they are not committing a sin is that it wouldn't be rational for them to accept the Christian faith merely on the say-so of the Spaniards: indeed, he argues, it would be "foolhardy and imprudent" for them to do so, given their overall evidential situation.

3.2.1 Justified Belief under Bad Ideology

Because we are dealing with prejudice, it will be plausible that many of the socio-epistemic contexts we will be considering will be in the grips of ideology in the relevant sense. This means, concretely, that there will be limits to the evidence that subjects will have access to. But from the point of view of the normative epistemology that we aim to articulate here, this alone doesn't seem to raise any special concerns. After all, *anyone's* access to evidence will be limited in some way or other; moreover, all anyone can ever do is just to process that evidence in accordance with the relevant epistemic norms. (There is an interesting parallel here to something we observed with respect to endogenous non-ideality: we can certainly imagine a socio-epistemic context with a less restricted information-economy than this one. In this sense, this socio-epistemic context is decidedly non-ideal. But at the same time, it is highly doubtful that we could truly imagine an "ideal" socio-epistemic context, one with no restrictions on information flow, no institutional boosting of certain kinds of information, certain authorities, etc. It is doubtful that any complex society could exist which did not provide institutional imprimatur to certain authorities, certain kinds of information, etc. That is to say, any society will—for good or ill—deploy methods for controlling the flow of information, not necessarily in the blunt form of outright censorship, but more often in subtler forms of boosting certain signals, while dampening others.)[23]

In a recent paper, however, Amia Srinivasan (2020) appears to cast doubt on this line of reasoning. Proposing a form of "radical externalism," she argues that the epistemic situation of subjects in societies permeated by pernicious ideology, at least with respect to relevant domains of cognition (i.e., the domains of social cognition directly or indirectly affected by the ideology), is essentially analogous to that of the envatted brains we briefly considered in chapter 1. Consider Radha, a woman in rural India who is regularly beaten by her husband, and who comes, after thorough reflection, to believe that her beatings are well-deserved, and that it is a husband's role to discipline his wife (2020: 398–399). Srinivasan asks:

> Is Radha's belief that she deserves to be beaten justified? I think the answer
> is: surely not. For Radha's belief is not merely false, but moreover the

---

[23] I will revisit this point toward the end of chapter 6.

product of a convincing, and systematic, misogynistic illusion: that it is men's place to subordinate women. This illusion [. . .] ensures that Radha has no dependable access to the moral facts of her situation. Radha, despite her own best efforts, is tragically cut off from moral reality.

Radha's false belief is hardly her fault; it is not only explained but obviously excused by the patriarchal illusion of which she is a victim. Radha is doing, we want to say, the best she can, given her own distorted epistemic connection to the world. Her belief is eminently understandable; we would be naïve to expect anything better of ourselves in Radha's position. And yet none of this is the same as saying that Radha's belief is justified. Indeed, once we draw the distinction between justification on one hand, and excusedness or blamelessness on the other, it feels intuitive, I think, to say that Radha's belief meets the conditions for the latter, but not the former. Radha's belief is the product of a distorted relationship to reality: a relationship that excuses the falsity of her belief, but does not thereby render it justified.   (Srinivasan 2020: 399)

These bad ideology cases, Srinivasan argues (2020: 405–7) are analogous to brains-in-vats cases in the sense that the subject is systematically (and tragically) cut off from relevant aspects of reality, and is thereby deprived of the resources to form true beliefs. In such conditions, even impeccable reasoning from the available evidence will not bestow justification on the resulting beliefs. Putting ourselves in Radha's shoes, we could hardly expect to "do any better," epistemically speaking. As we have seen, we will certainly want to say that Radha is epistemically blameless and fully excused in believing as she does. But it does not follow that she would be justified.

This conclusion, Srinivasan argues, is fully compatible with the idea that our epistemology should be normative. If anything, externalism puts the normative focus in the right place. In cases featuring "subjects who exist under conditions in which pervasively false beliefs have the function of sustaining (and are in turn sustained by) systems of social oppression [. . .] the salient epistemological question becomes not whether subjects are blameworthy or praiseworthy for their beliefs [. . .] but how these beliefs relate to a system whose function it is to distort subjects' access to the truth for the purposes of oppressing them" (2020: 408).

The case of Radha is difficult in part because of its sensitivity and the self-harming nature of the belief in question. However, since Srinivasan's analysis is presumably meant to cover cases of ideology-infused belief more generally, we can substitute a blander case of prejudiced belief, such as someone who believes that women are less adept at math than men. Let's assume this belief is widely held in his society, and is reflected broadly in its institutional structure, moderating access to opportunity, etc. In the next few chapters, we will consider the epistemic standing of such beliefs simply on the merit of the available evidence. This is the challenge that is typically launched against prejudice, namely that it cannot rationally stand up to (the available) evidence. Srinivasan's challenge is more radical and deserves consideration in its own right: whatever their evidence is, and however they process that evidence, the result cannot be justified belief. This is because the evidence is provided to them under the aegis of a systematic and pernicious illusion—ideology—which distorts their access to the truth.

What should we think about this? As we have seen, my approach is fully compatible with the idea that "doing the best one can" with one's evidence, or more generally being epistemically blameless, can leave one well short of being epistemically justified. (If taking the opposite view is a hallmark of internalism, then my position is not internalist.) Srinivasan clearly has something stronger in mind. However, if evincing even perfect epistemic rationality will not guarantee that the output is a justified belief, then I can only conclude that our disagreement is primarily verbal and not substantive. Terminology can easily get in our way here. Even if we decide to withhold the term "justification" for beliefs formed under conditions of ideology, we will still need to draw a distinction—and a normative distinction, at that—between those who do and those who don't update their beliefs in light of the evidence available to them. Some people might simply and dogmatically form misogynist beliefs because they find it convenient or because it reinforces their social privilege.[24] Some might form the same beliefs by scrupulously reflecting on their evidence. Moral concerns aside, we will want to say that the latter are doing *something* right—epistemically speaking—which the former are not. After all, this is just the distinction between wishful thinking and evidence-based methods applied to the case of false belief rather than true belief. This marks a normatively important distinction: counterfactually, for instance, if the evidence had been good evidence, then the latter *would* have been justified, whereas the former would not.

One might insist that there is some further dimension of epistemic assessment on which neither the wishful thinker nor the victim of ideology qualify as "justified." In my view, nothing much hangs on this terminological

---

[24] See, again, Moody-Adams 1994 and Medina 2013 on "motivated" or "active" ignorance.

point. If externalists want to use some other term to mark that distinction, that is fine. Maybe they will agree to say that the latter is "epistemically rational" in forming her beliefs as she does, while the former is not. We will now have changed the labels but retained the underlying normative structure. The relevant point to consider, surely, is that even externalists must make room for a "guidance norm" (as opposed to a merely "evaluative norm") which will pretty much track with the traditional conception of epistemic justification, even if they call it by a different name.[25] On that norm, Radha may be doing everything right by her evidence, objectively speaking. In *not* forming the belief that she does, she would be guilty of neglecting or discounting relevant evidence.[26] There is, then, nothing in Srinivsan's argument to show that living under conditions of ideology precludes one from being epistemically rational, even in forming prejudiced beliefs. What remains is merely the question of whether we should call these beliefs "justified." But that can only be a verbal rather than a substantive issue.

3.3 Summary and Look Ahead

This chapter has sought to motivate and defend a non-ideal approach to epistemology by way of articulating two dimensions of non-ideality which must be taken into account by any viable approach to epistemic normativity. One of these dimensions concerns the intrinsic capacity limitations of the cognitive system that we are studying. Important insight into these limitations will plausibly come from strictly empirical (and in this sense "descriptive") approaches to the human mind, such as psychology (but also, neuroscience, cognitive science, etc.). The other dimension of non-ideality concerns the informational contexts that individual human beings operate within. All informational contexts have their limitations; some of these contexts will be doubly non-ideal in the sense that they carry the (often pernicious) imprint of human institutions and practices.

So far from compromising the notion of epistemic normativity, paying close attention to these dimensions of non-ideality offers the only sensible platform for saying what the relevant epistemic norms are. We cannot, that is, articulate epistemic norms for human beings assuming that they have unconstrained real-time processing capacities and always operate in a

---

[25] Again, see Simion et al. 2016.   [26] On this, see Srinivasan 2020: 407.

context of perfect information. Indeed, even reflecting in the abstract on the very idea of epistemic norms as governing the transition from evidence to belief requires us to recognize that certain adjustments must be made for the norms to be relevant: quite simply, evidence is an intrinsically uncertain pathway to belief; only finite minds should ever avail themselves of it. Once we do start adjusting for cognitive finitude in this way, there is just no reason why the particular parameters of adjustment—which concessions to non-ideality we must make—shouldn't be made to fit the situation of human cognizers, since it is ultimately to them that we presume to apply the norms in question.

In the following chapters, we will switch to considering the consequences of the second dimension of non-ideality. I will argue that many people will in fact find themselves in socio-epistemic contexts where there is plenty of evidence to support prejudiced beliefs. Even if we assumed that in a situation of perfect information, no one would be warranted in holding any such belief, that is not the situation in which people are called upon to form their beliefs. (In fact, given their cognitive finitude, it plausibly *couldn't be* the situation in which they form their beliefs.) And once prejudiced beliefs enter into our cognitive economy, they can change the epistemological landscape in dramatic ways. To test the conviction that prejudice is always epistemically irrational, our investigations should proceed along two distinct but complementary pathways. Along one pathway, we will consider the *acquisition* of prejudiced belief: how could anyone ever come into possession of a prejudiced belief if not by taking an epistemic wrong turn somewhere? Along the other pathway, we will consider the *maintenance* of prejudiced belief: regardless of how one came into possession of these beliefs, there appears to be plenty of contradictory evidence on offer in anyone's normal course of experience; so, how could anyone remain prejudiced without violating canons of epistemic rationality?

These perspectives are often conflated in the literature, even though they raise importantly different epistemological concerns. In the next two chapters of the book, a detailed case will be made that in neither of these two dimensions—acquisition or maintenance—does prejudice necessarily correlate with culpable epistemic wrongdoing, or, more generally, with a morbid and dysfunctional cognitive outlook.

4

The Epistemology of Prejudice Acquisition

Our ordinary ways of thinking and talking about prejudice conceal an important but unresolved duality. In standard contexts, "prejudice" is clearly a term of disparagement. It is, in a phrase going back to Bernard Williams (1985), a "thick concept," i.e., a concept that is at once descriptive and evaluative. Unlike, say, "hero," the evaluative component here is clearly negatively charged. But what exactly do we mean to disparage when we call something a prejudice? It is not uncommon to hear people speak as if beliefs were prejudiced simply in virtue of their contents. On this sort of thinking, maybe we can imagine that we are in possession of a list of prototypical exemplars of prejudiced beliefs—e.g., "Muslims are terrorists," "women are overly emotional"—and then judge other potential candidates by how well they match with the prototypical exemplars. The problem with this sort of "extensional approach," however, is that it doesn't even begin to connect with questions about epistemic rationality, simply because it makes no mention of evidence and epistemic processing. So if what we mean to disparage when calling something a prejudice is at least in part the believer's epistemic grounds for holding the belief, then we would need to move beyond a merely extensional approach. That is, we would need to supplement an intensional perspective, which defines prejudice in terms of characteristic errors in epistemic processing.[1]

Many philosophers appear to have no qualms about moving between these perspectives. For illustration, take Miranda Fricker, who writes: "We must surely start with the presumption that, at least as regards explicit prejudice, we are epistemically culpable for allowing prejudice into our

---

[1] A telling analogy might be drawn here with our concept of "superstition." We can certainly make an illustrative list of "popular superstitions." But we wouldn't have gotten to the core of what is distinctive about superstitions—and what merits the disparaging tone—until we ask questions about people's epistemic grounds for holding these beliefs.

thinking" (Fricker 2016: 36).[2] This superficially simple statement conceals precisely the kind of duality I have in mind: it is assumed that we *know* (at least to a tolerable degree of precision) what prejudiced beliefs are, independently of any epistemic considerations; secondarily, we can say, *of* these beliefs, that our analysis must surely start from the presumption that whenever someone holds one of them, they are epistemically culpable for doing so.

It is fine, of course, to adopt as a working hypothesis the assumption that there is a tolerable degree of alignment between our extensional and intensional characterizations of prejudice: these, then, are beliefs that no one can rationally hold, because they could never be adequately supported by evidence. But sooner or later, we will have to subject that assumption to systematic scrutiny. This is the task of the present and following chapter. Our first approach to the issue will be through the lens of acquisition: how could people come to hold prejudiced beliefs in the first place? What sort of evidence (if any) can they presume to draw on? Can such evidence ever in fact support the beliefs in question? By contrast, the following chapter will consider epistemological questions regarding prejudice maintenance: regardless of how one came into possession of one's prejudices in the first place, we can ask how anyone can be justified in retaining those beliefs in the face of the massive amounts of counterevidence which, after all, seems to surround us?[3]

4.1 Acquisition by Induction

Prejudiced beliefs are not hardwired into the human mind;[4] whenever there is prejudice, that belief has been acquired at some point. Belief acquisition

---

[2] "Explicit prejudice" is presumably meant to mark a contrast with the phenomenon of implicit bias. For more on the distinction between prejudice and implicit bias, see section 2.3.

[3] The familiar distinction between propositional and doxastic justification might shed some surprising light on this. The standard motivation for drawing the distinction is to point out that even though there is evidence available to justify a particular proposition, this does not mean that *you* are justified in believing as you do, since you might still have failed to consult this evidence, or otherwise reasoned incorrectly from evidence to conclusion. (For an overview, see Silva and Oliveira forthcoming). What we are considering now would be something like the flipside of this: propositionally, it is certainly plausible that the belief is amply defeated by the evidence. But as we saw in section 3.2 above, it does not follow from this that *you* are unjustified in believing as you do, since you might not have rational access to all that evidence. So, while the belief is not supported on a global view of the total evidence, it can nonetheless be supported by the subset of the evidence that the subject is able to make use of.

[4] It is conceivable, of course, in light of the argument of chapter 2, that the need to conduct one's social cognition in terms of in-group and out-group categories *is* hardwired into the

provides a natural starting point for an inquiry into the epistemology of prejudice: taking some sort of extensional characterization of prejudice more or less for granted, is it true, as Fricker stipulates, that we are always "epistemically culpable for allowing prejudice into our thinking"?

One common critical perspective on the acquisition of prejudice approaches it in terms of simple inductive scenarios where subjects are presumed to start with no relevant information whatsoever, building their generalizations from scratch. (As we shall see later, this constitutes a highly restrictive picture of the range of available evidence. Nonetheless, it is instructive to see where the epistemology of prejudice can take us even given such restrictions.)

Consider an example: Johnny is a fourth grade student who notices (correctly, let's assume) that the top students in his math class are all boys. He infers from this observation that girls are comparatively less adept at math than boys. If you were to ask him who he would turn to for help on a math puzzle, Jim or Jenn (neither of whom he knows), he would naturally respond "Jim." It appears that Johnny holds a prejudice against girls. This prejudice shows itself in the way that he would treat arbitrary girls, even ones that he doesn't know.[5]

I think we can all agree that there is something not quite right about Johnny's belief. But in what sense "not quite right"? From a *moral* point of view, it is fairly easy to substantiate the intuition: his prejudiced belief against girls is demeaning and might feed into a pattern of wrongful treatment (marginalization, neglect, denial of opportunity, etc.). We'll hold off on further discussion of these moral considerations until the last two chapters of the book. Our present concerns are epistemic, not moral: can we give similar substance to the presumption that Johnny has also done something *epistemically* wrong in forming the belief that he does? It is one thing to point out that Johnny's belief is, as we presume, false; that's certainly a way of giving substance to the claim that something is "not quite right" about his belief. But it is not the perspective taken in this book: the "not quite

---

human mind. But that is not to say that the specific categories in terms of which these judgments are framed would be hardwired: clearly, they are not.

[5] For now, I will set aside lingering suspicions that Johnny may also have some rather subtler information at his disposal, namely that his math teachers are all men, that they display a preference for boys, etc. Incorporating these sources of evidence will make things more complicated, but certainly not in a way that favors the standard view of prejudice-in-acquisition.

right" must be understood in terms of the beliefs' standing with respect to evidence, not with respect to its truth.

4.1.1 Inductive Overreach?

One common view would have it that Johnny is guilty of what might be called "inductive overreach." The problem is not that Johnny doesn't have *any* evidence, because clearly he does. Rather, the problem is that the evidence in his possession is not sufficiently strong to support his inductive generalization. Moreover, this evidence provides him with no warrant to believe anything about *Jenn's* mathematical abilities in particular. The problem, then, of prejudice-in-acquisition, would be something like an innate tendency to "overgeneralize" on insufficient evidence. Consider, to this effect, psychologist Gordon Allport, whose influential book on prejudice marks the starting point of serious inquiry into the matter:

> A prejudiced person will almost certainly claim that he has sufficient warrant for his views. He will tell of bitter experiences he has had with refugees, Catholics, or Orientals. But, in most cases, it is evident that his facts are scanty and strained. He resorts to a selective sorting of his own few memories, mixes them up with hearsay, and overgeneralizes. No one can possibly know *all* refugees, Catholics, or Orientals. Hence any negative judgment of these groups *as a whole* is, strictly speaking, an instance of thinking ill without sufficient warrant.   (Allport 1954: 7)[6]

I do think this perspective captures an important feature of common thinking about the epistemology of prejudice. And certainly, if we could say that no one could be justified in holding a prejudiced belief unless they knew every person within the relevant group, then we could indeed expect a nice alignment of our extensional and our intensional categorizations of prejudiced beliefs. The problem, however, is that this approach would also render unjustified a whole host of other, perfectly commonplace inductive beliefs.

By comparison: Johnny notices (correctly, let's say) that the tallest students in his class are all boys. He infers that boys generally grow taller than

---

[6] "Thinking ill of others without sufficient warrant" is the central element of Allport's definition of prejudice (see Allport 1954: 6*ff.*).

girls. If we were to ask him who is likely to be taller, Jim or Jenn (neither of whom he knows), he would naturally respond "Jim." In other words, if we approach the question simply as a domain-general question about inductive justification, it is by no means obvious that Johnny's evidence *is* insufficient. In structurally comparable inductive scenarios, that is, we seem to have few qualms about drawing such generalizations from limited observational evidence. Quite simply, no general theory of induction will attempt to specify a minimum bounds of information that should lead a rational agent to favor one hypothesis over another. *Any* bit of information worth its salt will favor one hypothesis over competitors. (In fact, this is pretty much how we define the notion of information, as opposed to mere noise, in the first place.) An epistemically rational agent will promptly adjust his beliefs accordingly (where "belief," as we saw in section 1.5, is understood simply as credence distributed over the relevant propositions). To put it in slightly different terms, if we thought about Johnny's epistemic state-space in terms of a competition between two hypotheses regarding the comparative mathematical aptitudes of boys and girls, then his observations *should* lead him to favor the hypothesis that girls are less adept than boys over the hypothesis that girls are equally adept as boys. If he didn't come to favor the first hypotheses over the second, then he would essentially be guilty of throwing away evidence for no good reason. This would precisely be an instance of the sort of epistemic irrationality that we are concerned with: but in this case, the irrationality leads to a *failure* to adopt a prejudiced belief in a case where the evidence, on balance, supports it.[7]

(Before moving on, let us note in passing that it is a separate question just *how much* the information garnered in these observations should lead Johnny to favor the first hypothesis over the second. This is not best understood as a question of what he should believe given his evidence, but of what degree of confidence he should have in that belief, given the evidence. It is certainly true that Johnny may be guilty of overestimating the significance of the evidence, and thereby becoming too confident in his generalization. But at the same time, he can be said to believe that

---

[7] I do think we can make sense of the idea that we can reserve a degree of praise for a person who would staunchly refuse to update his belief on this kind of information. But unless he were in possession of better evidence from other sources, this praise would presumably have to be a kind of *moral* praise, not a form of *epistemic* praise. This raises the specter of potential conflicts between our moral ideals and our epistemic ideals, which will become a central theme later in this book.

girls are less adept at math than boys, even while adopting a relatively wide range of credences in that proposition. We will return to these issues in section 4.3 below.)

4.1.2 No Justified Induction Whatsoever?

But maybe the point is more radical than that. Perhaps the problem is not that people tend to overgeneralize on their inductive evidence, but the fact that they are generalizing at all. On such a view, Johnny's observations of individual instances should be presumed to provide *no* information whatsoever supporting any kind of group-level generalization. Does anyone hold such a view? Consider the oft-heard slogan "you don't know me!" (as discussed, for instance, in Moss 2018a).[8] Taken as an epistemic (as opposed to a moral) injunction, "you don't know me!" seems to imply that since you don't know *me*, you also have no epistemic right to believe anything about me. Your observations of other people, even people who belong in my broad social category, have no epistemic bearing on my case. In fact, if we go back to Allport, we can find a similar idea embedded already there: *strictly speaking*, Allport writes, no one could be warranted in holding these views about Catholics, Orientals, or whatnot, simply because no one could possibly know *every* person who falls under that classification. A strict reading of this line of reasoning would seem to suggest that there can be no epistemically justified inductive generalizations whatsoever in the domain of social cognition.

But once the claim is made explicit in this way, we can immediately see how startling it is. Inductive generalization is the lifeblood of all empirical cognition. It would remarkable if there were any significant domain of human cognition in which induction could be shown to be inherently epistemically unreliable. Are there really no true, inductively supported generalizations at any level of abstraction about particular groups of human beings and their interests, proclivities, aptitudes, and so forth? Imagine an impressionable young traveler on his first Inter-Rail trip through Europe writing postcards home: Dutch people speak excellent English; Danes are gregarious, and so on. We can certainly grant that these beliefs

---

[8] For more discussion of the presumptive "right to be treated as an individual," see Lippert-Rasmussen 2013; Eidelson 2013.

are supported only by weak inductive evidence. But that they are inductively supported generalizations at all can hardly count against them.

If such observations literally provide *no* information that could support an inductive generalization, then the situation is essentially akin to what we should believe about the outcome of a sequence of tosses of a fair coin. In coin toss situations, we know (or presume to know) that past outcomes have no bearing on future outcomes; no matter how many observations we make, we will still have no grounds for favoring one hypothesis (heads) over another (tails). But coin tosses are *designed* to have a random outcome, and that's how we know that we should resist our inductive impulses even in a case where a first series of observations skews in favor of heads.[9] What would be our grounds for thinking that similar restrictions apply in social cognition?

Returning to Allport's contention, consider someone who starts out with an open mind, but then goes on to have a series of negative encounters with Catholics in his neighborhood. The issue at stake is whether his retaining an open mind here—steadfastly continuing to reapply the principle of indifference—isn't just a matter of him throwing away information for no good reason. (What precisely his updated probabilities should be is, as before, a delicate matter: but what is at stake at this point is simply whether these experiences should have *any* bearing at all on what he should expect from future encounters with Catholics.) And it is hard to say, from a strictly epistemic point of view, why he wouldn't be entitled—indeed required—to assume that these experiences provide him with evidence—albeit weak and defeasible evidence—about his neighborhood Catholics as such. (Let's say our subject is alive to the possibility that there might be sociological or historical reasons why his neighborhood Catholics like to keep to themselves; or he might be alive to the possibility that there are psychological reasons why their behaviors and body language seem so alienating to him. But even taking these issues into account, he should *also* update on the information he gleans from his experiences.)

Perhaps the thought is that, well, people are different, and maybe there is just too much underlying variability in human traits (behavior patterns, cognitive performance, etc.) for such generalizations to find any traction. To

---

[9] Of course, even this is an idealization: consider a situation in which tossing the coin immediately produces a very long sequence of heads. Even if you start with the assumption that the coin is fair, there must come a point at which you should start drawing this assumption into doubt, as evidenced precisely by the fact that inductive generalization would provide much more successful bets than repeated applications of the principle of indifference.

be sure, there is variability in human performance. But then again, there is variability in any complex natural system; so far, this fact shows only why it is *induction*, and not deduction, that is the mode of generalization under consideration. Moreover, there is no reason to think that our inductive generalizations couldn't be sensitive to this kind of variability. Variability is not chaotic: it can still fall within what statisticians call a "normal distribution." Normal distributions have consistent statistical features: it may be more likely, for example, that instances will fall toward the center of the distribution. Assume that we settle on some social category (say, British people) and we start inquiring into the hypothesis that British people drink more than other Europeans. The question of whether British people drink more than other Europeans is not a question about whether there is some unique amount that every British person drinks, nor is it a question of whether there are (some) Germans who drink even more than Brits. It is, rather, a question about whether the center of the normal distribution of British people's drinking habits is different than that of other Europeans. And while observing the drinking habits of some number of British people provides only limited information regarding what we should expect of some random future British person, it is hard to deny that it provides *some* information. After all, there exist empirically grounded generalizations about these sorts of things. We generally trust these generalizations when we find them, for instance, in statistical yearbooks.[10] We fully expect that policymakers will take these generalizations into account in their decision-making. So our general cognitive habits simply do not support the idea that there could be a blanket epistemic ban on induction in social cognition.[11]

---

[10] For an illustrative example, see http://www.euro.who.int/en/health-topics/disease-prevention/alcohol-use/data-and-statistics.

[11] One worry one might have here turns on the very real possibility that the problem isn't induction in social cognition quite generally, but rather that gender (or race, etc.) is simply the wrong category on which to center that induction; it is no more revealing of cognitive abilities than eye color or height, let's say. Even while I acknowledge that this is a genuine worry, I want to make two quick points in response: first, we can take a variety of positions on the question of whether there exist innate gender differences in aptitude, even while recognizing that social circumstances can *make it true* that gender will be an important predictor for aptitude, by way of inculcating prejudiced stereotypes or providing boys and girls with unequal opportunities. But secondly, this worry is neither here nor there with respect to the present point, which is rather whether Johnny has *reason to believe* that gender is a relevant categorization for inductive purposes. And if gender is indeed the most salient predictor of mathematical aptitude that he can find, then he arguably does have such reason.

4.1.3 The Viability of Induction in Social Cognition

Perhaps the problem with this inarticulate skepticism about induction is best seen if we momentarily switch the valence of the example from negative to positive, from *thinking ill* of others to *thinking well* of others. Is it specifically *thinking ill* of others which carries this kind of epistemic restriction? By contrast, assume that Johnny has had several positive experiences with his neighborhood Catholics, noting their friendliness, generosity, and eagerness to help. Is he now epistemically misguided to think that these experiences constitute evidence which should incline him toward believing that he can rely on future encounters with neighborhood Catholics to provide a friendly smile and a helping hand?[12] In fact, wouldn't we somehow hold it against Johnny if he failed to take epistemic note of these facts?

Once again, this is fully compatible with the idea that induction provides only a relatively weak grounds for believing anything about future encounters. And so, one should be open to the possibility that not every person who falls into the stereotyped category displays the property in question, or displays it to the same degree. This, I take it, is the truth behind "you don't know me!" Insofar as the evidence you would garner from actually speaking to me is significantly stronger than any background inductive information you have, you shouldn't form a belief about me on those grounds alone. But weak or strong, the inductive evidence is still evidence. And simply in virtue of being evidence, it will provide some measure of support for one belief over another. The requirement of being "open-minded" in one's interactions with other people must be made consistent with the idea that there can exist useful and epistemically warranted inductions in the domain of social cognition. Otherwise, we would simply lack a plausible account of the foundations of social learning.

Maybe what is problematic about people's inductive habits is often not that they tend to extend their generalizations too far, but that they invest *too*

---

[12] One might worry that changing the valence of the judgment switches the topic altogether. This worry can be easily substantiated from a moral point of view (cf. Fricker 2007, Blum 2004, Beeghly 2015). But it is more difficult to see how it could be substantiated from an epistemic point of view. For a simple example: quite often the judgments in question can be explicitly comparative, in which case the negative judgments will just be a flipside of the positive judgments. So if I come to think that Hondas are more reliable than other mid-priced Japanese cars, I will also be disposed to think that Toyotas (etc.) are less reliable than Hondas. Norms of coherence seem to require nothing less. In any case, we will return to possible interactions between moral and epistemic norms in the final two chapters of the book.

much confidence in these generalizations, relative to the strength of their evidence. Effectively, this would mean interpreting Allport's "thinking ill of others without sufficient warrant" not in terms of whether one has evidence to think ill (or good) of these others, but rather in terms of whether one has appropriately adjusted one's credence to one's evidence. But this does not in any way render prejudiced belief a peculiar case: this requirement attaches to the product of any inductive generalization. There are general epistemic norms that can tell us about this. "Sufficient warrant" would speak to the appropriate degree of confidence. But this does nothing to preclude the idea that someone could hold a (false) *negatively charged stereotype* with the appropriate level of confidence, and we would still naturally classify his belief as a prejudice. But in virtue of holding a well-evidenced belief with the appropriate level of credence, his belief is presumably epistemically justified. And so we cannot say that prejudiced belief is necessarily an expression of epistemic irrationality.

One's credence will of course bear on the question of how open one will be to new evidence acquired in encounters with other individuals falling under the same classification. Even if we concede that someone is justified in holding a prejudiced belief, we should still require of them that they recognize the defeasibility of the underlying generalization and thereby display appropriate openness to new evidence. This points toward the question of how anyone could be justified in *maintaining* their prejudiced beliefs in light of such evidence. This is the topic of chapter 5. Notice, for now, that even someone who *does* adjust his credence appropriately in light of the strength of his evidence could still *believe* the proposition in question, and could, thereby, be said to be prejudiced. But we have failed to find any grounds for holding on to the idea that he must also have committed some sort of epistemic error in coming to believe as he does.

4.2 Acquisition by Testimony

Johnny, as we have seen, believes that women are less adept at math than men. Presumably, we are free to describe Johnny's epistemic situation any way we want; contrary to widespread views about the epistemology of prejudice, there are plausible epistemic contexts in which even Johnny's very limited first-personal experience with girls in his class could be sufficient to justify a belief of that sort. But how plausible is the assumption that this is the only kind of evidence that he has to go on?

The epistemology of prejudice is part of *social* epistemology, first, in the trivial sense that the phenomenon we are concerned with arises in the context of social cognition, i.e., thinking about other people, and, in particular, thinking about them through the lens of their group membership. But second, the epistemology of prejudice is part of social epistemology also in the sense that the relevant evidence goes beyond what individuals can glean by way of personal experience, and also includes elements of social learning. Strikingly, however, many contributors to this discourse persist in considering the question of the epistemic standing of prejudiced belief very much in terms of an *individualistic conception of evidence*. Here is Allport again (1954: 7):

> Sometimes, the ill-thinker [i.e., the prejudiced person] has no first-hand experience on which to base his judgment. A few years ago most Americans thought exceedingly ill of Turks—but very few had ever seen a Turk [...] Their warrant[13] lay exclusively in what they had heard of the Armenian massacres and of the legendary crusades. On such evidence they presumed to condemn all members of a nation.

The emphasis on first-hand experience suggests that only evidence acquired by such experience could provide justification for "thinking ill" of Turkish people in general. What one might "have heard" of their role in the Armenian genocide, apparently, could not. A similar suggestion arises also in recent and more philosophically sophisticated discussions. Quassim Cassam, for instance, invites us to consider the award-winning British journalist Louis Heren, who believed that all politicians are "lying bastards." This certainly seems to have the right shape for a prejudiced belief. But whether it is a prejudice or not, argues Cassam (2016: 167–8), depends on the evidence that thinkers can call upon to support it. In Heren's case, given his extensive experience in working with politicians, the belief is not a prejudice but an "empirically grounded heuristic." Cassam doesn't assert, but certainly seems to imply, that anyone who held the same belief but didn't have a similar range of first-hand experience with politicians, would indeed be prejudiced. That is, Cassam presumably agrees that *there exists evidence* sufficient to justify the proposition *politicians are lying bastards*. But in order

---

[13] I propose to read this as "presumptive warrant," since (i) Allport doesn't actually hold that these beliefs are warranted in the context, and (ii) he is in the midst of articulating the claim that such evidence couldn't provide epistemic warrant in the first place.

for you or I to be (doxastically) justified in holding this belief, we would each need to have that evidence in our private possession. And the only way we could get hold of that evidence would be by first-hand experience.

4.2.1 A Literary Example

Can this be correct? Clearly, there will be cases where one *needs* information beyond what one can gain through first-hand experience. In addition to obvious cases, such as the fact that first-hand experience can tell you very little about things that happened before you were born, there are also subtler cases. Such experience takes time to accrue. Individually, they provide only a tiny, and perhaps a selective glimpse, of the larger body of evidence that bears on the matter. There can be significant *opportunity costs* associated with holding out for such evidence; other beliefs one might one want, for personal *and* epistemic reasons, to form might not be rationally available to one on a relevant time scale. Finally, one might also have serious doubts about one's ability to process or comprehend the significance of those experiences.

In such cases, one can plausibly think, "if only I knew more about what's going on here." Here's the rub: there *are* other sources of evidence available. We access them by routine, and use them to provide an interpretive framework for our individual experiences. Reaching for a broad term, we could call this form of evidence "testimony." As philosophers have long recognized, testimony is a fundamental channel of human learning.[14]

A literary example might help: Harry is 11 years old, and about to attend a new and highly selective private school of which he has very limited prior knowledge. Because he wants to hit the ground running, he is keen to know what is going on, as any alert student would be. As he travels to his new school on designated transportation, he chances into Ron, another first year student. Unlike Harry, Ron has older siblings who have attended the school; moreover, his family is deeply immersed in the cultural traditions that have shaped the school and its surrounding community. Ron is happy to pour from his knowledge. The student body, he tells Harry, is divided into four houses: Slytherin, Ravenclaw, Hufflepuff, and Gryffindor. Ron hopes to be assigned to Gryffindor, as all his family members have been.

---

[14] See Reid 1764, 1785 for the classic statement.

Specifically, he says: "you really don't want to be in Slytherin...Slytherins are slimy, they are."

What is Harry to do with this information? Can he just discard it? It seems he cannot: he knows that he himself starts from virtually no information, and he has reason to think that Ron is speaking from a superior epistemic position. Ron's testimony is not an "offering" that Harry is free to accept or decline at his whim. Testimony *is evidence*:[15] from the point of view of epistemic rationality, testimony is not merely something that one is *permitted* to take into account in forming one's beliefs; it is something one is *required* to take into account (unless, of course, one is in possession of "defeaters," i.e., specific reasons to disregard. Such defeaters, however, could only take the form of more evidence). In Harry's case, we can assume that Ron's testimony is true, and is offered from a position of genuine epistemic authority. But neither of these features are required. Ron could well be confused; his testimony would still be evidence that Harry is required to take into account.[16] And, of course, Ron might in actual fact be scarcely more knowledgeable than Harry; from an epistemic point of view, what matters is just that Harry *has reason to believe* that Ron is speaking from a position of knowledge (or at any rate, that he is relevantly more knowledgeable than Harry).

4.2.2 Beyond Individual Experience: Social Epistemology and Social Evidence

I submit that the common picture builds on a strikingly individualistic conception of evidence that is both psychologically implausible and also stands in stark tension with the broader philosophical motivations for thinking of epistemology under a social guise in the first place. Psychologically, it is extremely implausible that we all arrive at our prejudiced beliefs individually, by drawing (perhaps overhastily) on the random

---

[15] Let us not get sidetracked here by the so-called "assurance view" of testimony (see e.g., Moran 2005; Faulkner 2007), according to which the main epistemic point of testimony is not to provide evidence for *p* but to provide the hearer with a normatively underwritten assurance that *p* is true. We can agree with all essentials of the assurance-view while still maintaining that, whatever else is going on here, testimony *also* provides evidence for the proposition attested to.

[16] Those who are worried about admitting false propositions as evidence will hopefully be assuaged that here, what serves as evidence is not the proposition attested to, but the fact that someone, apparently speaking from a position of knowledge, attested to that proposition. The latter is both true and known to the receiving subject. For more on this, see 1.4.

bits of first-hand experience that is available to us. If that were the case, we would have a hard time explaining why so many prejudices are *shared* in any society. (The fact that they tend to be widely shared is presumably a reason why they are so damaging and systematic in their effect.) To adopt a phrase from Susanna Siegel (2017), prejudiced beliefs are often "culturally normal beliefs."[17] By invoking a notion of "culturally normal belief" in the context of an epistemological inquiry, I don't mean to suggest that it is the fact of normality itself which would justify people in holding these beliefs (or at least, provide them with an excuse), as though it would somehow be "unreasonable" (cf. Alston 1988, Medina 2013) to hold individuals to significantly higher epistemic standards than their peers.[18] Instead, the point is that culturally normal beliefs tend to be reinforced in formal and informal learning situations, so that part of the reason *why* they are culturally normal is that they are disseminated by explicit or implicit testimony. In this way, we are brought to consider that the evidence that supports the prejudice (upon acquisition) isn't limited to an individual's observations of people's performance in various scenarios, but also includes such things as *the fact that someone*—with suitable epistemic authority, let's assume—*told me* that this is the case. Quite often, we can assume, their authority bears some sort of institutional or para-institutional imprint, such as teachers, parents, or other caregivers.[19] More generally, and on empirical grounds, it should be no surprise that a deeply prejudiced society would be interested in disseminating and reinforcing its prejudices along such channels, say even to the point of incorporating them, explicitly or implicitly, in its school curriculum.[20]

Once we start thinking about prejudiced belief in these terms, we are looking at the question of epistemic justification in terms of a qualitatively different sort of evidence than we were previously. Now the question of justification is rather one about whether we could ever be in a position to

[17] We will revisit this notion in chapter 7.

[18] Cf. Rosen 2003 for an argument that seems to proceed along these lines. We will return to Rosen's argument in chapter 10.

[19] Drawing on Siegel 2017, one may also wonder whether children and adolescents may be able to draw inferences from established patterns of social interaction even without the support of explicit testimony. Such patterns provide plausible, albeit indirect, evidence about what "everybody knows," and should therefore, arguably, be granted some presumptive epistemic role in a properly social epistemology. I will develop some ideas along these lines in chapter 7. Meanwhile, see Begby 2018a for some cursory remarks.

[20] See, e.g., Engelbrecht 2006 for a study of South African school textbooks during the Apartheid and post-Apartheid era, and Bernier 2016 for a telling account of a mid-1950s history textbook used in Texas public schools.

justifiably accept such testimony. And it is hard to see how we wouldn't be. Our pervasive and justified dependence on others in forming our cognitive outlooks is well documented (see, e.g., Hardwig 1985; Fricker 2006; Goldberg 2010). Social cognition is hardly an exception: we would be hopelessly inadept at navigating our social worlds if we were not broadly epistemically entitled to take testimony on issues relating, say, to social facts, institutions, and norms. By way of example, imagine a precocious student, Johnny, who asks his teacher (c.1860) what justifies English colonial rule over India. His teacher cites chapter and verse from Mill's *On Liberty*: these "Barbarians" aren't cognitively capable of self-rule, and that's why it's appropriate for England to assume guardianship over their political affairs. Our question now is simply, why couldn't this constitute *a sort of evidence* which might contribute to Johnny's justification for believing that people from the Indian subcontinent are intellectually inferior, even in the absence of extensive individual experience with these people? After all, if Johnny is going to learn anything about world politics, it's going to be via channels such as this. Much of the information that will travel to him along these channels will be good information, even if not all of it is. This is reflected in the fact that he will rationally set his credence in anything his teachers tell him well below 1. But unless we credit Johnny with pre-existing epistemic resources to tell the good from the bad, we have no right to expect of him that he believe only the truths and discard the rest.

Of course, we might, in some sense, have *liked* to see schoolchildren in Colonial Britain, the American South in the pre-civil rights era, or South Africa during Apartheid manifest greater cognitive resistance to their indoctrination. But there is a systematic problem in the offing here: if we want to condemn prejudice on epistemic grounds in these scenarios, we run the risk of ruling out sources of evidence or modes of epistemic reasoning which serve us eminently well in other domains, and which no one should want to cast aspersions on in their broader application. In particular, the notion that epistemically responsible social cognition can only be based on individual experience cannot be right. Testimony is a pervasive source of learning, not least in the social domain. In deeply prejudiced societies, much of the testimony in question will carry prejudiced content. But unless we credit individuals with specific epistemic resources to discriminate among the good and the bad bits of the testimony that is offered to them, we have no grounds for saying that they are justified in taking the good bits only. In such scenarios, *not* taking the testimony on offer—the good *and* the bad—is essentially tantamount to a refusal to form one's beliefs in the light of the totality of evidence at one's disposal. But this is precisely an instance of epistemic irrationality, if anything is.

4.3 Summary

Assume, for the sake of argument, that our inquiry should start out with a non-exhaustive but illustrative list of "widespread prejudices" (perhaps indexed to particular societies). The thesis under consideration would then be that no one could hold any of *these* beliefs without thereby manifesting some manner of epistemic irrationality. That thesis could only be vindicated by taking a closer look at the evidential situation of particular people who might hold these beliefs. So far, we have considered the thesis in light of the *acquisition* of prejudice, and we have found no grounds for upholding the view that people couldn't find themselves (through no fault of their own) in epistemic situations where there was sufficient evidence to form the beliefs in question. This is so, whether we consider the matter in the form of induction from individual experience, or in the form of testimony from people who are apparently better placed than oneself. None of this is to say, of course, that plenty of prejudiced people might not, as a matter of fact, be exhibiting various kinds of epistemic irrationality. But it is to say that there is no deep, conceptual connection between prejudiced belief and epistemic wrongdoing. Whether particular people are irrational in holding their prejudiced beliefs is a matter that can only be assessed by taking into account the epistemic situation they find themselves in.

In the next chapter, we will turn from looking at the epistemology of prejudice acquisition to looking at the epistemology of prejudice maintenance. This perspective-switch brings a whole new raft of questions to the fore. In particular, and irrespective of whether someone was initially justified in acquiring a prejudiced belief (on the relatively scarce evidence that they would have had at the time), one might wonder how anyone could go on retaining their prejudiced beliefs in light of the apparently massive amounts of contrary evidence that surrounds us.

5

The Epistemology of Prejudice Maintenance

What we are justified in believing depends, in no small measure, on the evidential context we find ourselves in. I hope it will be granted, based on general considerations, that individuals may justifiably come to acquire a wide range of problematic beliefs, depending on the details of their evidential context. Moreover, I will hope it will be granted, based on the previous chapter's arguments, that some of these beliefs may well be prejudiced beliefs. We would be wrong, then, to say with Fricker and others that we are always "epistemically culpable for allowing prejudice into our thinking."

The concession that subjects may be justified in *acquiring* prejudiced beliefs helps move our focus on to the next assumption that tends to structure philosophical discussion about prejudice, viz. that no one could maintain such beliefs for long without ignoring or discounting contrary evidence, and thereby displaying some form of epistemic irrationality, such as cognitive inflexibility or dogmatic close-mindedness.

5.1 Cognitive Inflexibility and the "Prejudiced Frame of Mind"

Gordon Allport proposes this sort of cognitive inflexibility as a test for distinguishing mere "error in prejudgment" from cases of genuine prejudice. He writes:

> If a person is capable of rectifying his erroneous judgment in the light of new evidence he is not prejudiced. *Prejudgments become prejudices only if they are not reversible when exposed to new knowledge.* A prejudice, unlike a simple misconception, is actively resistant to all evidence that would unseat it. (Allport 1954: 9)

This quote sheds light on yet another layer in our commonplace ways of thinking and talking about prejudice. Immediately upon acquisition, a "false prejudgment" may not even constitute a prejudice. It *becomes* a prejudice only when the subject holding it manifests a disposition to retain it even in the face of significant contrary evidence. "Motivated believing" is a term that is often used to describe what is going on in such a situation: the believer manifests a bias against contrary evidence, because he is personally motivated to go on believing as he does. The motivated believer displays the broader intellectual vice of "closed-mindedness" (Cassam 2016; Zagzebski 1996). Transposed into the key of our current inquiry, we can say that he inhabits a "prejudiced frame of mind."[1]

An immediate problem with this sort of dispositional demarcation of prejudice lies in the supposition that prejudiced people, quite generally, will in fact have access to all the relevant evidence, and simply fail to make the appropriate use of it. In lots of cases, the evidence in question, even supposing it exists, might be beyond their epistemic reach.[2] They might, for instance, live in communities where such evidence is systematically suppressed. It seems we should want to know whether someone is prejudiced without having to settle complex counterfactual questions about how they would fare in evidential contexts fundamentally different from their own.

Another problem, bitterly familiar in real-world contexts, is that widespread social prejudice will often be causally implicated in creating downstream effects which in turn "render true" the prejudice, or at least appears to provide salient evidence in its favor.[3] Consider a feedback loop between the widespread prejudice "women are less adept at math than men" and the apparent fact that relatively few of the top talents in math programs are women. We want to say that there's a deeper structural explanation for why this evidence obtains. Moreover, this structural explanation gives rise to serious concerns about social justice. In a social context where no women are given opportunity or encouragement to pursue mathematical education, it likely will be the case that men are generally better at math than women,

---

[1] See also Appiah 1990 for a similar perspective.

[2] Or it might have been defeated through a move which I dub "evidential preemption," such as "the liberal media will tell you that *p*," uttered in a context where it's understood that what the liberal media tell you is not to be believed. I will examine evidential preemption in more detail in chapter 6.

[3] See, for instance, Haslanger (2011: 196–8), with reference to Ian Hacking 1999.

and all the extant evidence will favor this view. However, the structural explanation of why this fact obtains doesn't change the fact that it *is* evidence; nor does it change the fact that individual subjects will be required to make epistemic use of this evidence, as they will of any information available to them.

But even setting all these concerns aside, there is a deeper problem on the horizon. Allport argues that truly prejudiced belief is "actively resistant" to contrary evidence; moreover, this is where its irrationality lies. Now, it probably is true that once a prejudiced belief is acquired, it will tend to exert a significant degree of influence over the interpretation of new evidence. But importantly, this effect is not unique to prejudice. Rather, prejudiced belief embodies an underlying form of generalization—one that we put to wide use in a number of different contexts—which appears quite generally to show a significant degree of *rational* resistance to new evidence. This effect is largely neglected by philosophers who emphasize the supposed contrast between the inflexible dogmatism of the "prejudiced mindset" and the flexible openmindedness to new evidence which purportedly constitutes intellectual virtue.

5.2 Solomon Goes to University

An example will help fix our thoughts, and serve to connect this idea with the argument of the previous chapter. Consider Nomy Arpaly's example of Solomon, "a boy who lives in a small, isolated farming community in a poor country," and who "believes that women are not half as competent as men when it comes to abstract thinking" (Arpaly 2003: 103). Solomon clearly harbors a (false) negative stereotype against women. Nonetheless, and as Arpaly notes, this stereotype is not without evidential support. It appears that the stereotype is widely shared in his community, and we can assume that it has been repeatedly related to him by teachers and peers. Further, it may also be that women in his community have largely internalized the stereotype: as a result, Solomon may note—correctly—that none of the women he has encountered have ever displayed the aptitude in question. Both testimonial and individually acquired evidence, then, appear to lend a significant degree of support to the stereotype.

In light of this, both Arpaly (2003: 104) and Fricker (2007: 33–4) agree that Solomon is not unreasonable in holding his belief about women at this point. As Arpaly puts it (2003: 104), since Solomon has not been "exposed to striking counterevidence to it," his belief is not "*particularly* or *markedly* irrational." Following Allport, we may even be reluctant to call it a prejudice.

To see how this "false prejudgment" might transform into a prejudice, however, imagine that Solomon receives and accepts an entrance fellowship to a university. At the university, Solomon enrolls in a calculus class where he regularly interacts with women who display the relevant aptitudes. He is now in possession of the kind of evidence that previously eluded him, namely direct evidence of female aptitude in "abstract thinking." This new evidence, Fricker argues (2007: 33–4), rationally requires him to revise his beliefs about women. If he does not—if he persists in thinking that women are inferior to men in the realm of abstract thinking—*then* he is prejudiced. His stereotype will have transformed into a prejudice as a consequence of the changes to the evidential situation he is in. If he retains his previous belief even after being confronted with this new evidence, it can now only be because he harbors an irrational bias against female intelligence.

5.2.1 Social Stereotypes as Generic Judgments

This view can certainly claim a fair bit of intuitive support. Clearly, stereotypes are or embody generalizations of some sort. *Qua* generalizations, it is certainly reasonable to demand that they remain appropriately sensitive to new evidence. And here, as Arpaly and Fricker argue, is where Solomon's epistemic failing lies: he culpably fails to update his belief about female intelligence in light of new evidence.

But it matters deeply what *kind* of generalization we are talking about. Things would be very straightforward indeed if, for instance, stereotypes were simply universal generalizations. If so, Solomon would essentially be in the situation of the field biologist who, after encountering his first black swan, refused to give up his belief that all swans are white. But it is extremely implausible that stereotypes could embody universal generalizations in this sense. That is, it is highly implausible that common instances of stereotype judgments ascribe a particular property to every member of some group, or hold that every member displays the trait to exactly the same degree. For instance, if Solomon is appropriately sensitive to his evidence, he will long since have recognized that men and women alike display a *range* of abilities in virtually every endeavor they might apply themselves to.

This suggests that we would do well to look for a more appropriate model for thinking about stereotypes. One plausible model is that of so-called "generic" judgments.[4] As is widely recognized in the current literature, however, generic judgments display a peculiar kind of resilience in the face of apparently contradictory evidence.[5] As Sarah-Jane Leslie points out (Leslie 2008), we remain committed to the truth of the proposition *ducks lay eggs* even after being reminded that only female ducks do. Likewise, we might maintain the belief that mosquitos spread the West Nile virus knowing full well that the vast majority of mosquitos don't. Like any generalization, generic judgments are, of course, formed in the light of evidence, and must remain sensitive to new evidence. But the manner in which they are sensitive to new evidence differs dramatically from universal generalizations. In particular, it would be futile to attempt to falsify generic judgments simply by pointing to instances—or even a large range of instances—which fail to display the trait in question. Generic judgments are stereotypes in the truest sense: they hold that it is salient, relevant, and typifying of a particular group that it displays a certain trait, without necessarily committing themselves to particular details about just how many members of this group display this trait, or to what extent they do. Accordingly, it is perfectly consistent with maintaining a negative stereotype against female intelligence that one recognizes that not all women are equally obtuse, and indeed that some may be as smart as any man.[6]

---

[4] For philosophical perspectives, see Haslanger 2011, Begby 2013, Leslie and Lerner 2016. For perspectives from developmental and experimental psychology, see Rhodes et al. 2012; Hammond and Cimpian 2017.

[5] Leslie 2008, 2017.

[6] Haslanger 2011 also takes there to be a close connection between stereotypes and generics. It will be worth noting some important ways in which her approach differs from mine. First, Haslanger seems to offer the connection between generics and stereotypes as a reason to simply *avoid* using generics, or at least avoiding generics involving problematic categories such as race or gender. I have serious doubts as to whether this is feasible, and also whether the result of doing so would be as beneficial as one might think (cf. Ritchie 2019 for similar concerns). Second, Haslanger's analysis specifically concerns itself with problematic "essentializing" implicatures generated by generics. But by that token, the argument would only apply to the use of generics in communication (since implicatures are concomitants of speech acts), and would leave untouched the use of generics in cognition. Third, implicatures are highly context-sensitive, and it appears that one can generate similar essentializing implicatures also with assertions the eschew generics in favor of specific statistical operators (e.g., "a black male is seven times more likely to be imprisoned than a white male" will presumably generate implicatures about racist law enforcement in some contexts, but can equally well generate implicatures about deep-seated criminal tendencies in others). Finally, and despite real concerns about essentialization, I see no reason why Solomon's prejudice couldn't make room for the possibility that these "truths" hold only in virtue of contingent social facts, such as facts about education and socialization. In general, there is no reason to suppose that Solomon must believe that these discrepancies in intelligence are innate or otherwise biologically grounded. (Many thanks to Kelsey Vicars for discussion of these issues.)

5.2.2 Tallying the Evidence

If stereotypes behave anything like generics, then we must allow that Solomon's prejudice can embody a fair degree of flexibility in how it absorbs empirical evidence: for instance, Solomon might recognize that if both male and female intelligence falls on a range (i.e., there is no unique level of intelligence had by all members of either group), then it may be highly likely that some women are every bit as smart as some men. By contrast, if Solomon's stereotype displayed the extreme rigidity of universal generalizations—for example, if he held that there is no woman who is half as smart as any man—then he could maintain that stereotype only by culpably discounting evidence long before he enters the university. (For a simple example, assume that Solomon has a Cousin Bob whom he regards as particularly obtuse. Bob, Solomon reflects, is probably every bit as dim as most women. Accordingly, it is perfectly within Solomon's capabilities to recognize that *some men are as obtuse as some women*. If so, we should also expect that he is capable of drawing the inference that not all women are equally obtuse; rather, some women are more intelligent than others.)

Thus, to determine the exact nature of Solomon's prejudice, we need to move beyond Arpaly's quick gloss "women are not half as competent as men when it comes to abstract thinking" (Arpaly 2003: 103). To make the confrontation with new evidence as stark as possible, assume that Solomon's prejudice could be given some kind of quasi-statistical interpretation.[7] For instance, since Solomon is able to recognize that there is significant variation in intelligence within each group, men and women, he might be brought to recognize that his view plausibly entails that *women are typically (or on average) less intelligent than men.* For the sake of simplicity, let us assume that he believes intelligence displays some manner of normal distribution within each group, for instance as in Figure 5.1 below.

While this departs somewhat from the story of Solomon as presented by Arpaly and Fricker (most notably, perhaps, in substituting a more general notion of "intelligence" for a capacity for "abstract thinking"), it is also, I contend, a more faithful representation of the sort of prejudice that women

---

[7] This is for simplicity's sake only; it should in no way be taken to suggest that generic judgments in general, or stereotypes specifically, should be understood as covert statistical generalizations. For remarks on the complex relationship between generic and statistical generalization, see Leslie 2008.

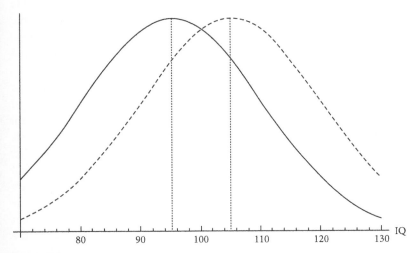

Dashed line = Male, Solid line = Female

Figure 5.1

have to contend with today.[8] Of course, Arpaly and Fricker are free to insist that Solomon takes an even dimmer view of female intelligence than the average male chauvinist does, in which case the values would have to be tweaked. But the point to note here is simply that, *qua* stereotype judgments, typical prejudices allow that a trait exhibits some manner of normal distribution within the targeted group. (As we have seen, if Solomon's thinking did not allow for this, we would not have to wait until he enters the university to charge him with epistemic irrationality; he would *already* be guilty of neglecting clear evidence that even within the female population he has encountered so far, some individuals are smarter than others.)

With this in mind, let us turn to assess the evidence that Solomon acquires when he enters the university and encounters highly intelligent women for the first time. This would, of course, constitute decisive counterevidence if prejudices were universal generalizations. But if the underlying logical form of prejudiced belief is something more akin to generic judgments, they will turn out to be rather more epistemically robust than this

---

[8] Indeed, the diagram is adapted from a popular website—http://www.iqcomparisonsite.com/—which claims to tell the unvarnished scientific truth about the comparative intelligence of various population groups. (I should emphasize that I am in no way endorsing the content of the graph, but precisely using it to illustrate what I take to be a representative instance of prejudiced belief.)

simple picture would suggest. For the evidence that he now acquires can be shown to be quite compatible with his prejudice—in fact, on plausible assumptions, it is even predicted by it. The reason is simple enough: the intelligent women that Solomon encounters at the university do not represent a random sample of the female population. Instead, they are a skewed sample, largely selected for the trait in question, namely intelligence.

Let us attempt to tally, in a rough and ready way, the evidence available to Solomon after he enters the university. There is, first, robust testimonial evidence from his upbringing that women are less intelligent than men. Second, there is empirical evidence from his interaction with women in his community which appears to confirm the testimonial evidence. Finally, there are the several positive instances of female intelligence encountered at the university. The question facing us is, does this last batch of evidence require him to reassess his prejudice against women? We can imagine Solomon reasoning as follows: while women are on average less intelligent than men, some women are more intelligent than others, and some are indeed so intelligent as to be the functional peers of all but the most brilliant men. Where might one hope to meet some of these women? At the university, of course! Thus, the current evidence is in fact predicted by his prejudice along with plausible background assumptions. As such, if he were epistemically warranted in holding his negative stereotype prior to entering the university, there is no clear reason why he should be required to revise it subsequently. Contrary to the common view, it is not the case that Solomon's previously acquired evidence is nullified as he encounters instances of intelligent women. Instead, it remains active, and reasonably controls his interpretation of the new evidence acquired. (The evidence that he acquires does, of course, require him to treat *these* women with due recognition of their intelligence. But this is a separate matter: for presumably one *can* treat individual women with due recognition yet remain prejudiced.)[9]

---

[9] It might be objected that this argument underestimates just how negative a view Solomon takes of female intelligence. But this will not help salvage the connection between prejudice and epistemic culpability. To see why, let us assume that Solomon took an *extremely* dim view of female intelligence, such that there was little or no overlap between the curves. Of course, now his new evidence would clearly require him to reassess his stereotype. Yet the fact remains that he can do this while retaining his belief that women are on average less intelligent than men. What the new evidence requires him to recognize is simply that the discrepancy is less pronounced than he previously believed. Thus, importantly, the resulting view is still prejudiced against women (albeit less prejudiced than previously). But Solomon is apparently epistemically justified in holding it: he has responded correctly to the new evidence that he acquires. And so, the common view has failed to establish a strict connection between prejudice and epistemic irrationality. (We will examine this point in more detail in section 5.4.1 below.)

Epistemically speaking, there need be nothing wrong with this line of reasoning: Solomon would be perfectly within his rights to deploy it. What it shows is that far from contradicting his stereotype, the new evidence is in fact predicted by it (at least when combined with independently plausible background assumptions). Accordingly, the new evidence is consistent with his prejudice, and does not, from the point of view of epistemic rationality, require a deep revision of it. (Of course, none of this is to say that real-life Solomons are likely to deploy this sort of reasoning in managing their epistemic affairs, as opposed to culpably relying on various kinds of biases to discount new evidence. But it is to say that, given a plausible elaboration of the story, Solomon could well be epistemically justified in maintaining his negative stereotype against women even after he enters the university.)[10]

For a contrasting perspective which is sometimes floated in these debates, consider the notion of "affected ignorance." Drawing on Aquinas (*ST* I-II, q. 6, art. 8), Michele Moody-Adams describes affected ignorance as a matter of "choosing not to know what one can and should know" (1994: 296).[11] Even if we suspected that many prejudiced beliefs might be held in place by such contrivances, there remains the question of whether all of them must. I think not. We really shouldn't be surprised to learn that prejudiced societies often take measures to shape the information environment in deep ways, thereby actively shaping what it is rational for individuals to believe as opposed to

---

[10] In a recent article, Jessie Munton (Munton 2019b) offers a different take on Solomon's situation. Similar to Haslanger 2011, she starts by observing that Solomon's belief about women is "true only in virtue of a particular set of facts about the social structure in which he and they are located, which deprives them of the opportunities required to develop such an inclination" (Munton 2019b: 7). This dependence on specific social structures and facts introduces a new source of epistemic error: "If Solomon is to appropriately reason with the statistic, he must represent, at least implicitly, the dependency of the regularity on that particular set of social structures and practices. Otherwise he is likely to expect the generalization to hold outside of the relevant social structures, and hence to draw erroneous conclusions from it" (Munton 2019b: 7). That is to say, in bringing his belief with him into the university setting, he is erroneously "projecting" his statistical generalization from one context to another.

There is much to be said in response to this. First of all, I do not think that statistical accuracy was what justified Solomon's belief in the first place. (That is, he could well have been justified in holding it, even if it wasn't accurate in any context.) Second, and relatedly, the failed projection from one context to another doesn't mean that his new belief is unjustified. Problems with projectibility are part and parcel of any inductive task: this is why induction is inherently risky, and why rational credence in inductive generalizations is always <1. It doesn't follow that all falsely projected inductive generalizations are unjustified. Finally, Munton's argument has no application to many standard cases of prejudiced belief (specifically, most of the examples we will be surveying in chapters 8–10), precisely because these do *not*, in any relevant sense, involve projecting from one context to another. Instead, the problematic reasoning there stays firmly in its home context.

[11] In a similar vein, see José Medina (2013: 39) on "active ignorance" and Charles Mills (2007) on "white ignorance."

merely relying on them to fall into substandard epistemic processing routines in a bid to not upset "the way of life they hope to preserve" (Moody-Adams 1994: 296). As I argued earlier (section 3.2), it is not my thesis that people in such situations would be *incapable* (as Moody-Adams seems to suppose) of lighting on the true beliefs. Rather, the problem is that they may have no *rational* path out of prejudice. Even if we did suppose that they engaged in scrupulous reflection on their own cognitive practices and commitments, there is simply no guarantee that the outcome would be significantly different. (One might still be tempted by the question: for specific individuals, are their prejudiced beliefs held in place by cultivated ignorance, or arrived at as a result of carefully weighing the evidence? As I hope will be clear by now, this is not a sort of question that we can answer on general grounds, without peering into that individual's mind. At best, we can make a careful examination of that person's actual socio-epistemic context, so as to determine whether their beliefs *would* be justified, if they had correctly availed themselves of the evidence at their disposal.)

5.3 Harry goes to Hogwarts

It will be helpful to contrast the example of Solomon with another case in which we might intuitively think that prejudice is not involved, if only because the belief in question is true. Apart from this fact, however, the cognitive and epistemic dynamics in play will be very similar. This raises the question of whether the mere fact that the belief in question is true should do anything to change our epistemic assessment of the believer, or, whether perhaps the believer in this case just "got lucky" that his evidence was good evidence.

With this in mind, let us return to the case of young Harry. In the previous chapter, we left off Harry's story after we had satisfied ourselves that he was really in no position to simply decline Ron's testimony that Slytherins are slimy. So far, this speaks only to the question of the acquisition of prejudice. As with Solomon, questions about the maintenance of prejudice arise most fully after he has arrived at his new school.

Harry cannot rationally decline the information that Ron offers to him, and he has, at the time in question, no other information with which to counterbalance Ron's testimony. How should we characterize the belief that he is required to form in his evidential situation? While Ron's testimony justifies Harry's belief that Slytherins are slimy, it would not justify Harry in attaching credence 1 to that proposition. Minimally, Harry must take into account the possibility that Ron might be misinformed, or that Ron's family attachments to Gryffindor have created an affectively motivated bias. He should probably also be open to the possibility that Ron is simply trying to manipulate him. But Harry can keep these possibilities in mind and still end up believing, and rationally so, given his total evidence, that Slytherins are slimy.

Let's say that on the basis of Ron's testimony, and the surrounding meta-epistemic considerations, Harry adopts something in the range of a .85 credence in the proposition that Slytherins are slimy. Let us assume (i) that he is right to assign this credence in the proposition, and (ii) assigning this credence amounts to "believing the proposition" by any sensible notion of belief. Credence-wise, it may, for instance, be no weaker than my belief that it will rain tomorrow, after looking at the tonight's cloud formation and reading the forecast. Even if my credence is less than 1, registering the fact that my information is incomplete, etc., we should still have no problem saying that I believe it will rain tomorrow. So, Harry comes to believe, as he epistemically should, that Slytherins are slimy.

Finally, Harry arrives at school and is enormously relieved to be assigned to Gryffindor rather than Slytherin. He has his first encounters with people in Slytherin. These encounters provide him with new evidence. Now, how should he process this evidence? Well, some of them are truly slimy. Clearly, this strengthens his credence both in Ron's testimony and in the belief that he acquired through it.[12] Some of them, though, don't seem so bad. Some encounters are perfectly neutral; others might appear to show Slytherins as rather quite personable. What should he think now? I submit that it would truly be epistemically irrational of him to simply discard his belief on these first encounters with apparently non-slimy Slytherins. He has reason to believe that Ron's testimony is ultimately grounded (via his older siblings) in a wider variety of experiences with Slytherins than he himself has had access to. In other words, his own first-personal experiences constitute a weaker evidential base than he can access via Ron's testimony. Moreover, he has plausible epistemic reasons to hold his belief at some distance from the contrary evidence: (i) he can think, in line with Solomon's reasoning above, that while Slytherins are slimy, not all Slytherins are equally slimy;

---

[12] For further reflections on this dual-aspect feature of testimonial evidence, see Begby 2020c.

further, (ii) he can reason that their sliminess manifests in different ways, and that I, Harry, lack the social acuity to tell which are the relevant contexts in which to judge them; finally, (iii) he can assume that Slytherins might have strategic reasons to appear to him as non-slimy, even though in fact they are. In other words, in light of what Harry can presume to know (given Ron's testimony), these encounters provide misleading evidence.

The example of Harry shows, just like the example of Solomon, how someone might be rationally required—not just excused or permitted—to retain his belief even in the face of significant contrary evidence. There is one difference, however, between the two cases, namely that Harry's belief is true (so we assume) while Solomon's belief is false. But what difference should this make to our assessments of the epistemic standing of the two subjects? In my opinion, none at all. Evidence is what justifies belief, and evidentially speaking, Solomon's situation is easily on par with Harry's.[13]

5.4 New Evidence in Light of Old Beliefs

Let us return to the case of Solomon. As *we*, with our settled convictions on the matter, look at Solomon's total body of evidence, we might have a hard time shaking the sense that it clearly decides the matter in favor of *our* belief that women are every bit as smart as men. And that it settles the matter *for us* is not in question. The common view goes farther, however, in holding that it must also settle the matter for Solomon. In assuming this further step, the common view fails to appreciate the degree to which what one already believes can rationally control the interpretation of new evidence.

For instance, in his discussion of the Solomon-example, José Medina argues that people who are brought up in deeply prejudiced societies under the cognitive sway of problematic stereotypes "are likely to develop

---

[13] One might object that the example is dubiously relevant, simply because the stereotype in question doesn't attach to "deep properties" that track individuals through many aspects of their lives, in the way that, say, race or gender does. This strikes me as false: individual lives at Hogwarts are very much formed by their identity as Slytherins, etc. Moreover, school identity plausibly serves as a very strong reinforcement mechanism, amplifying and streamlining certain kinds behaviors. We are free to imagine that even someone with only a weak disposition towards self-aggrandizing sliminess (perhaps Harry himself) could be assigned to Slytherin and thereby come to exhibit those properties in a much stronger way. Even if Harry were fully convinced that school houses constituted an entirely socially constructed identity, he might also believe that Slytherins come, by way of institutionally sanctioned mechanisms of socialization, to exhibit the relevant trait to a greater degree than others. And he would reasonably interpret his social experiences in that light.

epistemic habits that protect established cultural expectations and make them relatively blind and deaf to those things that seem to defy those expectations. In the first place, they will lack the motivation and intellectual curiosity to probe the evidence more fully, to ask about alternative explanations, and to find out more. In other words, the social imaginary produces a strong form of epistemic laziness that blocks evidentiary explorations" (Medina 2013: 67–8). But whether or not it *is* true that Solomon is engaging in this sort of active ignorance, I'm arguing that it *need not* be true in order nonetheless to produce effectively the same outcome. Given his epistemic situation as described in the example, we could in fact imagine Solomon being pleasantly surprised to discover so many smart women at the university and devote considerable epistemic resources to explaining how this might be. But given his intellectual starting point and given his evidence, it is not clear that any amount of openmindedness and intellectual curiosity should—epistemically speaking—lead him to form a substantially different belief.

It is by now a familiar insight from confirmation theory that people with different background beliefs ("theories") may reasonably differ in their assessment of the significance of new evidence.[14] The point can be conveniently stated in terms of Bayesian theory, although it by no means depends on it: the significance of new evidence to existing beliefs ("hypotheses") depends on the prior probabilities that one assigns to the evidence and to the hypothesis under consideration. As we have seen, Solomon might assign a very low prior probability to the hypothesis that women are as intelligent as men at the same time as he assigns a relatively high prior probability to finding evidence of female intelligence in a university setting. In light of these prior probabilities, his encounters with intelligent university women demand little if any adjustment to his background beliefs.[15] But with different background beliefs, the significance of the evidence might, of course, be very different.

These observations should clearly move us to ask how anyone could be epistemically entitled to hold such negatively charged background beliefs in the first place. And that was precisely the point of dealing with questions of prejudice acquisition and prejudice maintenance separately. As I argued in

---

[14] See Kelly 2006/2014 for an overview of the role of background belief in the assessment of evidence.

[15] In a similar vein, Harry can of course assign a low probability to the hypothesis that Slytherins are stand-up people, but a high probability to the hypothesis that they will try to come across to him as stand-up people.

chapter 4, there are many kinds of epistemic contexts in which subjects will be epistemically justified in acquiring prejudiced beliefs. As we have seen in this chapter, both Arpaly and Fricker materially agree that this is the case: Solomon's belief receives strong support from multiple evidential sources at the time in question; in recognition of this fact, their argument then changes to focus on the epistemology of prejudice maintenance. But as I have argued in this chapter, given Solomon's epistemically justified starting point, there need be nothing epistemically irrational about him retaining his prejudiced belief even in the face of the sort of evidence that we, putative straight-thinkers, would take to be decisive evidence to the contrary.

5.4.1 How Much Resistance?

But of course, while *some* degree of rational resistance to counterevidence is built into prejudiced beliefs, this resistance is not total. Allport's requirement of being suitably open to new evidence remains very much in force for any epistemically rational agent, whatever their starting point. I have argued that prejudiced people can often meet this requirement while still remaining prejudiced. But certainly, we can imagine *some* constellations of evidence that a prejudiced person might be confronted with, such that he would be rationally required to decisively change his mind.

Assume that in addition to the women he meets at the university, Solomon will also encounter women in more mundane, quotidian settings (coffee shops, public transportation, etc.). As is nicely pointed out by Paul Silva Jr. (Silva 2018), any information that Solomon gleans from these encounters cannot be easily "screened off" in the same way information gleaned from his encounters in the university setting can: whereas university women are selected for their intelligence, and in this sense constitute a biased sample, women in the more mundane settings must be presumed to constitute something much closer to a random selection. Assume now that Solomon overhears a conversation between two women on the subway, and is struck by how intelligent they both seem. He is now in possession of evidence which should lead to him downgrade, by however little, his cre-dence in the proposition that women are not as intelligent as men. But if Solomon leads a relatively normal life, and doesn't take steps to seclude himself from such evidence, then we should expect him to have a number of such encounters over time, each of which should contribute further to his loss of confidence in his previous belief. Reflection suggests that there must be some (finite) number of such encounters that Solomon could have after which he could no longer rationally sustain his belief that women are less intelligent than men.

I am happy to concede this point: in fact, I think it should be apparent that it essentially confirms the thesis of this chapter. First, it confirms that there need be nothing wrong, epistemically speaking, with Solomon's prejudice going into the situation. Second, it confirms that Solomon could respond correctly to a startling number of contrary bits of evidence while still remaining prejudiced. (On the order of hundreds, apparently: see Silva 2018: 14–16. And, of course, the more prejudiced you are initially, the more such evidence is required.) So it follows that a prejudiced person can meet the Allportian requirement of cognitive flexibility and openness to new evidence, while still remaining prejudiced. That is to say, even in cases where Solomon actively seeks out new evidence and adjusts his belief accordingly, he should— epistemically speaking—still likely end up with a sexist belief (albeit a somewhat less starkly sexist belief): he will simply think that the cognitive differences between men and women are less pronounced than he might have assumed initially. But clearly, this is consistent with his continuing to think that such differences obtain and remain significant. As a result, he remains prejudiced against women, even though he has done everything right by his evidence. Quite simply, given a prejudiced starting point, there is no obvious way that the mere idea of "responding correctly to new evidence" of female intelligence will automatically require Solomon to abandon his sexist belief.

But we can also use the occasion to pry a little deeper into the epistemic dynamics of Solomon's situation. First, should we accept, just as such, the assumption that these overheard conversations provide relevant evidence of intelligence? Presumably *some* conversations he overhears will do just that. But if Solomon's subway experiences are anything like mine, the vast majority of subway conversations he happens to overhear will be entirely inane (if only because of the topic of discussion). Of course, he might find that men are *as likely* to engage in inane subway conversations as are women. Far from supporting the hypothesis that women are as smart as men, this would rather go toward showing that subway conversations provide relatively poor evidence of intelligence.[16]

---

[16] This is, of course, another good Bayesian point: given his strong confidence in the relative intelligence of men over women, finding that men and women are essentially indistinguishable in terms of the quality of their subway chatter is reason to believe that this chatter is not a significant measure of intelligence.

Second, even if we were brought to concede that overheard subway conversations constitute evidence, we have not yet determined what the *relative strength* of this evidence may be. It is true, of course, that a large body of weak evidence can offset a smaller body of stronger evidence. But Silva's argument works best if we assume that Solomon meets with no other significant evidence during the relevant period of time. However, this seems implausible. Assume that Solomon is also active in other social venues, such as the chess club and the local film society. Solomon believes that members of these clubs are significantly smarter that average folks. He also notices, of course, that the overwhelming majority of members of both clubs are men. On his view, these unequal base rates are just reflections of the fact that men are, by and large, significantly smarter than women. Given this epistemic starting point, it is hard to deny that the conversations that he has in these clubs provide significantly *stronger* evidence of intelligence than conversations that he overhears on the subway. And presumably, he is significantly more likely to have these conversations with men than with women. So whatever evidence he accrues during his various subway rides needs to be continuously measured against, for instance, the evidence that he gets from engaging in conversations at the chess club or the film society. Even if his social life is limited, and he ends up *overhearing* significantly more conversations than he *engages* in, he might still believe (not unreasonably) that the conversations he engages in provide significantly stronger evidence than the conversations he merely overhears. And so, the epistemically beneficial effects of his random eavesdropping on the subway must be offset against the presumptively stronger, though more selective evidence that he receives through his social circles.

In brief, Silva's analysis of the positive significance of chance encounters with intelligent women seems to build on important idealizations regarding the kinds of evidential trajectories that prejudiced people are likely to meet with. There is nothing intrinsically wrong about that. But it is nonetheless worth taking a moment to explore its significance. In general, it doesn't seem unreasonable to suppose that a society which is deeply permeated by prejudiced beliefs may also be a society in which institutional barriers are set up to effectively preclude encounters of just this kind. For instance, it is worthwhile to take a moment to reflect on the fact that, as our lead example stipulates, Solomon encounters a significant number of female students even in the university setting. While this is something we take for granted now, it was a relative rarity in many Western societies until quite recently. Further, there is the assumption that Solomon is likely to have these random encounters with women outside the university setting. Again, that is something we take for granted, and which is plausibly supported by contingent features of the example which situate him somewhere in the contemporary United States. We are free to imagine some other person, raised into a similar epistemic situation, who is not so fortunate: Ahmed, for instance, though he has now moved from his home village to study at King Abdullah University of Science and Technology (KAUST), is rather less likely than Solomon to have random encounters with women as he ventures outside the campus.[17] (How he *would* respond to the contravening evidence that he doesn't have is a difficult question to answer: the cultural context in which he would plausibly have access to that evidence is so vastly different from the cultural context he was brought up in, that it may be impossible to resolve the counterfactual. This is, of course, one reason I resist Allport's view that the true mettle of the non-prejudiced mind is not so much *what one believes* as *whether one is adequately sensitive to contravening evidence.*)

5.5 Summary

The common approach to the epistemology of prejudice pivots on a stark contrast between, on the one hand, the flexible openmindedness in the face of new evidence which supposedly constitutes intellectual virtue, and, on the other hand, the dogmatic closemindedness of the prejudiced believer. In this chapter, I have argued that this contrast is illusory. In plausible epistemic contexts, a prejudiced believer can very well adjust to new evidence in precisely the way that our best epistemic theories prescribe, yet remain prejudiced.

To see how prejudices are capable of absorbing such contrary evidence, we must recognize that they paint a more complex picture of the world than the common view assumes. This is the insight that we gain from the realization that the logical form of prejudices is better captured in terms of generics than in terms of universal generalizations. If prejudices took the form of universal generalizations, they would be *epistemically fragile*; easy to

---

[17] Opened in 2009, KAUST was the first mixed-gender university campus in Saudi Arabia. In contrast to the extensive gender segregation enforced in Saudi-Arabian society at large (even after hopeful legislation cast in August 2019), the religious police do not operate on the KAUST campus and men and women are permitted to mix freely. According to a BBC report, "some Saudis are concerned the university will become an international bubble which will operate in another dimension to the rest of the country."

diagnose and dismiss, even from a first-person perspective. By taking this position, the common view unwittingly encourages the idea that we can know, simply by making sure we are correctly applying the canons of inductive inference, that our social cognition is free of prejudice. I believe this idea is misguided and pernicious: instead, it belongs precisely to the insidiousness of prejudice that they are *epistemically robust*, in the sense of being highly recalcitrant to apparent counterevidence and therefore often invisible to introspective reflection.

None of this is to deny that many instances of prejudice may (also) be held in place by the irrational contrivances of bias, motivated believing, affected ignorance, or similar mechanisms. It is, rather, to deny that they must *always* or *necessarily* involve some such distinctive and specifiable manner of epistemic irrationality. Though comforting, the common view of the epistemology of prejudice is false: many prejudices are epistemically on par with the social stereotypes that we all invest our trust in on an everyday basis, often without even recognizing them as such.

I conclude that neither in belief acquisition nor in belief maintenance need the prejudiced person's epistemic policies be significantly different from those we all deploy (justifiably, or so we must presume) in our everyday lives. And if the general outlook of this book is correct that epistemic rationality is a notion that primarily bears on process rather than product, then it follows that we have no good grounds for saying that prejudiced belief is necessarily a manifestation of some kind of epistemically irrationality. Considerations of epistemic luck may be relevant here: what distinguishes us from Solomon and his ilk may largely be a matter of our good epistemic luck, i.e., the luck of being bequeathed from early age with social stereotypes that are largely true (or so, at least, we like to believe).

6

Evidential Preemption

The conclusion emerging from the previous two chapters is that no good case can be made that prejudiced belief always exemplifies some manner of epistemic irrationality. This is so whether we consider the acquisition of prejudice or its continued maintenance in the light of contrary evidence. Specifically, when we consider the way in which different societies exert some degree of control over the flow of information, we can recognize that there may be nothing intrinsically suboptimal about the epistemic processing routines deployed by prejudiced people. Differently put, in a suitably warped socio-epistemic context, even flawless epistemic rationality could output prejudiced beliefs. Insofar as relevant notions of epistemic goodness attach to the process and not to the product (see section 1.2), we ought to conclude that their beliefs may well be justified in precisely the same way that we presume that the majority of our commonplace beliefs are justified.

The arguments so far provide something like a general theoretical template for understanding how even perfectly rational epistemic processes could give rise to prejudiced belief. The next three chapters provide significantly more detail by outlining specific social and institutional mechanisms by which prejudiced beliefs might be boosted, disseminated, or insulated from contrary evidence. It is important to note how these mechanisms can be in place to a greater or lesser degree also in societies that we may not immediately think to classify as deeply prejudiced, such as our own.

We will start by considering a commonplace but understudied argumentative maneuver which I call "evidential preemption." It is a central thesis of this book that testimony, though often a beneficial epistemic mechanism, can also serve as a crucial vehicle for the propagation of prejudiced belief. Evidential preemption, as I will explain, is a subsidiary mechanism which tacks naturally on to testimony, and which may serve to effectively "inoculate" recipients against future contrary evidence. In this way, evidential preemption sheds a starker light on the confrontation of prejudiced belief with new evidence: in some cases, meeting this new evidence may actually *not* require you to reduce your credence at all; in fact, in certain circumstances, it might even license you to *increase* your confidence in the prejudiced belief. This apparently paradoxical effect arises from a perfectly general socio-epistemic mechanism, one that is frequently deployed also in perfectly benign circumstances. I will argue that evidential preemption has significant explanatory power not only with respect to the epistemological resilience of prejudice, but also with respect to a range of other troubling socio-epistemic phenomena, such as conspiracy theories, echo chambers, and "fake news."[1]

6.1 Evidential Preemption: The Very Idea

Evidential preemption is not uniquely identifiable by any particular type of linguistic expression, but is perhaps most easily recognizable in sentential constructions such as:

(i) "My opponents will tell you that *p*; but I say *q*."[2]

While certainly not new, variations on this maneuver appear to have entrenched themselves in recent politics and public life. For a representative example, consider Bill O'Reilly commenting on the 2015 State of the Union Address:

> Wages have fallen significantly during President Obama's tenure. He will tell you that's because he inherited a terrible recession but I'll tell you the wage situation is due to the expansion of high-tech in the marketplace when machines replace people and the high cost of doing business in the U.S.A.

---

[1] Finally, we can also note that evidential preemption puts more pressure on the widely accepted notion that beliefs are justified or not in light of the "evidence available to the agent" (see section 3.2 for more detail). Evidential preemption shows that evidence can be "available" in some relevant sense (for instance, in being widely broadcast), even as many subjects will not be in a position to make good epistemic use of it. In this way, I believe evidential preemption can add a significant dimension to analyses emphasizing "affected ignorance" (Moody-Adams 1994) or "active ignorance" (Medina 2013), as discussed in sections 5.2.2 and 5.4.

[2] Typically, we may take it that *p* and *q* are in some kind of apparent tension, so that the speaker can rely on the hearer to recognize that rational commitment to one proposition would prima facie exclude rational commitment to the other (e.g., "My opponents will tell you that I am too young and inexperienced to be a leader, but I say, this country is ready for change.").

In a similar vein, here is Newt Gingrich, writing for the American Enterprise Institute in 2010:

> Washington is developing plans for your retirement savings...They will tell you that you are "investing" your money in U.S. Treasury bonds. But they will use your money immediately to pay for their unprecedented trillion-dollar budget deficits, leaving nothing to back up their political promises.

We can ask: what is the purpose of these moves? In particular, why would a speaker spend valuable airtime not just broadcasting their own take on how things are, but also advertising others' conflicting points of view?

I am interested in determining what role these sorts of utterances play in communication, in particular in testimonial exchange. As such, it might be helpful to begin by contrasting (i) with the following sort of case:

(ii)   "p, although some folks think that q."

Here, readers familiar with the work of H.P. Grice might be tempted by an analysis which foregrounds the *cooperative character of communication:*[3] in uttering (ii), I might be signalling to my hearer that though *I* believe that p, this is not a widely shared view, and that the hearer would do well to adjust his credence accordingly. This is a familiar enough phenomenon, and there are standard templates in epistemology and philosophy of language that can help us make sense of it: for instance, following the so-called "assurance view" of testimony,[4] we might think of it in terms of the speaker asserting that p, but then immediately moving to cancel out the "assurance" that usually travels along with it—i.e., the invitation to believe p based simply on speaker's testimony which is the normal concomitant of assertion.[5] In less theoretically laden terms, then, uttering (ii) would essentially amount to saying something like "p, but don't take my word for it."

I have no doubt that this analysis is appropriate for a number of cases which share surface properties with the ones that I am bringing to attention here. But there is an *antagonistic* element to (i) which this rather optimistic analysis seems unfit to account for. For neither O'Reilly nor Gingrich are seeking to temper the confidence that their audiences might take in their

---

[3] See Grice 1989.   [4] Cf. Moran 2005; Faulkner 2007.   [5] Cf. Goldberg 2015.

claims, by pointing out that apparently reasonable people hold opposing views: to the contrary, they are seeking to undercut these opposing views, but apparently without having to resort to offering additional argument, evidence, or proof.[6]

How might this maneuver help them achieve this end? In what follows, I will analyze the epistemological consequences of evidential preemption under two distinct modes, which I will call, respectively, preemption by neutralization (section 6.2) and preemption by source discrediting (section 6.3). I will argue that in many cases, either mode of evidential preemption can succeed in materially affecting the evidential situation that the audience find themselves in—or more precisely, the situation that they will find themselves in once the future evidence is disclosed. In this way, evidential preemption can affect not just how people will be *psychologically disposed* to respond to future evidence, but also how it will be *epistemically rational* for them to respond. Before this, however, it will be helpful to have a brief look at the psychological motivations underlying the production of testimony in the first place.

6.1.1 Motivating Testimony

In introducing evidential preemption, it will be helpful to note that assertions, at least of the sort that is typically of interest to epistemologists, are typically "motivated," in the simple sense that the speaker is not just looking to fill the airwaves, but is aiming to redirect an inquiry, persuade an audience, disseminate a significant truth, and so forth. Recognizing this motivation is presumably key to explaining why speakers would ever be moved to make

---

[6] This antagonistic element may also help shed some light on when evidential preemption is likely to be a viable strategy and when it is not. For instance, if someone were to say "others will tell you that one should start buttoning one's shirts from the top, but I say it's best to start in the middle," the utterance might, at best, be understood merely as expressing the speaker's idiosyncratic preference. Similarly, if someone said "others will tell you that Elvis was born in Tupelo, but I say he was born in Jackson," the attempt to persuade might well backfire, causing the hearer to be *less* inclined to accept the testimony than he might otherwise be, simply because of the added rider about what others will say. What such examples would lack, in my view, is some plausible back story about why others would be wrong about such a trivial fact, or why it should be in their interest that I be misinformed about it. By contrast, when we deal with ethically or politically charged content, this back story is often not far to seek. Indeed, in our highly polarized and politicized information economy, such antagonistic interactions are legion, and in many places, are virtually assumed by default. Evidential preemption, I believe, can be expected to work best in contexts where such antagonism is part of our common understanding of what is at stake.

assertions at all, in light of its associated risks: as epistemologists have recently pointed out, assertions are governed by norms, such that if one's assertion were shown to be wrong or unfounded, one would thereby have rendered oneself subject to possibly significant social sanction.[7]

This observation brings to salience a point that has not received a lot of attention in the relevant literature: in standard cases of testimonial transaction, it is clearly not a matter of indifference to the speaker which belief the hearer ends up endorsing as a result—rather, the speaker asserts that p *because* he wants us to believe that p.[8] In particular, the world being what it is, testifiers will often recognize a distinctive interest in "safeguarding" their testimonial contribution against future contrary testimony from other parties. For instance, my testifier might understand that I am subsequently likely to meet with other apparently equally knowledgeable and sincere people who will gladly testify that not-p (or testify to some further proposition q, which is clearly in conflict with p). He understands that I will then be in a predicament broadly akin to that recently described in terms of the epistemology of expert disagreement: at that point, I will be in possession of two bits of contrary evidence in the form of testimony from apparently equally knowledgeable sources.[9] In the absence of an independent reason to favor one expert over another, my only rational recourse might be to cancel my belief in p and retreat to a position of suspended belief.[10]

Given my (original) testifier's interest that I maintain my belief in p, what options are open to him? One way to control the flow of information is, of course, to try to prevent my exposure to the contrary testimony in the first place. But this can be a costly and resource-draining endeavor; moreover, it carries its own risks in cases where the defensive bulwark is breached. So here is a subtler strategy: he can instead say something like the following: "my opponents will tell you that q; but I say p."

It is my thesis that this rather innocent-looking move can actually succeed in shaping the hearer's future epistemic situation in a rather dramatic way. If so, this is clearly troubling, and we would do well to develop an understanding of how it might work.

---

[7] For contrasting perspectives on the substance and consequence of the "norm of assertion," see, e.g., Lackey 2007, Weiner 2007, Brown and Cappelen 2011, McKinnon 2015, Goldberg 2015, and Begby 2020c.

[8] Whether he wants us to believe that p because he sincerely has our epistemic well-being in mind, or because he wants to manipulate us is not relevant at this point: as I will argue later, evidential preemption can occur in both kinds of cases, to similar effect.

[9] Cf. Goldman 2001 and Coady 2012, chapter 2, for discussions of these issues.

[10] See Elga 2007 and Christensen 2007 for articulations of this sort of view.

6.2 Preemption by Neutralization

I have introduced the topic by highlighting the speaker's motivation for resorting to evidential preemption. By contrast, most discussions of the epistemology of testimony are focused on the recipient's perspective, on his or her reasons for accepting or declining the information that is offered through another's testimony. As we move on, it is worth noting that our appreciation of the problems raised by evidential preemption does not seem to depend on whether we favor one or another of the standard approaches to the epistemology of testimony. As virtually anyone working in this area will agree, I can, in favorable circumstances, be epistemically justified in forming my beliefs based on what other people tell me. Where philosophers disagree is on the question of how exactly to specify these circumstances. On non-reductionist views, I can be justified, at least in some situations, in forming beliefs simply on another's say-so. On the contrasting reductionist view, I can only ever be justified in light of some previous bit of epistemic legwork, for instance in reasonably assigning a relatively high degree of confidence in the speaker's competence and sincerity.[11] Both accounts can be satisfied in the cases I am interested in, for typically, reductionist accounts concede that the epistemic processing in question can be quite minimal: in order for me to form the belief that p on the basis of another's say-so, I must have reasonably determined that the speaker seems knowledgeable and sincere, and I must have considered p in light of other things I presume to know about the situation.[12] But the evidence to support those assessments can be overall quite weak, so long as there are no apparent defeaters.

To align our inquiry with these well-known approaches, then, assume that the hearer is in a recognizable and common epistemic predicament, i.e., he has an interest in knowing whether p, but lacks either the intellectual capacities or the worldly wherewithal to determine whether p for himself. Now here is an apparently knowledgeable and sincere person who is keen to

---

[11] The broad distinction between reductionist and non-reductionist approaches to the epistemology of testimony goes all the way back to Hume 1748 and Reid 1764, 1785. Few today would endorse a strongly reductionist approach to testimony: see Coady 1973, 1992 for a powerful case against. But see, e.g., Fricker 1994 and Lackey 2006 for sophisticated attempts to incorporate some of the motivations for reductionist approaches into a viable, critical account of testimony. The examples I give in the following satisfy the constraints stipulated also in these more demanding approaches.

[12] See, e.g., Fricker 1994, 2006; Lackey 2006.

offer testimony on the matter.[13] Assume that appropriate epistemic conditions are satisfied, and that it is reasonable for the hearer to form the belief that p in light of the testifier's say-so: that is, the hearer has determined that the speaker is well-positioned to offer testimony regarding p; in the absence of defeaters, the testimony furnishes him with an epistemic justification for believing that p.

But here's the trouble: the speaker does not just offer testimony that p, but also issues a warning that others will try to persuade him of an opposing viewpoint. What is the hearer to do with this extra information? It is one thing to observe that the speaker might be working on him psychologically to be disposed to maintaining a belief in p even after being confronted with contrary testimony, hoping, perhaps, to exploit well-known mechanisms of familiarity bias.[14] But if our analysis were to stop with this observation, we would be missing sight of an epistemically significant dimension of the transaction. For the speaker may also have succeeded in materially changing the evidential situation the hearer will be in once the contrary testimony is offered to him. As I will argue, it does so by giving the hearer reason to believe that whatever information would be gained through that subsequent disclosure has already been taken into account in forming the belief that p.

Here is how: the testifier has a reasonable grasp of hearer's epistemic situation, and understands that by uttering p, he will put the hearer in an epistemic position where he is justified in forming the belief that p. Nonetheless, he also knows that contrary testimony will tend to erode that justification. In moving to preempt evidence from subsequent contrary testimony, the speaker is signalling to the hearer that even though the balance of evidence strongly favors p, the evidential situation relating to p is complex, with numerous factors counting both for and against. Others, who may appear knowledgeable and sincere, may believe differently, but they will be wrong. Evidential preemption, then, highlights one part of the total evidence—q—which will likely be made available to me at a later point, evidence which, if it were considered in isolation, would seem to indicate not-p. If that evidence were subsequently made available to me without forewarning, I would be rationally required to see it as cancelling out my reasons for believing that p. But now that the evidence has been preempted, the subsequent disclosure is neutralized and thereby rendered epistemically moot. I call this preemption by neutralization because it relieves the speaker

---

[13] Consider again the case of Harry and Ron, discussed in chapters 4 and 5.
[14] Cf. Heath and Tversky 1991.

of the pressure to provide further evidence against q, or even to go on record as denying that q is the case. The neuralization can be achieved simply by acknowledging that others believe that q, at the same time as one asserts that p.

Preemption by neutralization exploits an underlying general principle: in standard cases, whatever it is that justifies my epistemic trust in my testifier's assertion that p also justifies my epistemic trust in my testifier's assessment of the total evidence that bears on p. Differently put, maintaining one's epistemic right to believe that p based on another's testimony requires a positive epistemic commitment (i.e., not indifference) to the proposition that one's source is well-positioned to provide testimony that p.[15] This commitment need not, of course, be particularly salient in one's reasoning leading up to the decision to accept the testimony. Nor do we need to model this commitment in terms of a separate belief, with its own proprietary body of evidence bearing on it.[16] But the commitment would show itself nonetheless if, say, I were presented with a forced-choice bet on whether my testifier, whose testimony I have just accepted, is relevantly well-informed (Y/N). In such a case, I should clearly be more inclined to put my money on Y than N.[17] Conversely, if it were brought to my attention that I have reason *not* to trust my testifier's assessment of the total evidence that bears on p, then I should immediately recognize a reason to modify my confidence in my testimonially acquired belief that p.[18]

---

[15] This principle is "general" in the sense that variations can be given for any similarly structured epistemological product–process relation—be it testimony, perception, reasoning, or memory—where one's belief-formation is reliant on a particular information channel. For an influential articulation in the case of perception, see Wright 2004.

[16] Again, see Wright 2004, where considerable time is spent arguing that one's commitment to the "credentials" of one's sensory experience need not take the form a belief. Following van Fraassen (1980), he proposes instead to model it in terms of "acceptance": rational acceptance of P obtains when "one is warranted in acting on the assumption that P or taking it for granted that P or trusting that P for reasons that do not bear on the likely truth of P" (Wright 2004: 177). (Note that the distinction between belief and acceptance plays a significant role also in this book (see sections 1.5 and 9.1.3).)

[17] Which is not to say that I should put *all* my money on Y. I might, after all, have varying degrees of confidence in different testifiers, even if we restrict our consideration to those whose testimony I would be broadly inclined to accept.

[18] Denying this would amount to affirming something very much like a Moorean paradox: that is, it would amount to asserting that it is generally OK for me to hold that I am justified in believing that p on the basis of information provided through a particular channel while purporting to remaining neutral (or even skeptical) on the question of whether information that travels along that channel is generally worth trusting. True, some philosophers (e.g., Williamson 2011; Lasonen-Aarnio 2014) have argued that in certain cases, there need be nothing intrinsically irrational about believing that p while simultaneously conceding that one's evidence does not support p. Let us agree that such cases of genuine "epistemic akrasia"

If this is right, then I cannot generally be epistemically positioned so that I can accept my testifier's assertion that p, but remain free to decline the accompanying evidential preemption: the same conditions that would justify me in taking the assertion will also, in the absence of countervailing reasons, justify me in accepting the evidential preemption, insofar as it is essentially just presented to me as an articulation of my testifier's assessment of one specific part of the total evidence that bears on p. That is, the evidential preemption serves to signal to me that one particular bit of evidence bearing on p, which if taken in isolation would seem to render p problematic, has already been taken into account. If I were merely offered testimony that p, I would be bound to take subsequent testimony that q as throwing p into doubt. But if I am offered testimony that p plus a warning that others will say q, then I can be entitled to believe that q is consistent with p. (Why else would my apparently rational and well-meaning testifier nonetheless maintain that p?) I now have reason to believe that anyone who highlights q as a way to cast doubt on p is simply wrong or misinformed. Accordingly, when that bit of evidence is subsequently disclosed, its epistemic effect has already been neutralized.

6.2.1 Evidential Preemption in a Bayesian Framework

This intuitive account of what evidential preemption can accomplish can usefully be supplemented with a somewhat more technical rendering in terms inspired by Bayesian confirmation theory. Bayesian confirmation theory builds on the important insight that the significance of new evidence can only be determined against the background of the information that we already have in our possession, as reflected in our prior probabilities. In particular, conditionalization requires determining the unconditional probability of new evidence (i.e., ("P(E)"). All else being equal, the lower the probability of the evidence (given parameters $\{p, q \ldots n\}$), the greater its potential impact on what we should believe (or, to be more precise, the greater its potential impact on our posterior probabilities, i.e., our prior

---

are possible. But the basic cases of perception and testimony under consideration here don't fit the mould of any of the examples that have taken center-stage in these debates, such as improbable knowing or misleading higher-order evidence. (See Horowitz 2014 for critical discussion of these examples.)

probabilities adjusted in light of the new evidence).[19] By contrast, high-probability evidence is evidence that is predicted by, and therefore compatible with, what we already presume to know, and will therefore not require us to revise our beliefs to any significant degree.[20]

Stated in this framework, evidential preemption can be seen as an attempt to adjust an audience's assignments of probabilities to specific bits of future evidence in such a way as to neutralize their potential significance. If I were merely offered testimony that p, then subsequent testimony that q would constitute low-probability evidence, and would have a potentially significant impact on my confidence in p. By contrast, if I am offered testimony that p plus a warning that others will say q, then subsequent testimony that q constitutes high-probability evidence, which will have minimal (if any) impact on my confidence in p. In effect, I am not learning anything new— not acquiring significant new information—when others say that q. But new information is, essentially, the currency on which beliefs are to be updated. The preempted evidence has thereby been rendered epistemically neutral, insofar as it was fully predicted by my previous probability assignments. It is a moot point that the same evidence, given different probability assignments, would have a very different epistemic impact, counting strongly in favor of not-p. In our case, q's compatibility with p is secured by the justification for accepting p in the first place. If I were justified in believing p on the evidence I had at the time, then I am, all else equal, justified in continuing to maintain p even after the later testimony has been offered. That others will say that q is now, in effect, information that I have already conditionalized on. In this sense, evidential preemption can succeed in altering the audience's evidential situation in such a way as to materially affect what it will be rational for them to believe at some future time, not just what they will be psychologically disposed to believe.

6.3 Preemption by Source Discrediting

So far, the analysis has focused on cases where the speaker aims to undercut the force of future evidence by (partially) conceding the facts while

---

[19] I am here setting aside the difficult cases where my rational confidence in the original hypothesis is so high that I would have better reasons to dismiss the apparently contrary evidence than I have to dismiss the hypothesis.

[20] See, e.g., Bovens and Hartmann 2003.

preemptively *neutralizing* their epistemic significance. These are perhaps the most common cases, and also provide a clear and convenient platform for exploring the epistemological underpinnings of evidential preemption.

But it also seems that evidential preemption can do similar work in a more blunt way, by discrediting the source of the future evidence outright. For an important hint, we can return to the examples from Newt Gingrich and Bill O'Reilly. Both are concerned to preempt claims likely to emerge from the White House. They do so by providing an alternative hypothesis which undermines the credibility of the claims in question. But notice that neither Gingrich nor O'Reilly are particularly concerned to provide evidence for these alternative hypotheses. Nor need they, given the epistemic situation they are in: they know their audiences well, and they know that their audience combines an enormous confidence in them as political authorities with an extreme skepticism toward any pronouncement from the sitting Democratic president.[21] Indeed, the mere fact that their alternative accounts purport to unmask the Democratic White House as liars and manipulators is itself sufficient to boost the audience's confidence in their testimony.[22] Crucially, when the White House then subsequently goes on to make those very statements, their testimony is rendered epistemically inert: if anything, the utterance can create an ironic backlash, insofar as the statement can only confirm my original testifier's prediction. That is, the only new information that I would gain at that point is that my original testifier was right, as I already had reason to believe he would be.[23]

It will be tempting to think that this can work only because the audience is suffering from severe epistemic pathologies: they are willing to accept statements offered even by manifest charlatans so long as these statements confirm their bigoted opinion of others. This may be true of these particular cases. But I believe that in other cases, the overall epistemic situation of a hearer may be such as to render it quite reasonable for them to accept even a form of evidential preemption which works only by undermining the credibility of the source of the evidence.

---

[21] Consider Barack Obama's humorous quip: "And look, if I watched Fox News, I wouldn't vote for me. I understand. If I were listening to Rush Limbaugh, I'd say 'man...that's terrible.' Fortunately, I have more diverse sources of information."

[22] Donald Trump's "Crooked Hillary" epithet could obviously be seen to follow along these lines.

[23] In this sense, I hold that evidential preemption can also cast new light on the notion of "belief polarization," as discussed, for instance, in Sunstein 2002, Kelly 2008, Jern, Chang, and Kemp 2014, Singer et al. 2019, Dorst 2019, Nielsen and Stewart forthcoming.

For instance, this book has argued that many instances of prejudiced belief can be well supported by the available evidence, and, to that extent be epistemically justified. This is in sharp contrast with more common views which hold that prejudiced belief is always or necessarily the result of some sort of epistemic pathology or malfunction: the evidence to counter their prejudiced beliefs is readily available, but is either neglected, discounted, or inappropriately weighted.[24] I believe this view fails to take into account the degree to which testimony—in particular, testimony acquired during early childhood and adolescence—can reasonably come to shape people's cognitive outlooks. Once these beliefs are lodged in the mind, they can justifiably be maintained even in light of many kinds of counterevidence.

Consider, then, the epistemic situation of someone who has grown up in an enclosed cult-like community deeply committed to a variety of whacky conspiracy theories. While we may have a hard time seeing how anyone could justifiably acquire such beliefs in mature age, the situation is quite different for those who are exposed in a systematic fashion to such theories in early years. After all, it is not hard to find evidence for Chemtrails, for the fabrication of the Moon landing, and so on: one need only look to the skies on a clear day or consult the relevant websites.[25] For most of us, of course, such evidence carries very little weight in our overall epistemic assessment of the situation, or it is easily defeated by contrary evidence. But for someone to whom this is the only evidence, moreover evidence imprinted with the authority of peers and teachers in their community, the epistemic situation is significantly different. I take it to be quite clear that they can be justified in forming beliefs that are obviously false—indeed completely outrageous—to the rest of us.

6.3.1 Conspiracy Theories, Echo Chambers, and "Fake News"

Evidential preemption can play a crucial role in explaining the epistemological resilience not only of prejudice, but also of related phenomena such as conspiracy theories, echo chambers, and "fake news." For I take it to be a characteristic part of how such views are maintained in social settings that

---

[24] See chapters 4–5 for details.
[25] See Feldman (2009) for an articulation of such a low-threshold view of the nature of evidence, as well as my own discussion in section 1.4.

they not only provide the audience with a range of evidence relating directly to p, but that they also seek to preempt contrary evidence that the audience is likely to be confronted with at some point. Here, though, evidential preemption works not by indicating that the evidence is already taken into account, as in the cases we examined above. Instead, it works by directly discrediting the source. We know that we cannot insulate you from contrary evidence forever, so we preempt the future evidence by warning you, for instance, that the liberal media or university professors will tell you that q. But obviously, they will tell you that because they are part of the conspiracy, and so have no credibility on the matter. It is a blunter tool, to be sure, but the effect can be even more sweeping: if I am in an epistemic situation where the testimony of my peers and teachers rationally compels me to believe that p virtually no matter how outrageous p is, then it is hard to say why I should not also at the same time be rationally justified in taking on board their assessment of the credibility of various other sources. When that is done, then any evidence these sources will subsequently offer to me is rendered moot by preemptive discrediting: in fact, when the "liberal media" subsequently confirm the preemption by telling me just that, they are strengthening rather than weakening the evidential support for my belief that p. They are strengthening it, of course, not by providing direct evidence for p, but rather by providing evidence for the credibility of my testimonial source for believing p.[26] In a suitably warped socio-epistemic environment, then, evidential preemption can virtually inoculate an audience against future contrary evidence, insofar as any source that would seek to disclose such evidence would thereby show themselves to confirm my original beliefs.

We may put the point in terms of a distinction between first-order and higher-order evidence, which has recently come to the fore in the epistemology of disagreement: the epistemic grooming (as I will call it) that occurs in these contexts provides me not only with first-order evidence to believe a number of propositions; it also preemptively provides me with higher-order evidence about the credibility of a range of sources that would seek to contradict those propositions.[27] Transposed into this vocabulary, my thesis

---

[26] See Keeley 1999 for a perceptive analysis of the epistemology of conspiracy theories, one key point of which is their distinctive ability to convert prima facie contrary evidence into corroborating evidence.

[27] See, e.g., Feldman 2009, Kelly 2010, and Christensen 2010 for analyses of the interactions between first-order and higher-order evidence. In less favorable contexts, this sort of move might of course backfire spectacularly: if I say, "Roger Penrose will tell you that p, but I say q," in the context of a discussion of quantum gravity, a reasonable audience might instantly

is that if I am in an epistemic position where I am rationally compelled to believe the first-order evidence, then I am also in a position where I am epistemically justified in believing the higher-order evidence that travels with it (i.e., these other sources are unreliable because they are beneficiaries of the conspiracy and therefore motivated on non-epistemic grounds to deny these propositions).

These reflections have clear application to a socio-epistemic phenomenon prominently on display in contemporary US public discourse. In a recent and lucid analysis, C. Thi Nguyen has pointed out the difference between "epistemic bubbles" and "echo chambers."[28] Epistemic bubbles arise from the simple exclusion—inadvertently or no—of certain voices from a discussion. While we don't ordinarily choose our social circles with a view toward maximizing expected epistemic utility, we nonetheless rely on them for a number of important epistemic functions, such as providing information, confirmation, etc. An epistemic bubble is the non-intended by-product of this process. As a result, there is relevant information that is not being taken into account, simply because those who are in possession of the information are not given an opportunity to share it. Nonetheless, epistemic bubbles are fragile and can quite easily be "popped." Assuming that rational people generally prefer to form their beliefs in light of more information rather than less, pointing out to them that there is genuine information that they are missing out on should presumably motivate them to widen their epistemic circles. By contrast, echo chambers are much more resilient structures, where active measures are taken to ensure that the excluded voices remain excluded (Nguyen 2018: 6). And as Nguyen goes on to show, evidential preemption, in both forms that I have surveyed here, is a crucial mechanism for echo chamber construction and maintenance.

Admittedly, my analysis of the epistemic significance of evidential preemption has a whiff of rational reconstruction, and it is important not to lean too much on its explanatory potential as a psychological mechanism by which people form their political beliefs or broader epistemic dispositions "in the wild." But consider the phenomenon of "fake news." Drawing on Regina Rini's recent analysis (Rini 2017), one might well wonder whether much of what goes on in contemporary US public discourse is better

---

downgrade the credibility of my testimony, simply because I am signalling my disagreement with a manifestly superior epistemic source.

[28] See also Jamieson and Cappella 2008.

explained by a kind of "epistemic partisanship." Epistemic partisanship is a matter of assigning "greater credibility to a testifier *because* you know you share a political affiliation with her" (Rini 2017: 50). Notably, Rini argues that epistemic partisanship, like evidential preemption, is not intrinsically irrational. But everything has its limits, and our current susceptibility to fake news can be explained by our irrationally assigning too much credibility on such grounds.[29] I fully agree that many participants in US public discourse today are probably so set in their partisan ways that any rationalizing explanation will ring hollow. Nonetheless, I maintain that evidential preemption can play an important role in the explanation of how this state of affairs might have come about. Consider, specifically, the secondary sense of "fake news" which Rini registers in an addendum (Rini 2017: 59*fn*3): not, that is, the fake news of clickbait stories specifically manufactured for our credulous consumption (e.g., the infamous "pizzagate"), but rather the Trumpian manner of branding various news organizations wholesale as peddlers of fake news. At this point in time, of course, the temporal advantage provided by evidential preemption may no longer be particularly relevant; "fake news" serves as much as a ritual incantation, a call to arms, as an espousal of a superior epistemic vantage.[30] But at the same time, we may wonder how this situation came about. And here, it does not seem far-fetched to propose that endlessly iterated preemptions by source discrediting has played a significant role. After being subjected to repeated incantations of "the Democrats will tell you this" and "the mainstream media will tell you that," it is but a short inductive step to conclude that the next statement to come from those quarters will also be fake news.

Let us return to the question of epistemic justification. For instance, if we adopt something like a virtue-epistemological perspective,[31] we might observe that there's clearly a sense in which our current predicament is pathological when seen in the context of a larger picture of human flourishing: these people are obviously not leading healthy and prosperous

---

[29] Worsnip (2019) objects to Rini's analysis, citing a general epistemic obligation to "diversify one's sources." But arguably, merely exposing oneself to a greater variety of sources is unlikely to serve any epistemic benefit, unless there were also an added rider to remain "openminded" with respect to the likely accuracy of these various sources. But it's hard to see how this added rider could be consistent with the overarching epistemic requirement of total evidence. For clearly, I *have* epistemic reason to trust some sources more than others, even if those reasons, ultimately, turn out to correlate with my partisan affiliations.

[30] See, e.g., Hannon 2019.   [31] See, e.g., Battaly 2018.

cognitive lives.[32] This is, no doubt, an important perspective. Nonetheless, it seems clear that from the more circumscribed point of view of an evidence-centered normative epistemology, the question is really only one of how people could non-culpably get themselves into positions where this is a rational stance to take. Once we take into account the fact that they may well grow up in epistemically enclosed (or extremely polarized) communities, where they have been subjected to extensive epistemic grooming, it should be clear how they might. Here, evidential preemption provides an important part of the analysis of how such beliefs might entrench themselves in cognitive systems and come to acquire their distinctive resilience against counterevidence. Indeed, it is not hard to imagine that in a suitably warped socio-epistemic environment, evidential preemption can virtually inoculate an audience against future contrary evidence, insofar as any sources that would seek to disclose such evidence would thereby only show themselves to confirm my original beliefs.

6.4 Ethical Considerations

All the cases I have analyzed have a clear flavor of nefarious manipulation, for which the term "epistemic grooming" seems appropriate.[33] As such, it could be thought that though it might, given sub-optimal socio-epistemic circumstances, be rational for us to accept evidential preemption, the move itself is inherently manipulative, and should never form part of the communicative repertoires of well-intentioned people. In the closing section of this chapter, I want to draw this thought into doubt.

---

[32] But even here, things are not so simple. For instance, Cassam 2016 purports to offer a virtue-epistemological account of adherence to conspiracy theories in terms of intellectual character flaws. (For example, "Because he is gullible, dogmatic, closed-minded, cynical, prejudiced, and so on, he ignores important evidence which bears on his questions, relies on unreliable sources, jumps to conclusions and generally can't see the wood for the trees. The fact that this is how he goes about his business is a reflection of his intellectual character" (Cassam 2016: 165).) Needless to say, it is the contention of this book that such an analysis pays insufficient attention to the insidious epistemic mechanisms by which such beliefs often disseminate. In cases where dominant voices in the epistemic community can efficiently leverage resources such as evidential preemption, there may be nothing wrong, per se, with the intellectual character of the people who end up as believers. They are responding rationally to the highly constrained epistemic contexts that they happen to find themselves in.

[33] For another deployment of the concept of "grooming" in epistemic context, see Leydon-Hardy forthcoming.

It is a well-known fact that we are all, in different ways, less than perfectly rational,[34] and that we all suffer a range of epistemic blindspots and weaknesses.[35] Where these facts are known, it can be a perfectly reasonable strategy for concerned friends of mine to attempt to mitigate the effects of such vulnerabilities by preempting evidence that I will likely be confronted with at some later point. I take it that this is common in any learning situation. There is nothing nefarious, for instance, about an experienced cardiologist warning a colleague-in-training that relying too much on evidence from echocardiograms in diagnosing heart valve problems is likely to generate a large number of false positives, because varying degrees of backflow of blood can be noted even in perfectly healthy hearts.

More telling, perhaps, are cases where I aim to protect someone against the manipulative strategies of others. For instance, say I have a friend who I know to be epistemically impressionable and prone to conspiracy theories and other forms of quackery. I know that he travels in circles where ill-founded claims about the connection between vaccines and autism are trumpeted as scientific facts. It is perfectly reasonable for me to attempt to preempt that evidence by saying that it all stems from a falsified study. I may not provide further evidence for the claim that the study is bogus, either because I myself am unsure of the details, or because I doubt that such further evidence will be absorbed by my impressionable friend, who may lack basic training in statistics and experimental design. But even so, I rationally trust that the preemption will impact how he eventually approaches the inevitable disclosures, and I feel myself morally justified in deploying this strategy: after all, I am only trying protect a vulnerable friend from the manipulative epistemic agency of others.

In fact, it seems that both modes of evidential preemption that I have examined in this chapter can form part of reasonable people's discourse repertoires. That is, I can opt to concede certain facts while aiming to preemptively neutralize their epistemic significance: "Climate change deniers have begun pointing out that we may be entering a period of increased solar activity, and that this may have something to do with global warming. This is true, but these data are already taken into account in all standard models." Or I could seek to preempt the evidence by discrediting

---

[34] To forestall confusion, let me add that this is not the same as what I called "endogenous non-ideality" in chapter 2. Endogenous non-ideality places constraints on viable accounts of epistemic rationality. What is presently at stake is the various ways in which we might fall short even of a suitably de-idealized norm of epistemic rationality.

[35] See Ballantyne 2019 for a recent philosophical account.

the source outright: "Websites like truthseeker.org will say that the US government orchestrated the 9/11 attacks. But these guys are just crazy: look, they also argue that Elvis is still alive." Such counter-manipulative strategies, I think, can be in perfectly good ethical order. They show that there is nothing inherently nefarious about the resort to evidential preemption in ordinary human communication. In particular, it is important to recognize that such interventions *can* also serve to protect and enhance the target's overall epistemic autonomy.[36]

Zooming out to a larger, political perspective provides further support for this analysis. In brief, these people are typically participants in collective decision-making processes whose outcomes affect us all. As such, any community has a legitimate interest in exercising a modicum of control over the quality of information available to its constituents. Evidential preemption provides a means for achieving this, consistent with maintaining due recognition of the right to free speech.[37]

6.5 Concluding Remarks

While evidential preemption may seem like an innocent rhetorical flourish, I have argued that it can actually mask a significant epistemological device: it can materially affect not just how people will be psychologically disposed to respond to your opponent's subsequent assertion that *p*, but also how it will be epistemically rational for them to respond. In many circumstances, evidential preemption can serve to manipulate an audience's future epistemic situation by neutralizing or altogether undermining evidence that has yet to be disclosed to them.

Evidential preemption provides a new dimension to our analysis of the confrontation of prejudiced belief with new evidence. Previously (chapter 5), we have assumed, with the standard view, that exposure to contrary

---

[36] For a fuller discussion, see Begby 2020a, section 4. In this sense, evidential preemption differs in important ways from phenomena such as "gaslighting" as discussed in Abramson 2014 or the "predatory grooming" discussed in Leydon-Hardy forthcoming.

[37] In this way, my analysis may be seen to yield a surprising affinity with Rae Langton's analysis of the phenomenon of illocutionary silencing (cf. Langton 1993; Hornsby and Langton 1998). Whereas locutionary silencing corresponds to impositions on free speech more traditionally understood, illocutionary silencing works in a more nefarious manner by manipulating the audience's ability to engage in the proper uptake of the speech act. Nonetheless, our analyses depart on a crucial point: whereas Langton (et al.) appear to believe that illocutionary silencing is inherently problematic, I have argued that evidential preemption can serve a vital and well-justified role in safeguarding an epistemic community against motivated misinformation.

evidence always requires the epistemically rational agent to reduce his credence in the relevant proposition. The point at stake there was simply that in many cases, even correctly adjusting for this new evidence is likely to leave the agent with prejudiced beliefs intact. Evidential preemption shows that agents in fact aren't always required to reduce their credence in light of the new evidence. In the cases that I have dubbed preemption by neutralization, they have grounds for believing that they have already conditionalized on this evidence, and therefore would be irrational to do it again. In the cases I have dubbed preemption by source discrediting, exposure to new contrary evidence can have the paradoxical effect of increasing my rational confidence in the contested belief, because it increases my rational confidence in my testifier's overall epistemic standing.

Nonetheless, and like testimony itself, evidential preemption is a socio-epistemological mechanism which is neutral in its own right, and should be counted as good or bad only in its specific deployments. What is crucial, however, is that from a *consumer perspective*, there may be no way to tell the good deployments from the bad. This serves as a further reminder of the significance of exogenous non-ideality: in a suitably warped socio-epistemic context, even flawless adherence to the principles of epistemic normativity could serve to steer one's beliefs farther away from the truth.

7

Common Ground

The Peculiar Epistemology of 'Culturally Normal Belief'

The basic orientation of the project so far has been to start from a characterization of prejudice as a cognitive attitude, specifically a belief, held by individuals. We then observe how this attitude tends to spread from person to person by mechanisms of overt communication such as testimony, eventually affecting, in potentially very severe ways, the life quality of the people who are targeted by these attitudes.

When we raise concerns about prejudice from the point of view of epistemic rationality, we will typically be operating within this basic framework. We are asking how it could be *individually rational* for people to hold these kinds of beliefs, and in particular, whether they could ever be justified in retaining these beliefs in the face of the significant contrary evidence which appears to surround them. In the previous chapter, we investigated one significant mechanism—evidential preemption—which helps explain how people can rationally retain their prejudiced beliefs even in the face of significant contrary evidence. Prejudice, then, is not something that we can hope to fix simply by confronting people with relevant evidence: there is also the further question of what they are rationally able to do with this evidence. The fact that there is, in some sense, *available evidence* to counter these beliefs does not mean that individuals will be able to rationally *avail* themselves of it.

While this individualist orientation is very useful for bringing traditional philosophical concerns into focus, it shouldn't be our only framing of the issues. True, my account has made significant moves to place the problem of prejudiced belief in a social context. But so far, we have mostly thought about this social embedding in terms of how testimony provides a source of evidence for individual thinkers. In this chapter, I will, in a tentative and exploratory fashion, attempt to lift the lid on a rather different angle on the problem, one that can potentially contribute significant insights on the persistence of prejudice in our social lives, but does so while partially (and in some cases, perhaps even wholly) dislodging the phenomenon from the beliefs of individual subjects.[1] Prejudice, I will argue, can come to take on a life of its own in governing our social interactions. As such, it can continue to hold sway over our shared lives even after we have effectively stopped believing in them.

7.1 Stereotypes as Social Scripts

We have defined prejudices in terms of stereotypes. Stereotypes lead a double-life of sorts. On the one hand, they are beliefs held by individuals. But on the other hand, it is a central feature of stereotypes that they also tend to have a certain social currency. They are, to borrow a phrase from Susanna Siegel (2017), "culturally normal beliefs." When one person holds them, it is likely that many do. Moreover, the fact that they are widely held is a crucial part of the story of why it would be rational for any one of them to hold them.[2] In this guise, stereotypes can take on a somewhat different hue: they are not just detached intellectual attitudes, but also play a significant role in giving shape and structure to our social interactions.[3] Even if people are rarely brought to assert what apparently "everybody knows," a perceptive bystander can nonetheless make reasonable inferences about what these people believe by observing how they act together.

One way of putting this point is to say that an important role of stereotypes is to provide us with mutually assumed *social scripts*, which help provide normatively laden templates for structuring our social interactions.[4] Psychologists frequently tout the cognitive necessity of stereotyping, as did we in chapter 2. But we might also point out that they are necessary for social interactions: without the ability to assume a fair amount of mutual knowledge about social roles, we would be forced to improvise from scratch

---

[1] See also O'Connor and Weatherall 2019 for a different angle on the importance of emphasizing social mechanisms in the dissemination of false belief.

[2] See 4.2.2 for a fuller discussion.

[3] Including, of course, avoidance behaviors, i.e., the choice to interact as little as possible with certain people.

[4] See, e.g., Schank and Abelson 1977. For philosophical analysis, see Bicchieri and McNally 2018, Hesni (MS). Similarly motivated approaches to understanding the complex interrelations between social norms (broadly speaking) and individual cognitive commitments to these norms can be found in, inter alia, Haslanger 2011, 2019; Witt 2011; Davidson and Kelly 2018; Kelly forthcoming.

our social interactions every time we meet someone we don't already have an extensive track record with. Given our cognitive finitude, we could not sustain the kinds of social lives that we do, were it not for the fact that we can rely on mutually assumed social scripts in our interactions. (Indeed, we can ask how one would build the relevant kind of track record with individuals in the first place, without relying on such scripts.)

My claim, then, is that stereotypes play an important part in these social scripts, and also that, in return, these social scripts play an important role in reinforcing and sustaining the stereotypes.[5] (That there should be this parallel between the role of stereotypes in the space of cognition and in the space of social agency should hardly be a surprise. We think in order to act, and we act in order, among other things, to secure channels of information feeding into further thought.)

Banaji and Greenwald provide a nice way to capture the way that these stereotype-based social scripts structure our interactions:

> In a department store to make a purchase, you readily surrender your credit card to a total stranger whom you categorize as a *salesclerk*. You trust this to be [...] someone who will not surreptitiously record your account information and then sell it to an identity thief.
>
> Entering a medical clinic, you assume the obedient role of *patient* (another category). Even though you may never have seen any of the medical staff before, you unquestioningly follow the instructions of people who are dressed in ways that lead you to categorize them as *doctor* or *nurse*.
>
> (Banaji and Greenwald 2013: 79)

One way of putting these points is to say that the salesclerk, the doctor, and the nurse are strangers to us only in a mitigated sense: even though we don't know them *qua* individuals, we nonetheless know a good deal about how they will be disposed to act in relevant circumstances. The basis for this knowledge, as Banaji and Greenwald argue, is stereotypes.

But there is more to be said. These stereotype-infused social scripts don't just provide me with knowledge about how you are likely to act in context. Rather, one reason they provide such knowledge is that I can assume that you are also aware of the script, and will—at least in typical cases—be motivated to adjust your behavior accordingly. In other words, there is a

---

[5] Cf. Turner et al. 1987.

central element of reflexivity involved here, which makes the scenario importantly different from, say, the way in which a zookeeper in training is instructed to approach a dominant male Orangutang. We will shortly look more closely at this element of reflexivity in light of philosophical and psychological notions of "common ground." But before we get to that, we must ask some further questions about what motivations people might have for assuming their roles in playing out these social scripts.

The question of motivation is crucial, but also very complex: we may not expect a single answer for all contexts. But in general, we can look for some kind of incentive, positive or negative, offered to participating individuals willing to play their part. Some of these incentives may classify as internal, some external. One obvious reason that people might be motivated to play their role is because each sees the social interaction as rewarding in its own right. This would be a prime example of an internal motivation. In other cases, a participant may have no internal motivation per se, but is offered an external reward—for instance, a salary—to play their part. This is presumably what is going on in many of the cases where our interactions are structured around expectations relating to your professional role as sales-clerk or nurse.

However, sometimes neither of these kinds of positive rewards—internal or external—are on offer. Yet people seem willing to play their part anyhow. Why is that? One possibility is that pressures of social conformity are simply so strong in human psychology that we are loathe to violate social expectations even in cases where there is nothing in it for us. But we should not overlook the power of negative incentives, in the form of social sanctions, in holding these structures in place. These sanctions need not be particularly punitive in order nonetheless to have an appreciable impact on our social interactions. For instance, in violating script-based expectations, I risk being branded as "difficult," "awkward," or downright "clueless." This may affect my opportunities to benefit from other social interactions further down the line.[6] (In other cases, of course, the sanctions can be very punitive indeed, such as when the scripts encode thickly moralized conceptions of hierarchical social roles.)

---

[6] I suppose we are all familiar with particular individuals who seem to willfully flout these role expectations all the time, and apparently do so without suffering significant consequences. In those cases, however, they are in an important sense just signaling their transition to a different role, for instance the role of the irreverent colleague or the eccentric professor. One's being able to transition from one such role to another without suffering significant sanction is, in my view, a sure sign of social privilege.

The fact that social scripts are propped up by a system of incentives and disincentives—rewards and punishments—is hardly surprising. It is key to ensuring their continued relevance. It is also what makes these social scripts into *norms* (in the sociologist's sense, if not the philosopher's), rather than just observable regularities in social behavior. *Qua* norms, they can be presumed to have a degree of resilience that mere regularities do not. Before moving on, we should note two things in brief: first, what is being offered through these incentives is not in general *epistemic goods* (except perhaps incidentally, in cases where the social relations they underwrite are structured around learning, such as in an apprenticeship). Therefore, my claim is not that it would be specifically *epistemically rational* for individuals to comply with these norms. Rather, norm compliance should be seen in terms a more broadly *prudential* form of rationality. Nonetheless, the fact that so many of us do prudently shape our behaviors in this way, I will argue, also has downstream epistemological consequences that are often over-looked in the literature.

Second, emphasizing the role of incentive structures in explaining the resilience of social norms is not to say that these norms couldn't also be 'internalized' by other psychological mechanisms (see, e.g., Kelly forthcoming), serving as a separate causal pathway for norm-maintenance. In other words, it is not as if we need to picture individual agents as continuously engaged in cost-benefit analyses aimed at deciding whether they have prudential reason to comply with the norms. Nonetheless, the incentive-structures can still have an important role to play in explaining why *these* are the norms that would get internalized in the first place. And additionally, it is clear that we *do* in fact sometimes engage in precisely such cost-benefit analyses, deciding perhaps that the sanctions are not sufficiently punitive so as to deter me from violating the role expectations that are placed on me. When a critical mass of individuals reach this conclusion at more or less the same time, it can precipitate a massive restructuring of our social environment.

7.2 Common Ground

It is a significant part of the functionality of these social scripts that they are not only known to (virtually) every properly socialized agent, but also, *reflexively known*—i.e., I not only know it, but also know that others know it. This element of reflexivity suggests that the phenomenon might be usefully analyzed in terms of a conception of "common ground." However, as we shall see, it will have to be a conception of common ground with certain important modifications.

The coinage "common ground" is typically associated with the work of Robert Stalnaker (1978), though it was intended as a systematization of previous notions of "common knowledge" or "mutual knowledge" developed by David Lewis (1969) and Stephen Schiffer (1972). These standard notions of common ground primarily earn their keep in the analysis of linguistic interactions, though they should also apply, *mutatis mutandis*, to other kinds of coordinated behavior. The details can get forbiddingly complex, but we can get away with the bare bones, focusing in particular on a pair of ideas.

One idea is the requirement of reflexivity, which we have already made mention of. In the basic case, the propositions in common ground are not merely the intersection of the beliefs of the conversation partners. There is also the higher-order requirement that each partner represents the other partners as believing what is in the common ground. In other words, a proposition p is part of common ground only if I believe that p, I believe that you believe that p, and so on for the other participants.[7]

A second key contribution is the study of the mechanisms by which propositions are added to or subtracted from the common ground. Most directly, the speech act of assertion constitutes one party's bid to have a proposition—the proposition asserted—entered into common ground. If the assertion is not explicitly gainsaid or in some other way resisted by the other participants, we can henceforth assume that this proposition is now part of common ground.[8] But assertion is only one mechanism by which this might happen: presupposition is a more indirect way of achieving the same aim. "Presupposition accommodation" (Lewis 1979) occurs when I assert a proposition whose truth implicates some further proposition which has not been asserted, and so is not (yet) part of common ground. This happens quite frequently in linguistic interactions. If I say, "sorry, I'll be late, my car broke down," then the proposition *NN owns a car* is not generally taken to

---

[7] Notably, Stalnaker (e.g., 2002: 715ff.) takes a more relaxed stance here, holding that propositions can be in the common ground simply in virtue of being "accepted," even if they are not believed. This is a welcome amendment: acceptance, it will be recalled, featured importantly in our analysis in chapter 1 and will feature again in chapter 9. That said, Stalnaker's notion of acceptance is not precisely what I have in mind: on Stalnaker's view (2002: 716), acceptance is a broad class of propositional attitudes which includes belief. By contrast, on my view, belief and acceptance are categorically different sorts of attitudes.

[8] Cf. Begby 2020*b*.

be part of the asserted content. But my interlocutor adjusts on the fly, entering it into the common ground anyway.

7.2.1 Toward a Less Restrictive Account of Common Ground

There is much to learn from this sort of account. But it remains a very restrictive, and in many ways abstract account. As Mitchell Green (2017) points out, however, to observe that it is abstract in this sense is not to offer a criticism: rather, we should see it as a challenge to develop the account, modify it for further applications, and so forth, all in the general spirit of the basic idea.[9] This is what I will take myself to be doing in the following.

One modification will come from explicitly emphasizing the ways in which common ground is not simply a feature of linguistic interactions. In particular, we also respond to a variety of non-verbal cues to add or subtract from common ground.

Relatedly, we must query the idea that the elements of common ground are exhausted by propositions. For instance, skills and motor routines might also be part of common ground: how one comports oneself on a crowded sidewalk, or the proper handling of chopsticks.

In making these modifications, we might eventually have to move in the direction of a more holistic conception of common ground altogether: it may be that we cannot exhaustively list the elements of common ground; moreover, we must be open to the idea that the logical interrelations between these elements cannot be mapped in as clear and perspicuous a manner as we might have hoped on the idealizing assumption that common ground is fully propositional.

For our purposes, however, the most important development will come from looking again at the idea that the elements of common ground can only play their role in virtue of being *believed* by all participants to the conversation.[10] Typically, the worries that are voiced in this area concern our

---

[9] The restriction to considering common ground exclusively in terms of propositions added or subtracted by way of explicit speech acts is very much in the nature of an idealization, useful in order to see how far we can go with certain kinds of analytical tools (i.e., those of formal semantics and pragmatics). The answer, surely, is impressively far. But this is not to say that for other purposes, we would not do well to loosen these restrictions.

[10] As we have seen, Stalnaker (2002: 716) does not specifically require that participants *believe* the propositions in question. But he does require that they be united in treating them "as true for some reason."

ability to fulfill the reflexive (higher-order) condition on common ground, i.e., what I believe about what you believe.[11] In what follows, we will let that angle lie and focus instead on the first-order thoughts. That is, we will ask whether it is true that *I* need to believe the elements of common ground in the first place. Elements of common ground, I argue, can continue to play their functional, coordinating role even if *no one* believes them, so long as one has reason to believe that others believe them.

To develop these modifications, there is no need to start from scratch. Instead, we can take our bearings from the account of the eminent psycholinguist Herbert Clark (in particular Clark 1996). The starting point of Clark's account is the set of assumptions that people must make about each other in communicative interactions, including but not limited to linguistic interactions. We identify our communication partners as belonging to groups, and presume to draw information from their group membership about what they are likely to know, what they value, what interests them, and so forth. Obviously, there is no one group to which any person belongs, and by nesting these group ascriptions one can arrive at an increasingly more expansive and refined body of assumptions about the person in question.

Nationality	Scot, Frenchman, Spaniard, Finn
Residence	American, Westerner, Californian, San Franciscan
Education	college graduate, psychology major, Yalie, Oxonian
Occupation	physician, lawyer, plumber, ophthalmologist, bricklayer, cowboy
Employment	Stanford employee, Stanford psychologist
Hobby	birder, philatelist, baseball fan
Language	English speaker, Japanese speaker
Religion	Christian, Protestant, Mormon, Baptist, Southern Baptist
Politics	Republican, Democrat, liberal
Ethnicity	Black, white, Chicano, gypsy
Subculture	drug addict, Hell's Angel, thief
Cohort	teenager, senior, baby boomer
Gender	man, woman, boy, girl, he, she.[12] (Clark 1996: 105)

---

[11] See Clark and Marshall 1981 for an overview.

[12] We can note that the list is dated, for instance, by the absence of a "they" category, as well as trans- or non-binary gender categories. But that's indeed part of the point: this is not an exhaustive ontology, but a body of shared assumptions. As such, we should expect that it will be highly specific to time and place.

If my communication partner is aware that I am categorizing him in this way, then these assumptions can serve as the common ground of our communication. Obviously, there will be uncertainties about the exact perimeter of what is common ground between us (e.g., granted, he is a Spurs fan, but has he heard the latest Harry Kane injury update?). We can then use communication to probe these limits. But in making these communicative moves, we are obviously taking a lot of other things for granted as untested common ground.

This suggests a very different, but to my mind, rather more plausible picture of how communication works. Instead of using explicit communication to add propositions to our common ground by piecemeal accretion, we use verbal and non-verbal cues—gender, age, ethnicity, clothing, hairstyle, etc.—to project wholesale large bodies of assumptions on each other, and then use explicit communication to probe specific parts of this presumptive common ground. On the basis of these projections, we engage in extensive "audience design": there are things that we would say to a Canadian and expect to be understood without further ado which we wouldn't say to an American, simply because we can assume that there are things which every Canadian knows, but not every American does. In the words of Clark and Schaefer (1992: 257): "speakers tailor utterances for particular addressees [. . .] The form these utterances take depends fundamentally on what speakers take to be their common ground with the addressees."

We are now in a position to see that what is projected on the other in these cases is essentially a holistically integrated set of stereotypes.[13] Most immediately, perhaps, they are stereotypes about what the other person will believe (e.g., that Justin Trudeau is the current PM of Canada). But also, they may be stereotypical assumptions about what the other person will value, and, importantly, how they will interact with others. Which is just to say that a significant part of the functional role of common ground is its power to give content to the expectations that shape our mutual interactions. Without these assumptions, as we argued earlier, we would be forced to improvise our mutual interactions from scratch every time. This would not only be inconvenient. It would arguably make it impossible for us to have the kinds of social lives that we depend on having every day.

---

[13] Notice, for instance, the similarity to Banaji and Greenwald's "Six Dimensional Person Category Generator," which we explored in section 2.2.1.

7.3 Common Ground without Belief

We have talked about stereotypes as a necessary starting point for social cognition. But it would be a mistake to think about social cognition merely as a domain of detached intellectual interest. Instead, it is deeply bound up with action, and, in particular, with coordinated social action. As such, it is plausibly part of the functionality of these stereotypes that they be widely known. Only in this way could they serve the role of providing us with a wide range of social scripts for shaping our mutual interactions.

But this raises an interesting possibility. Many accounts of common ground assume that each participant *knows* the propositions that make up common ground (hence "mutual knowledge").[14] But this is clearly too strong: knowledge is factive, and even mutually assumed false (first-order) beliefs can play the same coordinating role. Truth, quite simply, plays no significant explanatory role here.

But even if we relax this notion, and talk only about "mutual belief," we may well be building into our model more than is strictly speaking needed. That is, I can be motivated to act in accordance with these social scripts even though I don't actually believe in the underlying stereotypes, or in any other way endorse their content. What might motivate me to act in accordance with scripts that I don't endorse is precisely the risk of social sanction that comes with violating the script or even just explicitly raising questions about its validity.[15] Since I have reason to assume that *you* (and many others) endorse the script, I also have reasons to act as if I do, even when in fact I don't. The sanctions might not be particularly forbidding in all cases—say, the risk of being branded as "socially awkward," "difficult," or even "bitchy." But the point remains that whenever there is any cost associated with norm violation, there will be at least a minimal incentive to comply. Even though I don't perceive the terms of cooperation to be particularly beneficial for me, I might, for a combination of internal and external reasons, see them as more favorable than no cooperation at all. I might also evaluate my own

[14] Cf. Mallon 2016: 433: "a social role is created when a kind representation becomes widespread, common knowledge in a community. A social role in this sense exists in a community when ideas about the membership conditions for the role, about the permissions, duties, and other norms attaching to role members, and about role-typical properties, become something everyone in a community knows, knows that everyone knows, and so on."

[15] This is not, of course, to say that it is always prudent to play along with expectations. See Hesni (MS) for perspectives on when and how to "disrupt" social scripts.

standing in such a way that I don't favor my chances of getting a good hearing were I to try to renegotiate these terms. (One might think that it's always a good thing for relatively privileged people to signal their willingness to renegotiate these terms: consider, for instance, the professor who insists to his undergraduates that "we can all be informal here." In some cases, this might be welcome, if the trappings of traditional formality genuinely get in the way of us accomplishing what we jointly need to accomplish as professor and student. But in another way, it might be unwelcome: given that the professor comes into the situation with significantly more power, the student might not favor the prospect of "renegotiating" the terms of their social interaction. In some cases, it can be better to stick with the somewhat unfavorable social script that one is given than to petition for a new one, given the risks involved.)

But, of course, once we recognize this fact, we can also see that the other party might be in the exact same position. When this happens, we would be in a situation where these stereotypes can continue to govern the terms of our social interaction even though neither of us endorse their content. The reason is that both of us believe (or suspect) that the other endorses their content. If there were a way of asking outright, it would be relatively easy to determine that this is not the case. But asking outright is itself a way of revealing that one does not endorse the script, which therefore risks the same kind of social sanction.

In such cases, then, all participants might in an important sense be cognitively ready to "move on." But since stereotypes play the double role also of shaping our external social space, we can be prevented from doing so. By way of serving this externalized function, stereotypes can exert a significant "inertial force" on our patterns of social interaction.[16]

As a result, we could theoretically have a "prejudiced society" without individual prejudiced believers. Writ large, this is probably no more than a theoretical possibility. But in particular local contexts, we can plausibly see something very much like this at work. For instance, religion is a major factor shaping the social life of people in many parts of the United States. It is taken for granted that everyone believes, and many social activities will be organized in or around the schedule of the Church. No one, for instance, would organize a community sporting event on Sunday morning. The question that is bound to strike any casual observer of these practices is

---

[16] See Haslanger 2007 for an example along these lines.

"do they *really* believe, or are they just playing along?" The fact that they are all so willing to comply with Church-related restrictions on behavior is evidence that they do believe. But it is perfectly conceivable—and perfectly consistent with this evidence—that most or all of them actually don't. They might even suspect that others are in the same position. But at the same time, and given the potential social sanctions involved, it might just be easier to go along with the established routines than to ask the critical question, *why are we doing this*?

For a more problematic example, one that bears more directly on the epistemology of prejudice, consider the notion of "perceived electability."[17] Let's say our country has never had a female head of state, partly as a result of a long history of institutionalized sexism. Along comes a female candidate who I believe is highly qualified, and indeed among the best candidates in the field. I would be happy to cast my vote for her. But at the same time, I believe that others will not vote for her, simply because she is a woman. Not wanting to waste my vote on an "unelectable" candidate, I decide to go with someone I think has better chances of winning. But of course, a significant number of others might well be reasoning in the exact same way. If we had a way of signaling this to each other prior to making our decisions, our female candidate might well have been competitive. But instead, we all mold our behavior to fit the standard social script according to which women lack essential leadership qualities, even though none of us fully endorse the underlying stereotype. In doing so, we are also facilitating the continued suppression of the very evidence that would actually demonstrably problematize the underlying stereotype, namely a record of female politicians competently performing the duties of public office.

Here, we can see the outlines of a strictly social and interactional model of the persistence of social prejudice, one which makes no strong assumptions about the "prejudiced mindset" of the individual agents who participate in these social interactions. In these kinds of settings, the task of explaining the persistence of prejudice takes on a rather different hue: we may no longer be stuck with explaining how it can be rational for people to continue believing

---

[17] This phenomenon is now finally receiving critical scrutiny in mainstream media (though perhaps not to the point of scrutinizing their own role in sustaining it). See, for instance, "Whites (and men) only? Harris goes there on the 'electability' argument" (https://www.cnn.com/2019/05/06/politics/kamala-harris-joe-biden-electability-race/index.html), "A gay president? The majority of Americans believe the country isn't ready" (https://www.cnn.com/2019/05/04/politics/poll-of-the-week-gay-president/index.html?no-st=1572367243), "Many Democrats love Warren. They also worry about her" (https://www.nytimes.com/2019/08/15/us/politics/elizabeth-warren-2020-campaign.html).

these things, for in some cases, they may not have these beliefs at all. When it comes to the separate question, why do they nonetheless act *as if* they believe them, we have a different sort of answer at our disposal: they act as if they believe them, because they believe (truly or falsely) that others believe them, and because of the way the social incentive structures are set up, it's easier to continue to act in compliance with our social scripts than to ask critical probing questions about their underlying rationale.

7.4 Many Pathways to Belief

So far, we have considered the possibility that stereotypes can continue to supply us with social scripts even though no one actually endorses their content. With this, we have a different way of framing our approach to the question of prejudice: not every approach to the prevalence of prejudice need suppose that people are "prejudiced" in such a manner that we have to ask how it could be rational for them to go on believing as they do.

But consider how these kinds of interactions will look to children or adolescents who are being gradually inducted into these practices. After all, they are in no position to tell whether people actually believe these things or are merely acting in accordance with the scripts. Nonetheless, it's presumably a reasonable default inferential rule that *if* people consistently act in accordance with the script, then they endorse it. And if they endorse it, there is good reason to believe that it is true. So I should believe it too.

This serves as a reminder that there are many ways to come by our social beliefs. We might come by some through our own base-level observation and induction. Others we come by through explicit testimony from peers or recognized social authorities. But these aren't the only ways. Human beings are extraordinarily sensitive to the "unspoken rules" of social interaction, as well as the institutionalized and semi-institutionalized facts about social roles. Even from early years, it seems that we are able to draw productive inferences about what others believe from how they act together, or, often as relevant, how they *don't* act together: i.e., why persons of backgrounds A and B are never enrolled in the same school, why certain sports seem to be reserved for people of a certain background, and so forth. No one *tells* you that it is so, let alone why it must be so. But one can nonetheless observe that it is, and draw apparently reasonable inferences from it.[18]

---

[18] See, e.g., Haslanger 2018, 2021, for a development of this kind of perspective.

The situation here is in important ways redolent of what Susanna Siegel (Siegel 2017) has recently called "the problem of culturally normal belief." To see the nature of the problem, Siegel introduces us to Whit, a late-teen boy who has grown up in an ethnically homogeneous white community in contemporary United States, and who develops the predictable racial attitudes as a result.[19] These racial attitudes are "formed and maintained in a casual way that is more like absorption than deliberation. Since many beliefs formed in this way are clearly well founded, in certain social and psychological contexts, racial attitudes formed in the same way might seem to be their epistemic equals" (Siegel 2017: 172).

Nonetheless, it is part of Siegel's contention that Whit's racial attitudes are irrational, despite the fact that they constitute the "socially normal response to one's social environment" (Siegel 2017: 172). That is, Siegel fully concedes that "casual absorption of culturally normal beliefs" is in many cases a perfectly fine route to forming one's own outlook. But Whit's case is different. In brief, his belief is irrational in virtue of inheriting the irrationality of the culturally normal beliefs that he draws upon.[20]

I very much agree with Siegel that socially accepted patterns of action and interaction can provide individuals with something like a non-overt form of testimony even in the absence of explicit assertion. What should we think, then, about the claim that in certain cases, but not in others, subjects will be doing something wrong, epistemically speaking, in forming their beliefs in light of this testimony?

Siegel writes:

When everyone in the neighborhood drinks from the faucet without a second thought, one casually assumes that the water from faucets is safe to drink. That assumption is well founded, as are many other beliefs acquired in the same casual way. By comparison, Whit's dispositions to be suspicious and distrustful of black men, to feel discomfort sharing public spaces, are as natural to Whit and his friend as the presumption that their water is safe to drink.   (Siegel 2017: 186)

---

[19] Siegel 2017: chapter 10.
[20] I take it that the irrationality here does not lie in the specific content of Whit's racialized attitude, or even just the fact that it is racialized at all. Rather, the problem is that attitudes absorbed from one's social environment in this way can never be rational if they weren't rationally held to begin with.

So far, so good. Whit arrives at his belief that Black men are to be avoided in very much the same way that he arrives at his belief that the water is safe to drink. But while the latter belief is rational, the former is not. The difference does not lie in anything having to do with the relative quality of the inference from evidence in the two cases; rather, it lies solely in the fact that the social-level hostility to Black men that he observes in his culture is itself ill founded. This ill-foundedness "can transmit from the social-level testifier to individuals" (Siegel 2017: 187), thereby rendering his belief irrational.[21]

"Ill-foundedness" is a technical term, and it's not immediately apparent how Siegel intends for it to map on to more familiar (though of course still controversial) epistemic notions such as justification, epistemic responsibility, etc. She is quite clear, though, that ill-founded beliefs are irrational beliefs.[22] To the contrary, I think there are plenty of cases where individual subjects can be perfectly within their epistemic rights to absorb even ill-founded beliefs from their social environment.

Consider, for example, the widespread belief that MSG (*monosodium glutamate*) is bad for us. This view is now widely discredited, but like many dodgy "scientific facts" of yesteryear, it has proven hard to dislodge once it has become part of "common knowledge." Notably, though, the problem is not simply that bad science lies at the heart of the case.[23] There's a plausible account of the origin of this belief suggesting that the scientific community's willingness to accept it in the first place was in part a result of racism or xenophobia (and even more so for the general population's willingness to accept it).[24] That notwithstanding, I hope we can agree that

---

[21] Nonetheless, note that, according to Siegel, this transmission can be blocked in cases of explicit assertoric testimony. Consider the case in which Whit's mother believes—irrationally—that the water is not safe to drink and explicitly tells Whit that this is so. In that case, Siegel argues (2017: 186), the ill-foundedness of the mother's attitude does not affect Whit's epistemic standing to believe as he does. I think this admission clearly delimits the range of application of Siegel's argument, as I have argued elsewhere (Begby 2018a).

[22] Where she apparently departs is on the question of whether irrational beliefs are also blameworthy beliefs. We can set that aside here. But see Begby 2018a, with response from Siegel (2018).

[23] As, for instance, in the case of another ill-founded but by now culturally normal belief, namely that spinach is significantly richer in iron and other nutrients than other leafy, green vegetables (cf. Sutton 2010 for an account). Despite its ill-foundedness, I take it that many of us are not markedly irrational in continuing to believe in the power of spinach, after observing its widespread veneration in our culture.

[24] See Barry-Jester 2016, drawing on Mosby 2009.

MSG is bad for you is something like a culturally normal belief in most Western societies. Even in the absence of explicit testimony, we can plausibly "absorb" this belief by observing people's evident concerns about whether their food contains MSG, not to mention the fact that Asian restaurants will often—to this day—continue to advertise their food with "No MSG."

To see how—despite the ill-foundedness—it may not be an irrational belief, we can ask, *what else should they believe*? The worry here is that we would be counseling people to disregard what they have every reason to believe is evidence. I assume that refraining from forming any belief is simply not an option. One *cannot not* respond to the widespread MSG-scare and the "No MSG" signs in Asian restaurants as evidence, i.e., as grounds for some inference or other. But if it is evidence, what is it evidence for? Which inference is warranted? Presumably that MSG is bad for you. So, in the absence of countervailing evidence, one can rationally come to form the belief that MSG is bad for you even though there is clear ill-foundedness in its aetiology. Otherwise, we would be committing the epistemic error of disregarding evidence.

But there is now a final twist to consider. As the argument of this chapter shows, we can apparently have "culturally normal beliefs" without believers. Whether by "casual absorption" or by inference from social facts and patterns of interaction, Whit could nonetheless end up with the same beliefs. In that case, how do we substantiate the assumption that he is irrational? His attitude can't be irrational in virtue of inheriting the irrationality of others' beliefs: if these people don't actually believe it, then they are *ipso facto* not irrational in believing it. Maybe one could think that they are irrational to act as though they believe it, when in fact they don't. But this is too quick: it is clearly rational—prudentially rational—for people in certain social contexts to conceal their beliefs (think about the situation of Atheists in Saudi Arabia, or gay service personnel in the US military). Maybe we could think there's something "collectively irrational" about a society that organizes its operations in such a way that there's a significant gap between how people will act as if they believe and what they actually believe. But it's unclear how we should then transition from this charge of collective irrationality to the claim that a certain designated individual—i.e., Whit—is irrational in believing as he does. After all, he merely observes others going about their everyday business, reasonably infers that they hold certain beliefs, reckons that if they all believe it, there's a good chance that it's true, and thereby concludes that he should believe the same himself.

7.4.1 "Collective" Epistemic Responsibilities?

The question of "shared" or "collective" epistemic responsibilities does come up from time to time in the literature, so it might be worthwhile to take a moment to consider it in more detail. For instance, Medina (2013: 82) bemoans the "false dichotomy between the individual and the collective in discussions of responsibility." He argues: "It would be a fatal mistake to assume that our diagnoses and treatments of hermeneutical injustices have to choose between the individual and the collective level, without being able to operate at both levels simultaneously—and indeed... without being able to operate at a crucial intermediate and hybrid level: the level of *shared responsibility.*"

In general, though, I suspect that while it is easy to *say* "shared epistemic responsibility" or "collective epistemic responsibility," it is considerably harder to give any stable and determinate content to such notions. On the face of it, things might seem straightforward enough: for instance, at several points in this book, I have made passing reference to the notion of an "epistemic community." One might reason that, well, if there are epistemic communities, then there could be epistemic responsibilities that fall on them as such. One problem to be aware of here is that we run the real risk of idealizing on the epistemic agency of these communities (treating them as too integrated and too transparent in their component processes, and moreover presuming that they are empowered to act in ways that they are in fact not). But more fundamentally, there's a clear sense in which we would here still be operating with what is recognizably an *individualist conception of epistemic responsibility*: the only difference would be that we are now ascribing that responsibility to a singular collective agent, rather than to individual persons. It is not clear to me that this "levelling up" affords any new substantive insights or points us in the direction of new pathways for amelioration. In particular, it is not clear that the "epistemic community" is a sufficiently cohesive entity that it would make sense to "hold it responsible" for our collective epistemic failings.

Maybe a more promising direction would start from a distinction between "shared" and "collective" responsibility: if "collective responsibilities" are responsibilities that fall on us as a singular collective agent (a "group agent"), then shared responsibilities distribute over all of the individuals that comprise the group (though perhaps not in equal share). Now, it is certainly true that we often have moral obligations that we are unable to discharge unless a sufficiently large number of us act in concert.

This is often described as a matter of shared responsibility in the relevant sense.[25] Could there be a similar "shared responsibility" to overcome ignorance? Maybe. But then, if we fail, say because of complex coordination issues or because the ignorance is so deeply embedded in our school system, who is responsible? All of us? But arguably, none of us individually may have been in a position to do any better, epistemically speaking.

Medina is sensitive to these concerns, of course, and also offers a different framing of the problem which is designed to bring such structural issues to the fore. He writes (2013: 251–2): "Assuming shared responsibility for *epistemic* harms brings together the subjective and the structural in a particularly perspicuous way. On the one hand, . . . we cannot avoid taking into account the agent's subjectivity; and on the other hand, . . . epistemic responsibility cannot be properly identified and addressed independently of the agent's social position within structural processes and networks of social relations."

But to my mind, this precisely fails to accomplish what it advertises. We could take Medina as saying that in order to determine what their epistemic responsibilities are, we need to look to people's positions within the structural processes and networks of social relations. (For instance, Medina (2013: 158) speaks specifically about differentiated responsibilities attaching to our roles as parents and educators.) On its own terms, this seems reasonable, of course. But even as this gives us a sense of how larger social structures and processes are involved in determining our epistemic responsibilities, these are nonetheless fully individual responsibilities so far as Medina's account gives us any reason to suppose. The "shared" or "collective" dimension of epistemic responsibility is yet nowhere in sight.

That said, I do think we can make perfectly good sense of our intuitive habit of ranking communities as more or less openminded, tolerant, maybe even enlightened, and so on. Moreover, I do think distinctive patterns of epistemic failing are often rampant in deeply prejudiced societies. But in other cases, ignorance constitutes an emergent phenomenon: it arises out of patterns of individual action and behaviors none of which are "irresponsible," "irrational," or in any clear sense "substandard" when considered in their own right. It is true that some group-level agents are sufficiently cohesive that we can ascribe to them a full-voice sense of moral responsibility (and perhaps concomitant epistemic responsibility as well). States are

---

[25] Obviously, climate change action falls in this category, as do consumer movements such as the anti-sweatshop movements (cf. Young 2003).

an obvious example (and by extension, municipalities, provinces, etc.).[26] But then again, states have an exceptionally high degree of integration and formal institutional structure. Moreover, they are given a significant amount of coercive power, whose only plausible justification is that it is required to carry out these responsibilities. By contrast, I think it would be a mistake to work on the assumption that "epistemic communities" are always (or even often) similarly well-delineated entities. Of course, sometimes formal institutional structures—such as schools—play a significant role in anchoring our epistemic communities. If a particular school is peddling systematic misinformation, that is a serious concern. We then look to other institutional structures—curriculum review boards, for instance—to weigh in on the matter. But more generally, "epistemic community" denotes a looser, less formalized set of information sharing networks. I don't think there's a straightforward path to charging individual epistemic communities with failure to meet their epistemic obligations, where those obligations wouldn't ultimately fall on particular, well-positioned individuals within those communities (for instance, as Medina himself suggests, individuals acting in their capacities as parents or educators).

In brief, then, I do not think we significantly improve our understanding or explanatory leverage in such cases by appealing to some notion of "shared" or "collective" epistemic responsibility. On closer inspection, the best sense we can make of such appeals is that they will eventually turn back and distribute the responsibility over the individuals that compose the community.

7.5 Conclusion

Prejudices are (grounded in) stereotypes. These stereotypes don't merely serve as anchoring points in people's cognition; they also provide us with scripts helping to coordinate our social interactions. This chapter has sought to provide a different and novel angle on how stereotypes might come to have the social currency that they do, and in particular, why they are so resistant to change. On standard assumptions, the question of resilience is simply the question of why people have such a difficult time dislodging these stereotypes from their minds. Though it is most certainly tempting to hold

---

[26] Cf. Stilz 2011; Collins and Lawford-Smith 2016.

out for an explanation in the form of some kind of irrational resistance to counterevidence, it has been the burden of this book so far to argue that this temptation should be resisted.

In this chapter, however, we have considered the possibility that (part of) the problem may not be internal to individual people's minds at all. If stereotypes provide social scripts, there will typically be an incentive associated with complying with stereotypes in one's outward behavior, even when one doesn't actually endorse them. As such, they can continue to hold sway over our interpersonal transactions long after the individuals who take part in these transactions are cognitively ready to "move on."

These scripts have the force of norms. For instance, conceptions of manners would have dictated extremely stilted interactions between young men and women in the early twentieth century (at least if period novels are to be believed). We can assume that many of the interacting agents did not endorse the norms, nor was it in their best interest to endorse them. But it could nonetheless be in their best interest *to be seen as endorsing them*, on the assumption that everyone else did. And the fact that everyone believes that everyone else endorses them, gives everyone a reason to conform their behavior to the norms, which reinforces everyone's reasons to believe that everyone else endorses the norms. If there was a non-sanctionable way of raising the issue—*do we really think that these are good norms?*—then the trappings might fall away quickly. But the norms wouldn't have the force that they have if there were no sanctions for raising the question of their validity.

Because of this incentive-structure, I can have a motivation to play out the script even if I don't endorse it. But of course, the same can hold for you. So we are both playing out a script, and thereby enacting stereotypes that none of us actually endorse. Let's say that after many years of critical reflection on my own cognitive commitment, I have come to harbor various social-progressive beliefs. At the same time, I believe that such opinions are highly unwelcome in the social environment that I operate in. There will be an expectation of social sanction if one were even to broach the topic.[27] As a matter of fact, others have come around to similarly progressive views, but also hold similarly dim opinions about what most people believe. In such cases, common ground (or if one will: justified but mistaken beliefs about what in fact constitutes common ground) can exert a significant *inertial*

---

[27] I assume that conservatives and libertarians have something like this in mind when they warn against the putative "chilling effects" of excessive political correctness.

force on our social interactions—on the kinds of possibilities that will emerge on the horizon of collective action—even though the beliefs that presumptively make up the common ground are nowhere near as widespread as one might think. In the good case, then, common ground serves as a repository of resources for collective action; in cases where we tend to ascribe rearguard beliefs to others, it can be a drag on such action.

8
Automated Risk Assessment in the Criminal Justice Process

A Case of 'Algorithmic Bias'?

In our previous chapter, we found reason to move beyond the standard model on which prejudice is to be thought of primarily in terms of the cognitive attitudes of individuals. This is in no way to imply that the standard model is *not* useful, because quite clearly it is. Rather, the claim is that we should also supplement with models which explicitly recognize that the effects of prejudice can constitute an emergent phenomenon. On such a model, questions about individual epistemic rationality may not even arise, at least not in the form that has become familiar to us through the first few chapters of this book.

In this chapter, we will develop this perspective further with another case study. This case study illustrates how, in a deeply unequal and unjust society, even reasoning from known facts can, in an important sense, be prejudicial, or at least give rise to many of the same problems as explicitly prejudiced reasoning would. This happens when structural injustice is a major part of the reason why the facts are as they are. (In the previous chapter, we diagnosed the problem as at least in part "interactional" in nature. There, the interactions in question where interactions between individual persons. In this chapter, we will focus on interactions between major social institutions. I hope this illustrates one more sense in which simply levelling up from an "individualist" to a "collective" account of epistemic responsibility will not solve our problems (see section 7.4.1), unless we simultaneously imagine ourselves to be operating within very different institutional parameters than we do. But now, it should be clear, our problem is political as much as it is epistemic.)

We will frame this problem in terms of recent discussion about the use of so-called "automated risk assessment tools" in the criminal justice system. Often, these debates are cast around concerns about so-called "algorithmic bias."[1] While algorithmic bias is a genuine phenomenon and a relevant concern, I will argue nonetheless that by casting it in these terms, we can run the risk of obscuring the true source of the problem. At the deeper level, the problem concerns the appropriateness of reasoning from statistical facts (e.g., crime statistics) in cases where those statistics can be reasonably suspected to reflect contingent, often historically entrenched, structural injustices in our society. As I will argue, this problem has nothing in particular to do with algorithm-assisted reasoning and decision-making. Nor is it in any straightforward sense a case of bias, if that were taken to suggest that we might, at least in theory, hope that improvements to our epistemic routines could eventually serve to eliminate the problem. Instead, the problem is plausibly inherent in deeply unequal societies, giving rise to a potentially irresolvable dilemma at the intersection of ethics and epistemology: as Tamar Gendler has argued (Gendler 2011), structural injustice may force us into situations in which we can either satisfy our epistemic ideals or our moral ideals, but not both at the same time. The consequences of this dilemma will occupy us in much of the book's final two chapters.

8.1 Risk Assessment in the US Criminal Justice Process

At various stages of the criminal justice process, judges, members of parole boards, and others will be required to assess the risk that a particular individual will commit similar offenses when returning to society. This risk assessment is part of the determination of what kind of punishment (e.g., sentence, probation, community service) is appropriate to the case, the length of the sentence, or whether the subject should be eligible for parole.

To carry out an assessment of this form, one will naturally have to consult a broader range of evidence than was presented during the trial. Trial evidence is narrowly tailored to bear specifically on the question of whether the defendant was guilty as charged. But two people who are guilty of the same crime can nonetheless have very different risk of recidivism. We will shortly consider the *kinds* of evidence that might be relevant to assessing recidivism risk. But for now, notice that engaging in such assessment is an important, indeed obligatory, part of the correctional system's mandate: for instance, it is both socio-economically counterproductive and arguably also

---

[1] Or "machine bias": see Castro 2019 for a recent philosophical account.

unfair to give the same sentence to a first-time offender and to a repeat offender, even when they are found guilty of the same crime.

But even as it is an obligatory task, it is one that we are apparently rather bad at. In particular, there is a strong suspicion that judges' and parole boards' exercise of such qualitative judgment can be significantly influenced by racial prejudice and bias.[2] Given how bad we are at this task, and given the enormous personal and social costs of our failure, it is important to seek ways to improve. Since the 1970s, there has been a movement to systematize and give structure to such judgments by drawing on evidence-based tools from actuarial science, such as the "Salient Factor Score" (cf. Hoffman and Beck 1974; Hoffman and Adelberg 1980). I think the deployment of such tools can overall be called a moderate success. In particular, it can hardly be denied that such tools outperform unaided human judgment (often called "clinical judgment") in assessing recidivism risk.[3]

With the advent of new technology, the question naturally arises as to whether computerized, software-based solutions shouldn't also be incorporated into this process. If we accept the improvement brought about by the older actuarial systems, it is hard to see why one should be inclined to resist this move. After all, both are, in some relevant sense of the term, algorithmic tools, in that both serve to convert input information into an output score by way of some determinate process, relying as little as possible on qualitative human judgment. The technological platform as such—paper-based versus computer-based—seems, at best, peripheral to the epistemic, ethical, and legal questions at stake. In all their guises, these automated risk assessment tools essentially involve algorithms which take as their inputs various bits of information about the defendant—previous criminal record, education, employment history, family situation, and much else besides—yielding as output a precise numerical score indicating the defendant's risk of reoffense, as best as our evidence allows us to gauge. The deployment of such tools could be in the nature of "consultation" only, or it could fully replace human judgment. Either way, given the poor track record of human judges, and given the apparent success of such tools across a number of areas, it would seem that the question of whether we should consult such tools at all is as close as we will ever get to a socio-epistemic no-brainer: the stakes are

[2] Cf. Ayres and Waldfogel 1994; Mustard 2001; Banks et al. 2006.

[3] See Gottfredson and Moriarty 2006 for an overview. Similar (moderate) successes are also reported in other areas, such as mortgage lending (cf. Gates et al. 2002) and child protection services (cf. Hurley 2018).

maximally high, and these tools are quite simply part of our "best practices" for evidence-based decision-making in complex situations. We should no more rely on unaided human judgment in these tasks than we should, say, for calculating complex probabilities.

It is important to recognize that we are essentially engaging in a form of comparative assessment here: we may have (and probably should have) continuing concerns also about computer-assisted decision-making procedures. But a decision-making procedure need not be flawless in order nonetheless to constitute a significant improvement on any viable competitor. Here is one way to think about it. Lots of human decision-making requires us to execute important decisions on very limited evidence. The evidence is limited in part because there are strict limits to our processing capacities. Presumably, many such decisions would be better made if they were made on the basis of more capacious data. The obvious problem, then, is that humans would likely be very poor at processing this data, precisely because it is so large. When we run up against the limits of our information processing capacities, we tend to rely on heuristics. But these heuristics are notoriously biased, whether this is because they are influenced by explicit prejudice or by some subtler mechanism of implicit bias. But given these insights, a ready solution now stares us in the face: we can hope to move beyond our own processing limitations *and* our own biases by offloading the task to computerized algorithms which are presumably capable of greater objectivity than we are in at least two dimensions; both in terms of the amount of data that they can take into account, and in terms of the impersonality of its processing.

However, this rather optimistic piece of reasoning may seem rather naïve in light of recently mounting concerns about the social impact of "Big Data."[4] One central area of concern is precisely its impact on the criminal justice process. In 2016, ProPublica published a critical report on the Sentencing Reform and Corrections Act, still under Congressional review, which would mandate the use of these automated risk assessment tools at the sentencing stage in federal courts.[5] Against this background, and in light of the expanded use of such tools also in several state legal systems, ProPublica highlighted several individual cases where such tools have yielded results suggesting racial bias, despite the promise of greater objectivity in algorithmic decision-making. But additionally, they were also able to

---

[4]   See O'Neil 2016 for a popular overview.   [5]   Angwin et al. 2016.

retrieve large scores of data from a particular jurisdiction—Broward County, Florida—strongly suggesting that these biases are systematically patterned, and not confined to individual cases. The focus in the ProPublica story was on a particular assessment tool purporting to measure recidivism risk—COMPAS, by Northpointe (now Equivant). But there is no reason to think that the COMPAS system is uniquely flawed in this regard. Similar problems are likely to affect any such program.

In particular, ProPublica claimed to find that although there was no statistically significant difference in the COMPAS system's predictive success between White and Black defendants, there was a notable discrepancy in the errors observed. That is, COMPAS would wrongly place Black defendants in high-risk categories almost twice as often as White defendants; conversely, White defendants who did in fact go on to reoffend would much more often than Black defendants have been put in low- or medium-risk categories. In this sense, ProPublica's analysis seems to support the warnings offered in 2014 by then-Attorney General Eric Holder, that the resort to automated risk assessment tools in the criminal justice system might just serve to "exacerbate unwarranted and unjust disparities that are already far too common in our criminal justice system and in our society."[6]

8.1.1 Clearing Up Some Misunderstandings

Before going on to assess the merits of these allegations of "algorithmic bias,"[7] it will be helpful to clear up some potential misunderstandings. First, and most obviously, it is important to note that these risk assessment tools are not used at the verdict stage, i.e., in finding the defendant guilty or not guilty. Rather, what's of concern is their use subsequent to the guilty verdict, for instance in sentencing and parole hearings.

Second, the point of resorting to risk assessment tools at these stages is not to further penalize those who are found to be at particularly high risk of recidivism by *increasing* their sentences. Rather, it is to seek grounds for *reducing* the sentences of offenders found to be at low risk of recidivism. I take it that anyone with even a cursory knowledge of the US Criminal Justice

---

[6] https://www.justice.gov/opa/speech/attorney-general-eric-holder-speaks-national-association-criminal-defense-lawyers-57th.

[7] Note that ProPublica's article was part of a larger series called "Machine Bias: Investigating Algorithmic Injustice," other installments of which have detailed similar concerns about access to housing, educational grants, loans, credit ratings, and much else besides.

System's chilling tendency towards overcriminalization and oversentencing will find that such an aim is, considered in its own right, a welcome one. (It is welcome, we might add, both in terms of expressing a concern for the individual, and also in terms of the social costs—financial and other—resulting from the out-of-control US prison system.)[8]

Third, it is important to emphasize this latter point, because many might have concerns about the appropriateness of using risk assessment tools in any part of the criminal justice process. One might have these concerns because one thinks that only evidence which tracks the actual individual in question should play a role in that process. By contrast, these risk assessment tools necessarily draw on demographic evidence, including statistical evidence linking a variety of socio-economic factors to differential recidivism rates. Here, one might think that individuals who are found to have a high risk of reoffending are punished—unfairly—because of their demographic indicators, and not because of anything that they have done.

This concern, however, is somewhat misguided. At the verdict stage, it is certainly and obviously appropriate that evidence should be restricted in this way: only considerations that track the particular individual on trial are admissible in settling whether that person is guilty as charged. The fact that the defendant belongs to a demographic with higher crime rates precisely fails to track the individual in the relevant sense. But sentencing involves a forward-looking element that is not present at the verdict stage. We are not asking whether the defendant actually committed the crime, but how likely it is that he will commit similar crimes in the future. Since recidivism risk essentially involves projecting future probabilities, we cannot restrict ourselves to evidence that bears only on what this particular individual has done in the past. We are effectively asking, given what we know about this person's past record, what can we assume about his future? If we are to get any epistemic traction with this task, we must, by necessity, look to evidence that places this person and his past track record in larger context.[9]

---

[8] The United States accounts for no more than 5 percent of the world's population, but houses 25 percent of the world's incarcerated. It is far and away the world leader in incarceration (with Russia as a distant second). To a large extent, this is a recent development: the current total prison population of 2.2 million (with an incarceration rate of 716/100,000) is more than four times higher than in 1980. For updated statistics, see https://www.prisonpolicy.org/.

[9] Differently put: it would be a mistake to think of recidivism risk as an inherent property of individuals, one that we attempt to estimate by drawing on (at best) circumstantially relevant statistical evidence. Instead, recidivism risk is quite clearly a notion that applies to individuals in the social, economic, (etc.) situation that they would likely find themselves in once released. The same individual released into a different social situation (different work prospects, stable family situation, etc.) would likely have very different recidivism risk.

And so, we naturally come to look to crime statistics for demographic factors such as age, income levels, education, job situation, and so forth.[10] To require the courts *not* to consider this evidence at this point is effectively to require it to abandon this important part of its mandate, or else to try to fulfill it based on some other kind of "evidence," such as judges' "intuitions" or presumptive "insight into human nature." But this will not do: it should be in *everyone's* interest that courts find grounds for reducing the severity of sentences wherever possible (i.e., consistent with the constitutive aim of ensuring public safety). Moreover, it is imperative that they do so on the basis of the best evidence they can.

Much of the current criticism presents the deployment of risk assessment in particular in sentencing (as opposed, for instance, in parole hearings) as an entirely novel development.[11] But this is misleading at best: as Monahan and Skeem point out (2014: 158), reliance on some "inchoate notion of risk assessment" has been an integral part of criminal sentencing in many US jurisdictions since "shortly after the Civil War." What is new here is primarily a move toward formalizing the requirement of using actuarial risk assessment tools in sentencing (as opposed to simply relying on unaided human judgment), thereby broadening the range of evidence that is explicitly taken into account, and most recently, moving to incorporate computerized algorithms into the process. These developments may seem new in part because the use of risk assessment has been limited in recent decades by the trend of legislatively imposed requirements of "determinate sentencing" and "mandatory minimum sentencing." But presumably, anyone of a broadly progressive political mindset will agree that rolling back on minimum mandatory sentencing in favor of some form of qualitative risk assessment is potentially, on the whole, a very good thing. The introduction of such "tough on crime" legislation is deeply causally implicated in the emergence of mass incarceration (Monahan and Skeem 2016: 491), which is arguably one of the defining problems of social justice in contemporary United States. The resurgence of risk assessment in sentencing is often billed precisely as an effort to reverse this development.[12]

---

[10] See Slobogin 2018: 584 for a full list.

[11] See, for instance, Barry-Jester et al. (2015), writing for the popular website FiveThirtyEight: "Pennsylvania is on the verge of becoming one of the first states in [the USA] to base criminal sentences not only on what crimes people have been convicted of, but also on whether they are deemed likely to commit additional crimes."

[12] Consider, for instance, the following early instance: "In 1994, the Virginia legislature required the state's newly-formed Criminal Sentencing Commission to develop an empirically-based instrument for use in diverting twenty-five percent of the 'lowest-risk,

However, this rather hopeful analysis seems to ring hollow in the light of ProPublica's revelations. Mass incarceration is a hugely racialized problem in the United States.[13] And if ProPublica's numbers are correct, it would seem that White defendants now benefit from this new-found leniency much more than Black defendants. This is a significant cause for concern, and it is perfectly appropriate to ask how this bias creeps into what is after all supposed to be a more "objective" method of assessment. For instance, it is reasonable to ask whether it might, intentionally or unintentionally, have inherited the biases of the people who designed the algorithm. Unfortunately, this is a suspicion that we may not be in a position to confirm or disconfirm, since these algorithms are often proprietary and protected from view.[14] Even before delving into a deeper analysis, I think we can all agree that this is deeply problematic. Any public institution should strive for transparency in its decision-making. Reliance on proprietary algorithms appears to be a direct violation of that ideal of transparency.[15]

As I will argue, however, there is reason to think that the problem runs much deeper than this. Even if the algorithms used in risk assessment were made open to public scrutiny, there is every reason to believe that the epistemic and ethical concerns about algorithmic bias would still persist.

incarceration-bound, drug and property offenders to placement in alternative non-prison sanctions,' such as probation, community service or electronic monitoring. The risk assessment tool that the Commission developed relies on six types of risk factors: (1) offense type; (2) whether the offender is currently charged with an additional offense; (3) 'offender characteristics' (i.e., gender, age, employment, and marital status); (4) whether the offender had been arrested or confined within the past 18 months; (5) prior felony convictions; and (6) prior adult incarcerations" (Monahan and Skeem 2014: 159).

[13] Blacks and Latinos comprise 60 percent of the US prison population despite counting for less than 30 percent of the population at large. A black male is 7 times more likely to be imprisoned than his white counterparts. See also Alexander 2010 for an important analysis of the broader context.

[14] In response to criticism, Northpointe has meanwhile made public a sample assessment form: https://www.documentcloud.org/documents/2702103-Sample-Risk-Assessment-COMPAS-CORE.html.

[15] Cf. Cathy O'Neil's analysis (O'Neil 2016), on which opacity and the resultant lack of accountability is one of the chief problems associated with the use of "Big Data." Note, though, that this sort of criticism can easily be overstated: after all, it is not as if human judgment is particularly transparent either. (For discussion, see, for instance, Zerilli et al. 2018, Creel 2020.) For broader critical perspectives on the ideal of transparency, see O'Neill 2002 and Hood and Heald 2006.

8.2 Is It Really a Matter of Algorithmic Bias?

"Algorithmic bias" is a relatively novel coinage, and it is to some extent an open question what exactly we should mean by it. Intuitively, though, two things seem to be involved: (i) insofar as it *bias*, it should involve some kind of processing distortion resulting in skewed outputs, i.e., verdicts not reflecting the actual probabilities, (ii) insofar as it is *algorithmic* bias, we should expect it to have something to do with the fact that it arises in the context of algorithmic processing, perhaps specifically in terms of computer-based algorithmic processing. Further, I presume that any bias is corrigible, at least in principle. Accordingly, an optimistic approach might have it that the algorithms could be improved to the point where the bias is minimized or eliminated altogether. By contrast, a more pessimistic analysis would have it that the problem is endemic to algorithmic processing, and that the only way forward is for human cognizers, despite their known shortcomings, once again to take full charge of the situation.

If this is anything like what "algorithmic bias" is meant to bring to mind, then I will argue that framing our concerns in these terms is ultimately unhelpful and may only serve to obscure the deeper source of the problem. Given the task that the courts are set, given the institutional constraints that they operate within, and given contingent socio-historical facts about the United States, it is highly likely that any evidence-based decision-procedure, algorithmic or otherwise, will display essentially the same problems. As I will argue, this suggests that the problem is ultimately not epistemic in character, but rather moral and political.

Recall that ProPublica's conclusion primarily rested on the finding that Black defendants were almost twice as likely to be wrongly allocated to high-risk categories as White defendants found guilty of similar crimes. From a distance, this will certainly look like a manifestation of bias. But there is also a surprising, mathematical angle on which the problem comes to take on a very different hue. This has to do with the differential base rates between Black and White defendants. Everyone agrees that the COMPAS system's rate of *predictive success* for Black and White defendants is strikingly similar at around 60 percent. It is in terms of *predictive failure* that the discrepancies are telling: among subjects who did not, as a matter of fact, go on to reoffend, Blacks were almost twice as likely to be classified as medium- or high-risk. As has been pointed out in a paper by Jon Kleinberg et al. (2016), however, this disparity in predictive failure is in fact mathematically inevitable given the combination of equal predictive success and unequal base rates. In other words, if equal predictive success is the epistemic goal we steer by, then, given contingent facts about differential base rates, the apparent phenomenon that ProPublica calls our attention to is not, in fact, a genuine phenomenon at all. Rather, it is just the mathematical flipside of parity in predictive success.

For illustration, assume that 1,000 people are assigned a risk score of 7. Our base rates show a racialized pattern: let's say, of the 1,000, that 600 will be Black, 400 will be White. Now, we ask ourselves, for each of the two groups, how many of these did in fact go on to reoffend (within some specified time frame)? Analysis yields approximately 60 percent in both cases.[16] That sounds good: the system is apparently not biased; it has an equal success rate for both groups.

But now, let's ask what happens with the 400 people who did not reoffend? These are the ones who, according to ProPublica, are wrongly characterized as high-risk. But given the unequal base rates, it *must* be the case that Black people are overrepresented here: 40 percent of 600 = 240, while 40 percent of 400 = 160. This is just an illustration, of course, but we can already start to see how, when we put together the error rates for all of the medium- to high-risk categories, we should indeed expect to find that Black defendants are almost twice as likely to be mischaracterized as White defendants. Given the unequal base rates, it is mathematically necessary that meeting the benchmark of fairness in terms of parity in predictive success will mean that a significantly larger number of Black people will be wrongly assigned to higher risk categories.

We sometimes hear (e.g., Corbett-Davies et al. 2016) that there are differing, indeed competing notions of procedural fairness involved here. Even if it is true that we cannot satisfy both at the same time, there may be a moral case to be made for attempting to steer by an aim of parity in negative cases (i.e., predictive failure) instead of a parity in positive cases (i.e., predictive success).[17] But right away, we can see what would be the problem with such

---

[16] We can, of course, acknowledge that 60 percent predictive success is not tremendously impressive. But that is neither here nor there with respect to the present argument.

[17] I suppose one might be drawn toward such a view by some sort of vague ("intuitive") analogy with the well-known "Blackstone principle," according to which our criminal justice system should be significantly more willing to acquit the guilty than to convict the innocent. But whatever its merits as a general principle of jurisprudence, it has no clear bearing on the present case. These people have already been found guilty of whatever crime they were accused of. Now the question is, can we find any grounds for reducing their sentences? I don't think anyone would seriously propose, on analogy with the Blackstone principle, that we should rather give probation or community service to, say, ten high-risk offenders than a full prison term to one

a suggestion, relative to the present context of discussion: the whole point of seeking algorithmic assistance in our decision-making is to develop epistemic routines that will hopefully yield greater predictive success (with parity between categories). And given the unequal base rates, the parity in predictive success will necessarily produce matching disparities in failure rates, no matter how high or how low our actual success rate is. The idea that one might do better here by adopting a different notion of fairness, i.e., parity in predictive failure, makes very little sense: we would either be saying that we should attempt to fix the failure rate at a certain percentage, or that any reduction of the failure rate for one category (e.g., Whites) should be matched by a commensurate reduction in the failure rate for other categories (e.g., Blacks). The first would essentially constitute giving up on the aim of improving our epistemic routines altogether. But the second alternative is no better: the way to seek reduction in one's failure rate (for any category) is to seek an improvement in one's success rate. But once again, given the unequal base rates, there is no way to hold fixed one's parity in failure rates as one goes about increasing one's overall success rate.

Now, of course, we both can and should ask, why do these discrepancies in base rates obtain? And the answer, surely, will point to institutional racism, and to historical and ongoing injustices against Black people in the United States. But it's unclear what any of this has to do with "algorithmic bias,"[18] as though it was a problem of biased processing, one that we could hope to solve, or at least mitigate, simply by developing better algorithms. Closer reflection suggests that the problem does not lie in the algorithms by which we process the data. Instead, the problem seems to be in an important sense hard-coded into the dataset itself, by way of our long history of institutionalized racism. No amount of improvement in epistemic processing could make this problem go away.[19]

Still, it is important to make some distinctions here. Some of these injustices are, in an important sense, intrinsic to the whole institutional

---

low-risk offender. (This is, of course, compatible with saying, as we should, that prison terms in the United States are generally orders of magnitude longer than they should be.)

[18] See, for instance, the illuminating taxonomy of different notions of algorithmic bias proposed in Danks and London 2017.

[19] Notice, for instance, how algorithmic bias is often presented as resulting from bias inherent in the training data (see, e.g., Johnson 2020). The training data constitutes a limited subset of the complete data, and the algorithmic bias can arise if the training data is not a representative selection of the larger set. By contrast, the "bias" that we are currently debating would supervene on the whole data set, not simply on an arbitrarily chosen subset of it.

sector of criminal correction. From the sharpening of anti-drug legislation in the 1970s and the 1980s (i.e., "the war on drugs"), which had a highly disparate impact on the Black community, to the aggressive over-policing of Black neighborhoods,[20] discriminatory prosecutorial decisions,[21] etc., everything points to the fact that Black people are overrepresented in US crime statistics in part because the whole system exhibits deep racial biases.

However, there is reason to think that even if we could correct for these injustices, much of the problem would persist. The problems faced by Black people in the United States are not confined to the criminal justice sector. They are also marginalized in society at large, as a result of which they are on average poorer, less well educated, and suffer more from unemployment than White people. Sadly, these factors too are known—quite apart from questions about race—to correlate with criminal recidivism. Notice that the one factor that is not probed in these risk assessment tools is the defendant's race; this would constitute a form of facial racism that would immediately raise objections. Instead, what astounds here is the realization that given the United States' long history of institutionalized racism, one doesn't have to use race as a factor in order nonetheless to obtain essentially the same pattern of results. Instead, factors like income, education, family situation, etc., can effectively serve as "proxy attributes."[22] That is to say, given contingent socio-historical circumstances in the United States, poverty, lack of education, unemployment, and other factors that are independently known to correlate with criminal recidivism also correlate with race. (For an extreme example, consider how some of these algorithms will include home address as a risk factor, on the (not intrinsically unreasonable)[23] assumption that living in a high-crime neighborhood increases the likelihood of criminal recidivism. But many high-crime neighborhoods in the United States are 98 percent or more Black.)

Surely, this is a matter of justice, if anything is. But what is in question right now is whether there is pernicious *epistemic bias* at the heart of this problem, and so, whether we could plausibly hope to tackle the problem by improving our epistemic routines. As the analysis in this section suggests,

---

[20] This is one area in which actual algorithmic bias might well be in play: see the concerns raised about "predictive policing" systems in Lum and Isaac 2016, Haskins 2019, as well as the June 2020 letter circulated among mathematicians exhorting colleagues to boycott any further work with police departments in light of recent, highly publicized instances of police brutality against Black people in the United States (https://www.ams.org/journals/notices/202009/rnoti-p1293.pdf).

[21] Cf. Davis 1998, 2009.   [22] See, e.g., Johnson (2020: section 4) for a discussion.

[23] Cf. Stahler et al. 2013.

there is reason to think that there is not: instead, as I will argue in the next section, the problem is better understood in moral (and political) terms.[24]

8.3 Informed Decision-Making in Unequal Societies: The Problem of "Tainted Base Rates"

There is reason to think, then, that we should resist classifying our problem simply as an epistemic problem, which is what we seem to be doing when we are calling it an instance of "algorithmic bias." I have argued two things: first, that the problem isn't really one of *algorithmic* bias, as though it were specific to algorithm-assisted epistemic reasoning; second, it isn't, at a more fundamental level, a strictly epistemic problem at all, i.e., a problem resulting from biased epistemic processing, such that we could hope to do significantly better by improving our epistemic routines. In these cases, our epistemic routines—considered in their own right—could be improved indefinitely, while leaving the problem intact. This is because the problem isn't ultimately in the processing but in the phenomenon: given the history of institutionalized racism in the United States, the bias is essentially hard-coded into the dataset itself.

This argument does nothing to outline a resolution to the problem, but constitutes an attempt to seek a better understanding of its origin. In particular, this analysis suggests that there might be a genuine dilemma lying at the heart of the problem. I have already made brief reference to the work of Tamar Gendler (2011), and in what follows, I will refer to this dilemma as "Gendler's dilemma." Gendler's dilemma arises in situations—very common in deeply divided societies—on which it appears that we can either satisfy our epistemic ideals or our moral ideals, but not both at the same time.

Gendler's argument is framed in terms of the "cognitive costs of implicit bias." As we have seen (section 2.3), implicit bias plays no major role in this book. Nonetheless, the deeper problem that Gendler calls attention to, I will argue, is not strictly speaking about bias at all—implicit or explicit—but rather about *tainted base rates*. These are base rates—for instance in the form of crime statistics—which we would be epistemically irrational to neglect, but which we nonetheless have good reason to think are shaped

---

[24] See also Antony 2016 for similar ideas, but framed in terms of less dramatic examples.

by a history of social injustice (e.g., institutionalized racism). We are now confronted with a dilemma in the sense that what we ought to do epistemically speaking is at odds with what we ought to do morally speaking. The problem raised by automatic risk assessment tools in the US criminal justice process, I argue, is not just a particularly powerful illustration of Gendler's dilemma; it is also an instance of Gendler's dilemma *writ large*, affecting not just individual thinkers, but also social institutions.

"Base rate neglect" is a well-known epistemic fallacy on which subjects fail to properly incorporate information about underlying relative frequencies into their reasoning. A standard example is false positives from breathalyzers. Let's say a breathalyzer is 95 percent reliable, i.e., it has a 5/100 false positive rate. Assume that only 1/1,000 drivers on the road are driving under the influence. A driver is stopped and blows a positive breathalyzer test. We have no further information about the driver (age, gender, time of day, type of vehicle, etc.). Our question is simply: how likely is it that this person is driving under the influence? Many people will have their minds drawn toward the information about the breathalyzer's reliability, and will naturally answer "95 percent." In doing so, they have committed the fallacy of base rate neglect. Given the low underlying frequency of drunk driving (there's only a 0.1 percent chance that a randomly stopped driver will be driving under the influence), the correct answer is less than 2 percent.

Gendler calls our attention to a peculiar case which has subsequently become a focal point in much of the literature. The case involves the historian John Hope Franklin who is celebrating his receipt of the Presidential Medal of Freedom in 1995 by hosting a dinner at the swanky Cosmos Club in Washington, DC. As Franklin recounts, during this visit, another patron walks up to him, presenting him with her coat check. Apparently, then, the other patron mistook him for a staff member. It is easy to see what has gone wrong here: the patron (correctly) identified Franklin as Black, and (incorrectly) inferred that he must be a staff member (since most of the staff members are Black) and not another patron (since the membership of the Cosmos Club is overwhelmingly White). Even as our insides squirm over this faux pas, Gendler asks us to consider the epistemic situation of the lady with the coat check. Was she right to think that Franklin was a staff member? Well, her base rate reasoning is apparently flawless: the probability that a random Black man in the Cosmos Club is a staff member is, one would think, very high. If she didn't take this into account, she would be committing the fallacy of base rate neglect. From a narrowly epistemic point of view, then, it is unclear that she did anything wrong. Using known empirical indicators, she reasonably arrived at the belief that Franklin was in all probability a staff member.[25] Nonetheless, we seem to feel an intuitive resistance against reasoning from base rates in such cases.[26] The reason is that the base rates seem morally "tainted": they bear the imprint of White privilege.

Following the psychologist Philip Tetlock (Tetlock et al. 2000), Gendler calls this the phenomenon of "forbidden base rates." Tetlock's experiments show how base rate information that subjects would otherwise be perfectly happy to avail themselves of would suddenly be treated as "off-limits" once the correlation with race was revealed to them. As Gendler puts it, these subjects now "engaged in a kind of epistemic self-censorship on non-epistemic grounds." This form of self-censorship is epistemically costly in a "racially stratified society," in the sense that it leads subjects to "discount information that might be relevant to their full consideration of both background and foreground conditions" (Gendler 2011: 55).

Nowhere is this problem more acute than in reasoning about crime rates. As Gendler puts it:

> a person who has accurate statistical knowledge of demographic variation will, by definition, know about racial differences in crime rates. Whether or not one is aware of the precise statistics, to know nothing of these data would require one to cultivate ignorance about a striking feature of contemporary American society.   (Gendler 2011: 56)[27]

Even as one reasons—correctly—that these demographic variations are what they are only because of the history of institutionalized racism in the United States, this does nothing to change the fact that these are the base rates. Nonetheless, we can also surmise that making *epistemically* reasonable use of these base rates can only lead to further entrenchment of these

---

[25] This is not to say that she couldn't have been guilty of neglecting other sorts of evidence—e.g., if Franklin was a staff member, why was he wearing a tuxedo rather than a uniform? But presumably, there will be cases in which the base rates are sufficiently stark that it swamps the significance even of such individualized evidence. After all, seeing Franklin in a tux is evidence that not all staff members wear uniforms (on the presumption that Franklin is a staff member).

[26] Bear in mind, our question here is strictly epistemic: what should she *believe* about p given her evidence (including base rates)? The further question of how she should *act* given her belief that p raises separate issues that will only be addressed in chapters 9 and 10.

[27] Though Gendler does not comment on this, I would add that cultivating such ignorance would also plausibly entail cultivating ignorance about what *others* are likely to believe, and therefore to put a significant strain on one's social interactions with others. This is another cognitive cost of base rate neglect, which gives further impetus to the argument of chapter 7.

demographic variations. As Gendler argues, this points to a "perverse feature of the logic of discrimination, namely, its quasi-rational self-perpetuation" (Gendler 2011: 57). The cost "is profound": "living in a society structured by race appears to make it impossible to be both rational and equitable" (Gendler 2011: 57).

This, then, is what I call Gendler's dilemma. Gendler herself frames it primarily in terms of its bearing on the cognitive lives of individual subjects. To my mind, the problem presented by automatic risk assessment tools in the criminal justice process is, essentially, just Gendler's dilemma writ large, now occurring at the level of major social institutions, rather than simply at the level of individual thinkers.

As we have seen, engaging in risk assessment of this sort is an obligatory task, one that cannot be waived. Defendants with a low risk of reoffense *deserve*—as a matter of justice—that their sentences be reduced so far as is possible, consistent with the restorative aims of corrective justice and the goal of maintaining public safety. Our question is simply, how should this task be carried out? What is, as it were, the "epistemic best practice" here? The turn toward automated risk assessment tools is to a large extent motivated by the recognition that human judges are relatively poor at this sort of task. Specifically, there is every chance that their assessments will be shaped by prejudice and other forms of bias. Our problem arises through the discovery that the algorithms *also* seem to encode bias. What should we do?[28]

Probing deeper suggests that the problem may not ultimately be one of bias at all, let alone a distinctive form of algorithmic bias. Raising concerns about bias is, I take it, to raise concerns about epistemic processing: it is to suggest that the outputs of our epistemic reasoning don't accurately reflect the true probabilities. So here's our problem: which factors *do*, then, correlate with criminal recidivism? We *know* that a variety of socio-economic factors do. So if we're going to base our risk assessments on any sort of evidence at all, these must presumably be among the factors that we consider. But at the same time, we know that these factors in turn correlate with race. This correlation gives us pause, as it should. For we know that the reason there's a correlation between race and crime, as modulated by factors

---

[28] Notably, no one seems to be suggesting that we revert to unaided human judgment: as I argued above, even if far from perfect, the use of automated risk assessment tools can nonetheless be part of best epistemic practice simply in virtue of constituting a significant improvement on viable alternatives.

like poverty, unemployment, and lack of meaningful access to basic social goods such as health care and education, is that the United States has discriminated against its Black population throughout its history. The problem, as I have argued, is that the bias is encoded in the dataset itself, and not in the algorithms used to project probabilities based on the dataset.

The resulting problem is at once epistemic and moral. But in its strictly epistemic dimension, it is hard to see what is wrong with basing our judgments on these base rates; i.e., why this wouldn't be part of our "best epistemic practice" for carrying out the task in question. Recall, the legal system is charged with a mandatory task of assessing recidivism risk at various stages of the judicial process. Discharging this task requires consulting the best available evidence and issuing the appropriate recommendations. This task cannot be waived, even as we remain mindful of the fact that the indicators we (reasonably) take to be significant display a strong correlation with race. Of course, there is a sense in which one might *hope* that the legal system be brought to recognize that its evidence-base is tainted by a long history of institutionalized racism, and that it might accordingly be moved to mitigate these effects in its verdicts.[29] But under the separation of powers, it is crucial that the legal system operates on a narrow and highly specific mandate. The "hope" just touted would effectively constitute a proposal to expand that mandate well into the political domain. For obvious reasons, this is something many are wary of. Specifically, given the fact that the legal system itself has a long history of involvement in wilful perpetuation of these injustices, it is unclear why we should trust this institution to do significantly better than lawmakers in correcting them.[30]

---

[29] Notice, for instance, how section 718.2(e) of the Canadian Criminal Code instructs courts to consider, wherever appropriate, the use of non-imprisonment sanction. While this guideline applies quite generally for all cases, it is mandated that it be applied "with particular attention to the circumstances of Aboriginal offenders." Often referred to as the "Gladue principle," this was heralded as part of an attempt to combat the overrepresentation of Aboriginal subjects in the Canadian criminal correctional system. Empirical studies suggest, however, that the principle has not led to significant improvements on this score. On this, see, e.g., Welsh and Ogloff 2008, Roberts and Reid 2017.

[30] Consider, by way of illustration, the many critical responses to the College Board's recent announcement that it is adding an "adversity score" to its SAT test, in a bid to offset the effects of entrenched social privilege on college admissions. The factors reflected in the adversity score—drawn from census-provided "contextual data on the student's neighborhood and high school"—are, unsurprisingly, very similar to those that figure in assessments of recidivism risk: "typical family income, family structure, educational attainment, housing stability, and crime" (https://professionals.collegeboard.org/environmental-context-dashboard). While it has an outsize influence on distribution of social goods in the United States, the College Board is a

Shifting our focus to a notion of "collective epistemic responsibility" offers no clear outlook toward a resolution here. It is true that this is not a problem that we can hope to solve as individual persons. But it is also not a problem that we could look to individual *institutions* to solve: instead, the problem is structural and interactional. As the example of the branches of government illustrates, it is crucial to the way that we organize our social and political systems that we have a multitude of institutions, each with its distinctive mandate and associated powers. So it is to be expected that coordination problems will arise even at the institutional level. For a less stark illustration, consider the fact that Facebook apparently displays STEM related career ads to male subjects much more frequently than it does to female subjects (cf. Lambrecht and Tucker 2018). In light of persistent failures to open these career paths to women, we could think that such selective advertisement is a contributing cause to continuing discrimination. And maybe it is. But arguably, it can't be Facebook's problem alone to solve: in fact, precisely so as to mitigate these sorts of problems, Facebook has now taken the step of prohibiting gender-targeted advertising (i.e., you cannot choose to have your ads displayed only to this demographic rather than that). Nor is it the advertisers' problem to solve: the reason these discrepancies in advertising exposure obtain is, quite simply, that advertising to women is much more expensive than advertising to men. In other words, the advertisers might *want* to advertise to women, and may even prefer to, for precisely these reasons: but sooner or later, they will be outbid by more competitive advertisers.[31] Now, surely, we might want to say that we would be better off if we could somehow sort this problem out. We might even say that it redounds poorly on us collectively that we continue to have this problem. Yet the problem essentially involves coordinating the actions of different entities with different aims and incentives. Given the way the structure is set up, we can't expect them all to spontaneously shape their policies for the overall good. And given further concerns about political freedom, it is not clear that we would be better off if there were a single entity that was charged with coercively ensuring that we all coordinated our actions on this score.

---

private enterprise, essentially just offering consultation services (i.e., no college is required to take SAT scores into account). By contrast, the judicial system is a branch of the US government, operating under a strictly limited mandate.

[31] Thanks to Jing Hwan Khoo for pointing me toward this case study.

Meanwhile, the legal system is playing a recognizable part in maintaining a necrotic cycle: social and political marginalization leads to higher crime rates, which leads to harsher sentencing, which leads to further social and political marginalization, etc. When the relevant bias is effectively encoded into the dataset itself, via major social institutions and political history, the legal system's best strategies for "evidence-based decision-making," whether in the form of human judgment unaided, or assisted by computer algorithms, may only serve to further entrench the existing inequalities.[32]

8.4 Conclusion: Moral and Epistemic Normativity Redux

In my view, then, the challenges raised by automated risk assessment in the criminal justice system are not best framed in terms of "bias" (let alone a specific form of "algorithmic bias"), insofar as bias is to be understood in terms of flawed or otherwise compromised processing of data. Instead, I have proposed to frame the problem in terms of reasoning from "tainted base rates." As such, we can see how the problem involves the possibly irreconcilable pressures of moral and epistemic normativity. Understood simply in epistemic terms, there can be no serious claim that risk assessment in criminal corrections is a task not best carried out in light of evidence, and that (at least some of) this evidence will come in the form of correlations between recidivism risk and various demographic factors. Our unease only arises when these epistemic concerns run headfirst into moral concerns. While risk assessment is a recognizably epistemic task, it is also—in the larger picture—meant to subserve a moral aim, complex and multidimensional as that aim may be (i.e., balancing public safety, maintaining a sense of justice, plausibly aiming to restore convicted criminals to productive roles in society, etc.). By basing our judgments on the best evidence available, we risk compromising these moral ideals, insofar as we are foreseeably

---

[32] Notice, for instance, how Corbett-Davies et al. 2016 speak about the importance of seeking ways to "mitigate" the harm that arises as a consequence, say, by abolishing the bail system in favor of less imposing measures such as electronic monitoring. There's obviously much to be said in favor of such proposals. But notice that they precisely fail to address the underlying problem with racial disparities: now, we would instead be stuck with having to explain why a disproportionate number of Blacks are being subjected to the indignities of electronic monitoring. True, this might be preferable to discrepancies in bail or sentencing. But as a concern about structural injustice, moving to mitigate the consequences in this sense is precisely to leave unaddressed the underlying issues. (Moreover, given recent years' critical scrutiny of policing practices in the United States, it should hopefully be clear why discrepancies in electronic monitoring is not a trivial concern either.)

(if not intentionally) contributing to the vicious cycle of incarceration and social marginalization that afflicts many visible minorities in the United States. Conversely, if we decide to honor these moral ideals, it would seem that we are simply resolving not to base our epistemic reasoning on the total evidence available to us. In effect, we would be guilty of (willful) base rate neglect.

This is our dilemma. The sense that it is a *genuine* dilemma depends in no small part on the supposition, articulated but not defended in any great detail in chapter 3, that moral and epistemic considerations provide independent constraints on our cognitive lives. In the final chapters of this book, we will consider recent challenges to this supposition.

9
Moral Constraints on Belief?

So far as our argument up to this point has been concerned, it might as well be that our moral and epistemic judgments run on completely independent tracks. Whether we find some agent's doxastic state to be "good" in epistemic terms (i.e., justified) has no bearing on the question of whether we should also find it to be good in moral terms, and vice versa. There is a certain perspective from which this conclusion follows readily: true, it would appear that morality and epistemology share a basic normative vocabulary. But in itself, this is no reason to expect that there should be any significant interplay between the two domains. After all, other domains of philosophical inquiry may also share in this vocabulary—e.g., aesthetics—and there's no obvious reason to expect our moral judgments to constrain our aesthetic judgments or vice versa.

The assumption that moral and epistemic assessments exert no constraint on each other should not be allowed to go unexamined, however. Prejudiced belief causes harm. As we saw in the previous chapter, where this harm is pervasive and systematic—reinforced, perhaps, by major social institutions—it does nothing to quell our sense of moral frustration to learn that individual prejudiced believers may have done nothing wrong, epistemically speaking, in holding the beliefs that they do. In particular, this observation would completely fail to address the victim's perspective on the matter. So we will want to look again at the notion that there is no interplay between our moral and epistemic ideals.

In this chapter I will critically review two recent attempts to develop the idea that moral concerns can place significant constraints on epistemic normativity: moral encroachment (section 9.1) and doxastic morality (section 9.2). After concluding that neither can quite carry off the task that is ascribed to them, we will turn in our next and final chapter to examining the possibility that the interplay between morality and epistemology might in fact run in the opposite direction; i.e., that the range of our epistemic responsibility in an important way constrains the range of our moral responsibility. This would obviously constitute a very dramatic and in many ways unwelcome claim. It would seem to entail not only that we will ultimately be unable to mold our conception of epistemic normativity to fully fit our sense of moral rightness. It also seems to suggest that, in many cases, we will even lack crucial grounds for voicing our moral frustration at prejudiced belief.

After outlining this view in some detail in chapter 10, I will end the book by showing how the situation is nowhere near as bleak as it may seem. In particular, we will want to distinguish conditions that trigger *moral blame* from conditions that trigger a broader concept of moral responsibility. I argue that there remains an important sense of moral responsibility that can attach even to epistemically blameless agents. This form of responsibility may include an obligation to "make amends," for instance in the form of offering apologies, compensation, or in other ways to seek to undo the damage that one has caused. This distinction can provide a new, and in important ways a better, platform on which to vindicate the moral and legal standing of those who are victimized by prejudice.

9.1 Moral Encroachment

According to proponents of "moral encroachment," moral considerations can constrain what we ought to believe, where the "ought" is to be understood in epistemic terms, not simply in moral terms. In particular, moral considerations can contribute to "raising the epistemic bar" for justified belief, making it the case that a belief which would be sufficiently evidenced to qualify as justified in one context may no longer be justified once the "moral stakes" of the situation are taken into account.[1] These moral stakes are typically taken to consist in possible harms to the target of the belief. So, if adopting a certain belief might stand to cause significant moral harm to innocent (or undeserving) others, then the justificatory burden on that belief is correspondingly increased.[2]

---

[1] See, e.g., Pace 2011; Fritz 2017; Bolinger 2018; Moss 2018a; Basu 2019b. For discussion, see Begby 2018b and Gardiner 2018.

[2] It is crucial to adopt a suitably wide-ranging conception of "harm" here. In particular, we should be on guard against thinking of harm strictly in terms of, say, "physical harm." Instead, and following Feinberg (1984, 1988), I take harm to involve a setback to a person's reasonable and legitimate interests. "Harm" in this sense is a significantly broader notion than physical (or even psychological) injury (Feinberg 1984: 106). Even though we sometimes hear things like "the gunman fired two shots into the crowd, but luckily no one was harmed," this is not the sense of harm which is in play in this book: although none of the bystanders were injured, they were certainly harmed, inasmuch as they suffered an invasion of their legitimate interest in not being subjected to unwarranted risk.

To get a sense of how this works, it will be helpful to start with an appeal to the more familiar idea of "pragmatic encroachment."[3] In standard examples of pragmatic encroachment, we are presented with two evidentially identical scenarios, but with differing practical stakes. So, for instance, John might be justified on his evidence in believing that the last bus home runs well after midnight on a balmy summer evening, when he wouldn't much mind walking home anyway. But his belief might *not* be justified on a cold winter night, even though it would be supported by exactly the same body of evidence. In this sense, the practical stakes—roughly, the "risk" incurred in case one's belief were wrong—can encroach on one's epistemic justification. In a high-stakes case, one's belief might require more or better evidence in order to be justified.

Moral encroachment adds to this basic idea the thought that among the various practical considerations at stake in such situations, some may well be moral considerations. In particular, there will be situations in which one risks harming others' interests—and not just one's own—in forming the belief in question. (Let's say that in the second case, John has also promised his babysitter that he would be home by a certain time). In those cases, so goes the thought, one might not be justified in forming a belief on the basis of a body of evidence which nonetheless would be sufficient for justification in some other, morally inert context.

Before moving on, it might be helpful to note that this idea is compatible with at least one important motivation for evidentialism (see section 1.2.3). True, moral encroachment might require us to give up on simplistic characterizations of evidentialism, such as the notion that the epistemic standing of a belief supervenes on the total body of evidence bearing on that belief. But evidentialism can nonetheless survive in a subtler guise, as the thesis that only evidence can justify belief. Note, specifically, that these moral considerations aren't themselves "reasons for belief," in anything like the way that evidence is. So, *a fortiori*, they are not to be construed as "non-evidential reasons for belief" either. This is because moral considerations do nothing to increase or decrease the probability that a hypothesis is true. Instead, their role is that of contributing to setting the evidential threshold that a belief must meet in order to count as justified.[4]

---

[3] Cf. Fantl and McGrath 2002, 2009.
[4] Many thanks for Caroline von Klemperer for discussion of these issues.

9.1.1 Examples of Moral Encroachment

Many of the examples that motivate moral encroachment involve racial profiling and other forms of inference from statistical evidence.[5] I take it, however, that it's not strictly speaking the statistical character of the evidence which raises concerns in these cases. Rather, what seems problematic is a distinctive sort of inference from properties ascribed to typical members of a group to properties ascribed to an individual simply in virtue of his membership in this group. Statistical inference is one such inference, but by no means the only. Importantly, stereotype reasoning, which lies at the heart of the epistemology of prejudice, involves a very similar kind of inferential transition.

Moral encroachment differs in a crucial respect from the more flat-footed skepticisms regarding stereotype reasoning that we reviewed in chapters 4 and 5. Specifically, it does not commit to the idea that there is something intrinsically epistemically suspicious about all such inferences. Rather, it holds that these inferences can become epistemically problematic when the moral stakes are sufficiently high. So for instance, lots of people seem to believe that I must be an avid outdoorsman as soon as they learn that I am from Norway. Presumably, they entertain a stereotype of Norwegians as nature lovers. In the absence of further information—such as would be gained from observing my sallow complexion and slouchy posture—this inference is, I take it, no worse than the stereotype that it draws on. If the stereotype is epistemically warranted, then so is the inference, even if it should turn out to be false.

The Norwegian case is presumably relatively harmless, and won't raise many epistemic heckles. The cases that bother us are ones that involve problematic racial or other demographic classifications. Take, for example, the taxi driver who chooses not to pick up a Black passenger on the assumption that he will be a poor tipper (Moss 2018a: 198). Even if it were true that Black people generally tip less than other passengers, it may be argued that the driver has no right to believe of *this* person—though he is Black—that he will not tip well. The reason this belief is not justified, even if

---

[5] Some arguments presented under this rubric also involve cases of relations among intimates (cf. Schroeder 2018; Basu 2019b). However, the arguments they are meant to illustrate are often cases of the subtly but importantly different idea of "doxastic morality" which we will have occasion to look at below, in section 9.2.

similarly evidenced beliefs in other contexts would be justified, is that the taxi driver stands to harm the would-be passenger.[6]

To see how this idea is sometimes developed, consider how the degree of support that a statistical body of evidence provides for a hypothesis can be set arbitrarily high, short of 1. If we can find a case where we nonetheless would intuitively say that one should not believe a hypothesis that is, say, 96 percent likely to be true on our evidence, we will naturally ask why we should withhold belief here, given that the statistical evidence appears to be so compelling? (For instance, if you were investigating an electrical fault in your home, and you had isolated a possible cause to 96 percent probability, you would no doubt take that to be plenty sufficient.) Moral encroachment can then make a plausible case that the evidence, despite its strength, is insufficient because of the possible moral harm involved in forming the belief. In a morally inert context, or a less morally charged context, the evidence would have been sufficient.

Analogies with burden of evidence in criminal trials provide a neat illustration of the point (Moss 2018b, chapter 10). Burden of evidence in criminal trials is conventionally set to "proof beyond a reasonable doubt." On the face of it, this notion would seem to invite a specification somewhere along the credence spectrum, e.g., one has proof beyond reasonable doubt if one's evidence rationalizes a credence of, say, .96 or above. But legal practice resists this move, suggesting that there is no unique (rational) credence that satisfies the "proof beyond a reasonable doubt" standard.[7] The "prison yard case" provides a classic illustration:[8] there are twenty-five inmates in a prison yard, as shown on CCTV. One of them walks off camera, but we can't tell who it is. The remaining twenty-four inmates proceed to assault the prison ward, administering a severe beating. Common statistical reasoning would proceed as follows: we know the identity of each of the twenty-five inmates. So even though we don't know who walked off prior to the attack, we know that for each individual suspect, there is nonetheless a 96 percent probability that they participated in the assault. If that's the standard of proof, we should now have enough evidence to convict all twenty-five of

---

[6] Note that the harm could be greater or lesser. Some moral harm might come from believing of *anyone* that they are a bad tipper—middle-aged, suit-clad white men with horn-rimmed glasses, let's say. But the historical and social-institutional facts of marginalization make this harm particularly potent in the present case. Accordingly, its epistemic impact is comparatively stronger.

[7] For an overview, see Moss 2018b: 203–4 and Gardiner 2019.

[8] From Nesson 1979, and discussed at length in Moss 2018b: 204–7.

them. But moral intuition seems to balk at this reasoning, since we know for certain that one of them is not guilty. (If 96 percent probability does not seem sufficiently decisive, we can tweak the numbers further (1/100, 1/1000), all the while retaining our conclusion: in all these cases, the certainty of imposing unwarranted harm on an innocent person precludes a guilty verdict even though the statistical probability of guilt can be set arbitrarily high (short of 1).)

With this, let us return to the taxi driver who spurns a would-be passenger on account of his race. Let us assume for the sake of argument that the relevant statistical generalizations are true, and moreover, that they are known to the subject. It is not in question that these generalizations can lend a fair degree of support to the hypothesis under consideration.[9] Even so, the evidence seems intuitively insufficient to warrant belief about the particular individual in question. And a plausible reason it would be insufficient is that you have no knowledge of the particular person you are faced with, other than the fact that he is a member of the group in question. You have a justified belief in a group-level generalization; that generalization, seen from a purely statistical point of view, can support to an arbitrarily high degree the hypothesis that an individual who falls under the classification will display the property in question. But somehow that evidence seems insufficient to form the belief that *this* arbitrary individual will be a bad tipper. Why? Moral encroachment proposes that the reason we should withhold belief here is the possibility of moral harm to the target of the belief, the arbitrary individual in question. Note that while this argument is not explicitly couched in terms of the epistemology of prejudice, its relevance should be apparent. We could well be justified in holding all manner of stereotype generalizations involving social groups. What moral encroachment apparently draws into doubt is our epistemic right to infer from such generalizations that a particular individual has (or is likely to have) the property in question. What would block the inference is the (unwarranted) harm that the resulting belief might stand to impart on its target. This makes the belief not just morally problematic, but also epistemically problematic.

---

[9] Once again, note the difference from the more flat-footed skepticism we discussed in chapter 4, where what was in question was precisely whether information could carry over from group-level generalization to judgments about individuals at all.

9.1.2 Against Moral Encroachment

The subtlety in this position lies in the idea that we can grant that a body of evidence which renders a certain hypothesis *n* likely is sufficient to warrant belief in one case, but not sufficient in another. The difference between the two cases does not lie in the thought that we have some cryptic non-evidential reasons for belief in the second case but not in the first. Rather, it lies in the idea that the threshold for justified belief can change from context to context, in particular in light of what is morally at stake in the relevant context. When we factor in the potential for harm, we see that more is needed to justify forming the belief.

While I have quite a bit of sympathy with the motivations underlying this line of thought, it can be seen that the argument as stated trades on a distinction between credence and belief which cannot be accommodated in the theoretical framework of this book. Quite simply, once we have determined the degree to which our evidence supports our hypothesis, we will also have determined what credence we should have in that hypothesis. And once we have settled this, there is simply no further question about what we should believe.

On my approach, then, these arguments are not best understood as speaking to the question of what to believe at all. Instead, a better framework for thinking about this is in terms of a gap between belief (understood on the model of credence) and "acceptance."[10] As will be recalled from section 1.5, acceptance is essentially an executive decision to treat a proposition as sufficiently evidenced to act upon in a particular context, to provisionally close down further inquiry, etc. In psychological terms, it represents a very different function than mere belief. And precisely because it is an expression of executive control, it should be no surprise that moral norms might bear on acceptance in a way that they don't bear on mere belief. We are free to decline acceptance of propositions which we nonetheless deem to be highly probable on our evidence. Moreover, we are independently criticizable for the decisions we make in this regard. One ground for such criticism can certainly be epistemic. Nonetheless, epistemic considerations do not fully determine what it is reasonable for us to accept. (As I argued in section 1.5, we can even be right to accept propositions that we take to be highly

---

[10] See, in particular Cohen 1989, 1992. Bolinger 2018 offers an interesting application of acceptance to these debates. My own discussion is inspired by Bolinger's, but develops the point in a rather different direction.

improbable on our evidence, and in fact, significantly less probable than its competitors. But we couldn't straightforwardly be said to have made a decision to believe these propositions, even when we accept them.) In acceptance, then, as opposed to mere belief, we are made to answer to competing normative pressures: epistemic, moral, and more broadly prudential norms are now simultaneously in play.

Once moral encroachment is recognized as bearing on acceptance rather than belief, the contour of our problem shifts in important ways. Our taxi driver may well *believe* that his would-be passenger is less likely to tip well than others. If this belief is understood simply in terms of assigning a certain credence in light of his evidence, he can hardly be faulted for that. (After all, proponents of moral encroachment seem to agree as much.) What he can be faulted for, by contrast, is treating that belief as sufficiently evidenced for acting on in this particular context. Given the possibility of unwarranted harm, the bar for acceptance is higher than the bar for mere belief, which continues to reflect our best assessment of the evidence. (A fortiori, I believe this is the correct account also of more standard cases of pragmatic encroachment. For example, the person who decides that the proposition that the bank will be open on Saturday is not sufficiently evidenced to act on (given the associated risks) should still believe that the bank will be open on Saturday. After all, if he were given a forced-choice bet, where should we counsel him to put his money?)

On this understanding, moral encroachment fails to deliver the promised bridge between epistemological and moral normativity.[11] What it offers is not a moral constraint on belief formation, but a moral constraint on action (broadly construed, including the executive decision to treat certain beliefs as actionable). This is by no means a trivial point. To learn that one's acceptance-policies should be constrained by moral considerations is highly significant,[12] and can provide a further resource in our battle to limit the damages of social prejudice. But ultimately, it doesn't provide a moral

---

[11] See, for instance, Moss 2018b: 228–9.

[12] By contrast, see Peels (2016: 179–80): "Someone who believes on the basis of good evidence that *p* and has no reason to mistrust her belief that *p* clearly blamelessly acts on *p*, even if it turns out that *p* is false." This view is clearly too simple: I can believe, on excellent evidence, that *p* is true, but nonetheless recognize that I ought not act on the supposition that it is true, simply because of the risk of unwarranted harm befalling innocent others if the belief should turn out to be false. Notwithstanding the evidence, it would be morally reckless to act on the belief. Even so, these considerations have no bearing on the question of whether I should continue to *believe* that *p*. (For example, I might have excellent statistical reasons to believe that my current cough is caused by seasonal allergies and not by Covid-19. But for obvious reasons, I might nonetheless not be blameless in acting on that belief.)

constraint on belief, strictly speaking. Moss's analogy with burdens of proof in criminal trials bears this out: for instance, the jurors who acquitted O.J. Simpson for the murder of his wife might still *believe*—and probably *should* believe, epistemically speaking—that Simpson committed the crime, even if they didn't find that the belief was sufficiently well-evidenced for a criminal conviction.[13]

Now, we may note in passing that on Moss's view, moral encroachment attaches also to credences, not just to "full beliefs" (Moss 2018a: 184–90). How are we to take this argument? It is not, so far as I can see, a claim that, because of the moral stakes involved, the credence shouldn't be set where the evidence suggests that it should be set. Rather, moral encroachment makes it the case that such credences (even if correctly set in light of the evidence) would fail to constitute knowledge. This is not the place to develop a full case against the knowledge norm of belief.[14] Such notions might have a role to play in highly idealized approaches to epistemology. But in non-ideal epistemology, things seem importantly different. Quite simply, there are certain epistemic tasks, even high-risk epistemic tasks, that could not be carried out without resorting to statistical evidence. The cases of risk assessment in the criminal justice process reviewed in chapter 8 above, and which led us to consider Gendler's dilemma in the first place, are among them. When we are asking questions about the likelihood that *this* person will commit serious crimes in the foreseeable future, we can only turn to what evidence we have to settle the question of the likelihood that some person relevantly similar to this person—similar, say, in terms of age, social and educational background, employment history, and criminal record—would commit such a crime. And it is plausible that this evidence must, at least in large part, be statistical in character. Immediately, we might think that this means that we just shouldn't pass any judgment here at all (perhaps because, as Moss argues, our credence does not constitute knowledge). But that won't do: as I argued in chapter 8, these epistemic tasks can be obligatory. What this means is that in non-ideal contexts, we are sometimes *required* to pass judgment—and sometimes also to act on that judgment—on something less than knowledge.

---

[13] Differently put, they could agree that the evidence did not meet the burden of proof even as they also agree that it is highly likely on the evidence that he committed the murder.

[14] See, in particular, Williamson 2000, but also Hawthorne and Stanley 2008, and Gerken 2011 for interesting discussion, as well as my own remarks in section 1.4 of this book.

Finally, we should also note that even if we could fully endorse the idea of moral encroachment as a constraint on belief, not just acceptance, it would be overly optimistic to expect it to fully and finally settle the issues under consideration in this book. Our focus is on the epistemology of prejudice. Moral encroachment operates on a risk of harm to the belief target. It's certainly a fact about many prejudiced beliefs that they stand to cause significant harm, at the social and individual level. But it doesn't follow that any particular prejudice stands to cause much harm: after all, an individual believer's contribution to the harm might be virtually negligible. Moreover, the mere fact that the evidential bar for justified belief fluctuates with the moral stakes involved in adopting the belief in no way entails that one couldn't have evidence sufficient to meet that bar. While this is a perfectly general point, it is perhaps best gauged by considering the fact that the moral stakes involved in adopting a particular prejudiced belief might themselves fluctuate quite significantly. Let's say the belief targets a group of people that one is highly unlikely ever to interact with, directly or indirectly.[15] Consequently, one would assume that the risk of moral harm is significantly reduced. But the belief may be no less prejudiced for that. Or, as might well happen, the prejudiced belief is held by members of an oppressed and stereotyped group against the group that marginalizes them. Since the belief-targets are now significantly less vulnerable to harm, being members of the privileged social group, the effects of moral encroachment would be correspondingly reduced. But we would still want to know whether the beliefs in question are prejudiced beliefs, and, if so, how—if at all—they might be epistemically justified.[16] Quite simply, while our moral concern with prejudice is borne out of thinking about paradigmatic cases where prejudice is part of the apparatus that keeps the marginalized group in

[15] See Begby 2018b for further discussion. For instance, my kids are much enamoured of a book entitled *Ruthless Romans* (Deary 2010, vol. 22 of a series called *Horrible Histories*), which peddles exactly the sorts of stereotypes that you might expect from the title. I take care, of course, to point out to them that these "Romans" are not the same people as currently inhabit the city of Rome. But otherwise, I let them at it. Obviously, if I found them reading a similar volume targeting people significantly closer to us in time (say *Imbecilic Indians* or *Krazy Koreans*), my reaction would be very different.

[16] This is one reason to resist framing the epistemology of prejudice in terms of notions of "white ignorance," which as Mills argues (2007: 23) is to be understood as a matter of "privileged, group-based ignorance." (See also Medina (2013) for ruminations on "active ignorance" which ties these presumptive epistemic pathologies specifically to the machinations of social privilege.) As I argued in the Introduction, I am certainly in agreement that our moral concern should be drawn to situations where prejudice is part of a structural feature of social oppression and marginalization. But from a strictly epistemic point of view, the problem is of a more general sort.

place, this is hardly an intrinsic feature of prejudice as a socio-epistemic phenomenon.

9.2 Doxastic Morality

We have found that moral encroachment, while plausible on a certain construal, nonetheless fails to resolve the issues at stake in this book. It may be thought that another recent proposal can do better here. "Doxastic morality," as it is sometimes called, often trades on examples that are very similar to those that we have already explored in connection with moral encroachment, and is often not properly differentiated from it even by the people who advance it. But ultimately, as we shall see, there are good reasons to keep the theoretical accounts apart.

Basu and Schroeder provide a compact expression of doxastic morality in the following terms:

> First, doxastic wrongs are *directed*. When you wrong someone, you don't merely do wrong, you do wrong *to them*. Second, doxastic wrongs are committed *by beliefs*. So in particular, the wrong in a doxastic wronging does not lie in what you *do*, either prior to, or subsequent to, forming a belief, but rather in the belief itself. And third, doxastic wrongs are wrongs *in virtue* of what is believed. So a belief that is a doxastic wronging does not wrong merely in virtue of its consequences; the wronging lies in the belief, rather than in, or at least, over and above, its effects.
>
> (Basu and Schroeder 2019: 181)

Most centrally, then, doxastic morality pivots on the claim that there are moral norms that operate directly on belief, specifically on the contents of belief. This constraint would be separate from and independent of any other moral constraint bearing on belief *indirectly*, such as moral considerations pertaining to how we process the evidence, or the idea that in forming certain beliefs we would increase our risk of engaging in certain kinds of morally harmful behaviors, such as discrimination.

To illustrate the explanatory potential of doxastic morality, consider the following example from Rima Basu:

> *Wounded by Belief*. Suppose that Mark has an alcohol problem and has been sober for eight months. Tonight there's a departmental colloquium

for a visiting speaker, and throughout the reception, he withstands the temptation to have a drink. But, when he gets home his partner, Maria, smells the wine that the speaker spilled on his sleeve, and Mark can tell from the way Maria looks at him that she thinks he's fallen off the wagon. Although the evidence suggests that Mark has fallen off the wagon, would it be unreasonable for Mark to seek an apology for what Maria believes of him?   (Basu 2019a: 917)

In the previous section, I offered a re-reading of the intuitions that motivate moral encroachment by considering them in terms of acceptance rather than belief. Doxastic morality would seem immune to this maneuver precisely through the claim that one can stand to wrong another person *merely* in virtue of holding certain beliefs about them. For let us suppose that in the situation described, Mark is indeed entitled to feel resentment against Maria when he learns that she believes as she does. Of course, it is not *the learning of it*—by whatever mechanism that might occur—that he is resentful of. Rather, he is resentful of the thing that he learns, namely what Maria believes of him. This resentment is *apt*, Basu argues, only if he has in fact been wronged by Maria's belief as such. And insofar as we have agreed that his resentment is apt, we should presumably agree also that beliefs can wrong just as such.

9.2.1 A Closer Look

These reflections already suggest that doxastic morality is in fact a significantly stronger position than moral encroachment. Presumably, then, it will also require a different stock of arguments to support it. As I will show, it is not clear that such arguments are available.

Recall that we have framed the background concern in terms of potential conflicts between our moral and epistemic ideals. Along these lines, Mark Schroeder entertains the following line of thought:

if beliefs can wrong, then some beliefs must be wrong, and if this is so, there will be moral standards governing beliefs. But if there are moral standards governing beliefs, the worry goes, these standards will be orthogonal to the properly epistemic standards governing beliefs, and so these standards will come into conflict. Perhaps it will turn out that we are sometimes morally required to believe something that we are in no position to know or which is even highly improbable, on the evidence. Or perhaps it will turn out that sometimes even knowledge is morally wrong.   (Schroeder 2018: 116)

This would be the kind of reasoning that would lead to an acknowledgment of Gendler's dilemma. But on reflection, Schroeder argues, such apparent conflicts between what is morally required of us and what is epistemically required of us will turn out to be *merely* apparent:

> If the very same moral factors that make the human resources manager wrong the applicant and the father wrong his daughter also raise the stakes for how much evidence is required to epistemically justify their beliefs, then the moral wrongness of beliefs will guarantee an epistemic fault, even though some morally wrong beliefs are supported by evidence that would be sufficient to justify a belief about a different topic.
>
> (Schroeder 2018: 117)

Notice, however, how this sounds once again just like the arguments for moral encroachment. But as we saw, even if we were to acknowledge that moral considerations can serve to "raise the bar" for epistemically justified belief, this still leaves our account plenty short of *guaranteeing*, as Schroeder seems to suggest, that "the moral wrongness of beliefs" will also entail an "an epistemic fault" with these beliefs. We need to look farther, then, for an argument fit to establish this much stronger conclusion.

To my mind, the only way that we could establish a conclusion of this form would be to stand firm on the idea that one can wrong someone merely in virtue of the contents of one's belief. To see this, let us return to Basu's "wounded by belief" case, where the "aptness" of Mark's resentment is what serves as our grounds for concluding that Maria has wronged him simply in virtue of believing as she does. We can ask, is there really *no* constellation of evidence that Maria could possess such that it would fully warrant her in believing that Mark has relapsed into drinking? Assume, for instance, that Mark returns home only at 4 am on a worknight after attending a reunion with notoriously hard-drinking high-school buddies, he knocks over a lamp in the entry way, *and* he smells of alcohol. Now we can ask, quite irrespective of whether he has in fact been drinking, shouldn't Mark be brought to consider how things might look to Maria? Shouldn't he thereby recognize that the resentment that he might initially have been inclined to feel would in fact be quite *inapt*? That is to say, given her evidential situation, shouldn't Mark recognize that it is perfectly within Maria's epistemic rights to believe as she does?[17] Considered from the point of view of moral encroachment, at least, we must concede that, essentially no matter what the moral stakes of some situation might be, there will be some constellation of evidence which would be sufficient to justify the belief in question. If so, it is false to claim, as Schroeder does, that "the moral wrongness of beliefs will guarantee an epistemic fault" with those beliefs.

In brief, moral encroachment is designed to work on the transition from evidence to belief. If doxastic morality is to remain a recognizably independent position, we must take seriously the idea that the moral wrong in question would "not lie in what you *do*, either prior to, or subsequent to, forming a belief, but rather in the belief itself" (Basu and Schroeder 2019: 181). Specifically, the wrong cannot not lie in, say, jumping to conclusions based on contextually insufficient evidence; nor can it lie in the possibility that by forming a certain belief about you, I increase the risk that I will wrong you in some subsequent non-doxastic capacity, say, by discriminating against you in a hiring decision.[18]

9.2.2 Against Doxastic Morality

But is this a view we should take? Can we really make good sense of the idea that one might wrong someone merely in virtue of holding a particular belief about them, absent any consideration of the evidential context in which that belief is formed?

To begin, it is important to recognize that not all harms are wrongs. Wrongs are a subset of harms that correlate with rights.[19] That is, a harm

---

[17] Of course, this is fully compatible with the thought that once Mark presents Maria with *further* evidence—say in the form of his assurance that he didn't touch a drop—then she should change her belief.

[18] Could it be that we are supposed to understand Schroeder's resolution of the problem ("the moral wrongness of beliefs will *guarantee* an epistemic fault" (Schroder 2018: 117)) as running in the opposite direction, so that if we can't find that someone has committed an epistemic wrong, then we also cannot say that they have committed a moral wrong? This will not help either, as we shall see in chapter 10.

[19] One might object that adopting the language of rights is misguided here: aren't there, for instance, intangibles such as *respect*, which might be crucial to our social interactions but which nonetheless fall outside the remit of rights, strictly speaking? In response, I believe disrespect can cause real harm: lack of respect can undermine my public standing and my sense of self. In cases where that harm is unwarranted, it may amount to a wrong. (Note, for instance, Rawls's inclusion (1971, 1982) of "the social basis of self-respect" as one of the primary goods to which the theory of distributive justice should apply). As such, I have a legitimate and reasonable interest in others' showing me a basic sense of respect. (Though, presumably, not all cases of

amounts to a wrong only if one has a right to be protected against (or not be subjected to) such harm.[20] While there is no problem understanding how beliefs (and other doxastic states) can figure in the causal chain that precipitates harm, I don't think we can make good philosophical sense of the idea that one might have a perfectly general right against other persons that they believe (or not believe) certain things about one, just as such.

Remember that according to Basu and Schroeder, the wrong in doxastic wronging would be a wrong in virtue of what is believed, not in virtue of what happens upstream (i.e., in epistemic processing) or downstream (i.e., in action) from the belief. Accordingly, if doxastic morality were correct, it fundamentally shouldn't matter to the "aptness" of our reactive attitudes— blame, resentment, etc.—what the other's epistemic situation is. But clearly it does matter. Consider again the modified Mark-and-Maria case, where Mark has (perhaps inadvertently) put Maria in a position where virtually *all* of her evidence supports the hypothesis that he has been drinking. Maria's evidence, correctly processed, provides strong support for the problematic hypothesis, and thereby rationally requires Maria to believe it, even given moral encroachment. In consideration of Maria's evidential situation, Mark should recognize that he has no right to be resentful against Maria. Instead, he should take the opportunity to provide her with further evidence: "Hey, I know how this must look, but honestly . . . " Now, if Maria doesn't update her belief in light of this new evidence, then we can discuss the possibility that she might be wronging Mark. But in this case, the wrong wouldn't lie in *what she believes*, but rather in *how she processes the evidence*.

disrespect are wrongful, even when they are harmful: even if we agreed that all persons were owed, by default, a certain minimum of respect, one could clearly forfeit this right, for instance by one's own obnoxious and disrespectful behavior.)

[20] Here, I take my cues from Feinberg (1984, 1988). There are several reasons why not all harms are wrongs (cf. Feinberg 1984: 35): for one, I may simply have forfeited my right to be protected against such harm by my previous actions; or we may find ourselves in situations where not everyone's reasonable interests can be jointly satisfied, as in familiar moral dilemmas: we have two people in need of an antidote, but only one vial. But while we're on the topic, we can certainly wonder whether the converse also holds: do all wrongs involve harm? I believe that, on a suitably wide-ranging conception of harm (cf. footnote 2 above), this is a good working hypothesis. It is true that there are some puzzles involving putative cases of "harmless wronging" such as desecration of the dead or botched criminal attempts. I don't think there's any need to seek final resolution of these puzzles here: suffice it to note that it is extremely doubtful that defenders of doxastic morality would want to adopt this as their paradigm; instead, what is morally wrong about racist beliefs and other forms of prejudice is precisely the harm they stand to visit on their targets (on a suitably broad conception of "harm" as discussed above).

A closer analysis of another of the standard cases in the literature bears this out. As we saw in chapter 8, Gendler initially presented the dilemma that concerns us in terms of an anecdote about John Hope Franklin, the prominent African-American historian, who is mistaken for a staff member by another patron at an upscale D.C. social club. As Gendler points out (2011: 35*ff*), while this is no doubt a significant social gaffe, it is harder to say how the person who presents Franklin with her coat check has gone epistemically wrong in forming the belief that Franklin is (probably) a member of the waitstaff. After all, Franklin is the first African-American member of the social club while virtually all of its waitstaff is African-American. According to Gendler, then, the belief is (at least potentially) epistemically justified in virtue of being a correct application of the relevant base rate information.

On Basu's adaptation of the example (Basu, 2019*b*), however, the belief would not be justified, precisely because of the moral harm that it stands to cause. To paraphrase Schroeder, the moral wrongness of the belief will "guarantee" that it is also epistemically faulty, even though it is supported by evidence which would suffice for justification in some other, morally less exacting context (e.g., a context in which race has played significantly less of a role in determining social and economic standing than it has in the United States).

To see why this conclusion cannot be sustained, we can once again consider the distinction between belief and acceptance. What should we say of the patron who, considering his base rate information, determines that this person is (probably)[21] a member of the wait staff, but then decides *not* to act on that belief until he has further evidence (say, evidence of seeing this person wait on another table) precisely because of the risk of moral harm involved? To my mind, that person has done everything right. That is, he has done everything right epistemically, in forming the belief that is warranted by his evidence. But he has also done everything right *morally*, in determining that, though well-evidenced, the belief was not sufficiently well-evidenced to act on given the moral stakes of the situation. If this analysis is correct, it shows that the moral error in the original example would not lie in the formation of the belief itself. Instead, it would lie in the executive decision—"acceptance"—that the belief is sufficiently well-evidenced to act on in context.

---

[21] Basu doesn't foreground the probabilistic character of the problematic belief. But to my mind, it must certainly be a relevant feature of it, insofar as it is grounded in base rate reasoning.

9.3 Harms, Wrongs, and the Epistemology of "Moral Stakes"

Finally, let us consider an objection which attaches to moral encroachment and doxastic morality alike. Both positions unfold as though there were no serious epistemic concerns arising with respect to the subjects' appreciation of what is "morally at stake" in a situation. In effect, both positions assume that we could hold fixed the subject's understanding of what is "morally at stake" while leaving open the question of whether she should adopt a particular belief, given these moral stakes. In many cases, however, moral and non-moral reasoning will be deeply *entangled*, in the sense that we cannot give content to a subject's moral assessment of the situation without assuming a fair bit about her other doxastic commitments. In such cases, we cannot expect the moral stakes to provide an independent rational check on our belief formation policies.

In an obvious way, for instance, non-moral evidence can bear on the question of who the moral stakeholders in a situation are, even if we could agree on the relevant moral principles. For instance, Jeremy Bentham (1789) famously argued that the moral status of non-human animals is determined not by the question "Can they reason? nor, Can they talk?," but rather, "Can they suffer?" Clearly, however, this moral principle fails on its own to settle the question of whether some particular species has the relevant capacity. Instead, this question can only be determined by non-moral evidence: does it, for instance, have a neural system that responds relevantly to pain? Apparently, our best current evidence from neuroscience fails to settle whether invertebrates qualify for moral concern on this principle.[22] And so, even if we could assume that Bentham's principle is correct, we still wouldn't know what are the moral stakes involved in our treatment of them.

The lesson of this simple illustration transposes readily to cases of discriminatory treatment caused by prejudiced belief. Consider a case where, although one may be in an epistemic position to acknowledge that some person is *harmed* by one's forming a certain belief—in the minimal sense of suffering a setback to their legitimate interests—one may not be in an epistemic position to acknowledge that the person is thereby suffering an *unwarranted harm*, i.e., the kind of harm that constitutes a wrong. Let's say

[22] Cf. Crook et al. 2013.

someone charged with a hiring decision believes (falsely, but with epistemic justification) that Candidate A, being a woman, is less suitable for a certain position than Candidate B, a male. Now, the person doing the hiring is of course in a position to acknowledge that Candidate A will suffer a setback to her legitimate interests in being bypassed—it's not like she is formally unqualified and has no business applying for the position in the first place. But at the same time, he may not be in an epistemic position to acknowledge that this harm would constitute a wrong. So far as the headhunter is concerned, her right is simply that of being judged on her comparative qualifications, and to his mind, that is precisely what he has done. Essentially, if the headhunter falsely—but justifiably—believes that she is less qualified simply in virtue of being a woman, then his understanding of what is "morally at stake in the situation" will likewise be warped, but again, presumably with epistemic justification. Differently put, given his epistemic situation, we cannot rationally require him to have the right moral beliefs. And without those beliefs, it is hard to see how moral considerations—as *we* see them—could rationally encroach on *his* epistemic processing.

9.4 Summary

In this chapter, I have critically reviewed two recent attempts to develop the idea that there might be significant moral constraints on what we should believe. Neither of these will help fully resolve the issues that arise in the wake of the epistemology of prejudice. Moral encroachment has much to be said in its favor. But its conclusions are best understood as applying not to the question of what we should believe per se, but rather to the question of how well-supported a belief must be in context in order for us to act on it. And even as restricted in this way, moral encroachment cannot handle all cases of prejudiced belief: in some cases, the evidence will be sufficiently strong that it would meet the threshold for justification even taking the moral stakes into account. By contrast, doxastic morality fails to make good on the idea that beliefs can constitute wrongs in their own right. If we give up on that notion, the position is essentially indistinguishable from moral encroachment and subject to the same objections.

Finally, I have argued that both moral encroachment and doxastic morality turn on a problematic idealization, namely that there are no relevant epistemological problems bearing on one's (rational) assessment of the "moral stakes" in context. Rational agents cannot always be in an epistemic position to settle what the moral stakes of a situation are while leaving open the question of what they should believe, more broadly, on the basis of their evidence. Therefore, morality cannot always provide an independent constraint on our epistemic reasoning. This entanglement of moral and non-moral epistemology will form an important backdrop to the argument in the next chapter.

10

A Better Approach

Moral Responsibility despite Epistemic Blamelessness

In our previous chapter, we considered the possibility of countering Gendler's dilemma by developing the idea that moral norms could place serious constraints on epistemic processing. We concluded that neither of the proposals on offer are cut out for resolving the problems emerging from the epistemology of prejudice. In this chapter, we will begin by considering the possibility that the interplay between morality and epistemology may in fact run in the opposite direction. According to this view, ascriptions of moral responsibility depend on ascriptions of epistemic responsibility (but not the other way around): we can hold someone to moral account for the harmful consequences of their actions only if we can hold them epistemically responsible for knowing that their actions risked imposing wrongful harms in the first place (cf. Smith 1983; Rosen 2003, 2004; Zimmerman 2008; Sher 2009; Peels 2016). (Note, right away, how such a view seems to resonate nicely with the point made in section 9.3 about the entanglement of moral and non-moral reasoning.)

Now, if we were to accept this proposal at face value, it would appear to have potentially very dramatic consequences for our ability to address the social costs of prejudiced belief in moral terms. Since the overall contention of this book is that prejudiced people may in fact perfectly well be epistemically justified in their beliefs, it would now seem that we would also be barred from holding them morally accountable for the harms that their beliefs nonetheless cause.

However, the situation is nowhere near as bleak as it may seem. In particular, it is important to distinguish conditions that trigger *moral blame* from conditions that trigger a broader concept of *moral responsibility*, including a moral duty to offer apology, compensation, or in other ways to reverse the harm that one's actions have caused. As I will argue, moral responsibility in this sense can attach even to epistemically blameless agents. This distinction can provide a new, and in important ways a better, platform

on which to vindicate the moral and legal standing of those who are
victimized by prejudice.

10.1 From Moral Encroachment on Epistemology to Epistemic Encroachment on Morality

Consider, for a moment, a somewhat larger picture. Why are we concerned
with prejudice in the first place? Not simply, I gather, because we are deeply
concerned with people's epistemic virtue. Rather, we are particularly concerned with prejudice because of the personal, social, and political costs
associated with it. Prejudiced beliefs can cause us to bully, exploit, or
discriminate against specific people simply in virtue of their group membership. (Or it can cause us to turn a blind eye when others are engaging in
these behaviors, to much the same effect.) These consequences constitute
what I call "unwarranted harms."[1] Such harms violate the moral rights (and
in many jurisdictions, though sadly not in all, also the legal rights) of the
people who are targeted by the prejudice. In light of such harm, it is natural
that we move beyond considering prejudice simply from the point of view of
epistemology to also considering it in terms of moral responsibility.

But notice that in our regular discourse of moral evaluation, it typically
makes a significant difference whether a wrongful action was perpetrated
with knowledge or in ignorance. In brief, an action perpetrated in ignorance
may well incur a full or partial moral *excuse*, i.e., an exemption from moral
accountability. Notably though, it's not *simply* a matter of ignorance versus
knowledge, since we will also want to ask whether the agent *should* have
known (or could reasonably be expected to know, etc.) that his action was
harmful.[2] That is, we *do* differentiate between those who perpetrated an
action in ignorance and those who acted in full knowledge. But we also make
a further differentiation between those who should have known, even if they
didn't, that their actions were harmful, and those whose failure to know did
not involve any violation of epistemic norms. This is the distinction between

---

[1] "Unwarranted," to contrast with various kinds of possibly warranted harm, such as the
harm dispensed in legitimate self-defense, or in issuing fines or criminal sentences to white-
collar criminals.

[2] Consider how the law amends its notion of *mens rea* to also include recklessness and
criminal negligence, standards for which are generally determined with reference to a hypothetical "reasonable person." For more general considerations regarding "should have known,"
see Clarke 2014, Goldberg 2017.

culpable and blameless ignorance. In the latter case, but not in the former, the agent's bid for a moral excuse is significantly curtailed.[3]

Delineating, in general terms, the finer contours of what agents can be "reasonably expected to know" is not a topic for this book.[4] Instead, we will focus on the consequences of finding that someone's ignorance is non-culpable. In particular, in cases such as I have described, where a prejudiced belief is fully justified by any relevant epistemic norm, we seem to have an excellent candidate for a form of blameless ignorance. What should we think about the fact that such cases can nonetheless cause significant unwarranted harm?

10.1.1 The Excusing Power of Blameless Ignorance

Consider Gideon Rosen's example of the "Ancient Slaveowner." As Rosen observes, chattel slavery was essentially taken for granted in the biblical period. "No one denied that it was bad to be a slave, just as it is bad to be sick or deformed. The evidence suggests, however, that until quite late in antiquity it never occurred to anyone to object to slavery on grounds of moral or religious principle" (Rosen 2003: 64). Now consider the situation of a Hittite lord who "buys and sells human beings, forces labour without compensation, and separates families to suit his purposes" (Rosen 2003: 64). Without a doubt, his actions are morally wrong. But at the same time, it seems that the Hittite lord also *believes* that his actions are morally right. What should we think about his moral responsibility for the harms that his actions cause?

According to Rosen, the question of whether the Hittite lord is morally responsible for the harms that his actions have caused pivots on the question of whether he is epistemically responsible for knowing that slavery is morally wrong. To *us*, of course, it will seem *obvious* that slavery is morally wrong. But in his social context, it was apparently not obvious. Lots of otherwise sensible people failed to light upon that moral truth. Moreover, the moral permissibility of slavery is clearly presupposed in the major institutions governing his society. And in general, argues Rosen, one is not

---

[3] For a classic discussion, see Aquinas *ST* I-II, Q. 76.

[4] In fact, it pretty much follows from my account that there really couldn't be a perfectly general answer to the question of what people can be expected to know. Any plausible answer to such questions must be highly responsive to specific features of the subject's context.

the framework of social life.[5] One is obligated to reflect in "hard cases, in response to serious criticism, in response to known diversity of opinion and in response to perceived tension in one's moral view. But when what one takes to be a transparently correct moral verdict meets with no such friction, one is neither negligent nor reckless in failing to subject that verdict to special scrutiny" (Rosen 2003: 65).

The Hittite lord is certainly ignorant of the fact that slavery is morally wrong. But is he culpable for his ignorance? Rosen cites the following general principle: "X is culpable for failing to know that P only if his ignorance is the upshot of some prior culpable act or omission" (Rosen 2004: 301).[6] And Rosen believes we have been given enough detail on the case to see that he isn't culpable for failing to know that slavery is wrong. It's not that he *couldn't* have known that slavery is wrong. It is rather that we would be holding him to unreasonably high standards if we were to *demand* that he should know it.

Obviously, there is room for disagreement about this particular case. But surely, we can find *some* case in which a person is epistemically blameless in holding morally false beliefs. Our question, then, is what, if anything, finding that the person is epistemically blameless should tell us about his moral responsibility for the harms that his actions may nonetheless cause.

According to Rosen, the transition from questions of epistemic responsibility to questions of moral responsibility is governed by the following principle: "When X does A from blameless ignorance, then X is blameless for doing A, *provided the act would have been blameless if things had been*

---

[5] For the record, I think this principle is stronger than it needs to be, and potentially even false on its face. (Cf. Moody-Adams (1994) on "affected ignorance.") The point is rather that given the exogenous limitations on his epistemic context, there is no guarantee that even scrupulous reflection would eventuate in the desired conclusion.

[6] For the sake of completeness, we might also want to know what would happen if it was determined that the agent *is* culpable for his ignorance. In an earlier, pathbreaking paper, Holly Smith (Smith 1983) has argued that in cases of culpable ignorance, we should be open to the possibility that the agent's responsibilities extend no farther than to his ignorance itself, i.e., to his failure to inform himself as he should. (Smith calls this the "benighting act.") The fact that he goes on to cause harm to others subsequently (the "unwitting act," in Smith's terms) does not add to his moral responsibilities. This conclusion is supported in part by considerations of moral luck: whether the agent will or will not find himself in a situation where he acts in a harmful way is essentially a matter of moral luck. And moral luck should play no role in apportioning moral blame. So, in essence, we can acknowledge that there is a *moral duty* (not just an epistemic duty) to stay informed (and more generally, to adopt epistemically circumspect belief-forming policies), insofar as by being misinformed, we run a *risk* of causing unwarranted harm to others. What is in question now is whether, given that we have run afoul of the moral duty to stay informed, we are adding a second moral breach when the circumstances of action do in fact transpire.

for doing A, *provided the act would have been blameless if things had been as the agent blamelessly took them to be*" (Rosen 2003: 63n4). The Hittite lord is epistemically blameless for believing that slavery is morally permissible. If slavery were in fact morally permissible, then his actions of buying and selling slaves, etc., would be morally blameless. And so, the Hittite lord's ignorance of the moral facts apparently shields him from moral accountability.

The assumption underlying this conclusion is that it would be unreasonable to blame someone for doing the sorts of things that they blamelessly take themselves to be morally entitled to do. Say someone forms a belief that a certain kind of act is morally appropriate, even though in fact it is not. Our first question now is, is he epistemically culpable for forming the false belief that it is appropriate? If he is not, then he is also not morally responsible for performing the act in question. Otherwise we would morally require people to act contrary to their best judgment about what is morally required of them. Once we have conceded that they are entitled to these judgments, it would be quite unreasonable of us to blame them for acting in accordance.[7]

In slogan form, Rosen's view entails that "when a person acts from ignorance, he is culpable for his action only if he is culpable for the ignorance from which he acts" (2003: 61). Given the highly revisionist consequences of this position, it is perhaps surprising to discover that it is by no means an idiosyncratic view in the contemporary philosophical landscape: in fact, there appears to be an emerging consensus that one's moral responsibility is significantly (perhaps entirely) modulated by what one could reasonably be held to account for knowing.[8] Thus, for instance, Michael Zimmerman (1997: 423) holds that "one is culpable for behaving ignorantly only if one is culpable for being ignorant." In a similar vein, George Sher (2009: 19) writes: "when someone acts wrongly or foolishly, the question on which his responsibility depends is not whether he *is* aware that his act is wrong or foolish, but rather whether he *should* be (or, alternatively, whether a reasonable person in his position *would* be)." But finally, consider also Miranda Fricker, who figures prominently in other chapters of this book: "The question whether someone is morally blameworthy for an act or omission crucially depends on the epistemic question of whether there was

---

[7] Accordingly, Rosen ultimately proposes (2004) that it is only the "clear-eyed akratic"—i.e., the person who acts wrongly, knowing full well that his action is wrong—who can be held to the full measure of moral responsibility.

[8] Though see, e.g., Guerrero 2007, Fitzpatrick 2008, Harman 2011, and Mason 2015 for critical responses.

non-culpable ignorance in play" (Fricker 2016: 35). In all these cases, then, it would seem that we can hold someone morally accountable for the harmful consequences of their actions only if we can hold them epistemically accountable for knowing that their actions risked imposing wrongful harms in the first place.[9] This suggests a very different, virtually diametrically opposed picture of the relation between epistemic and moral normativity than we considered in chapter 9: in effect, we seem to have gone from *moral encroachment on epistemology* to something like *epistemic encroachment on morality*.

10.2 Epistemic and Moral Wrongdoing

Despite its apparently unsettling consequences, there does seem to be something highly intuitive about the view that one cannot be held morally responsible for things that one is in no position to know about. In particular, the examples that drive us toward this conclusion also provide further illustration of the idea that we explored in section 9.3, concerning the entanglement of moral and non-moral reasoning. Quite simply, we cannot generally assume that cognitive agents' best assessment of what is "morally at stake" in some situation is fully independent of what they can presume to know about the situation more broadly, given the evidence at their disposal.

One reason to be concerned about this conclusion, however, is that it apparently leaves us with nothing more to say about the situation of people who suffer harm by epistemically justified prejudice. In particular, if the prejudiced believers "have not done anything wrong," then apparently the people who are targeted by their prejudiced beliefs can't even claim to have been *wronged*. And if they haven't been wronged, then there is no compelling cause to redress their situation.

Fortunately, this is precisely what doesn't follow. The prejudiced believers may have done nothing wrong, *epistemically* speaking. But they may nonetheless have done something wrong in the sense of having violated others' moral rights, e.g., the right to be protected against discrimination. What determines whether some conduct is wrong in this sense is not whether the

[9] What primarily sets Rosen's view apart is the range of cases to which he believes this conclusion applies (e.g., the Ancient Slaveowner). But in terms of the conditional question—what should we think about moral responsibility in cases where *do* find that someone blamelessly (though falsely) believes he is in the right?—the underlying view is widely accepted.

agent was in an epistemic position to know that it was wrong, but rather that the victim has an objective right to be protected against such conduct.

This might seem puzzling, however. For how do we square this claim about a morally consequential objective right to be protected against certain kinds of harm with the idea of an epistemic constraint on moral responsibility? To move ahead here, we must begin by recognizing that moral responsibility is a multi-dimensional concept. In particular, we must distinguish the question of when moral blame is appropriate from the question of when agents can be held morally liable for the consequences of their actions. It may well be that conditions for moral blame depend on the agent's epistemic situation.[10] But the question of whether someone has been wronged by my action, and whether I can accordingly be held to account for the resulting harm, does not.[11] As I will argue, this distinction can provide an important, and in many ways better, platform on which to vindicate the moral and legal standing of victims of prejudice.

10.3 Dimensions of Moral Responsibility: Blame and Rectification

How should we conceptualize the idea of (epistemically) blameless wrong-doing, to which a substantial sense of moral responsibility might nonetheless apply? The overwhelming tendency in the literature is to focus on the dimension of moral responsibility that gives rise to various reactive attitudes, such as blame or resentment.[12] I am not going to argue that such reactive attitudes do not have important cognitive and social roles to play. What I will argue is that considerations of moral blame (etc.) in no way *exhaust* our concept of moral responsibility. In particular, we would do well to distinguish the question of when moral *blame* is appropriate from the question of when agents can be held morally *liable* for the consequences of their actions.[13] In what follows, I will argue that these dimensions can be

---

[10] Why should we even be willing to withhold moral blame in these cases? I will return to this question below.

[11] See, for instance, Quong (2015: 249) for a recent argument along these lines.

[12] For a classic statement, see Strawson 1962.

[13] Some contributors to the literature are, of course, fully clear on this distinction (e.g., Rosen 2003: 68n7). Nonetheless, they have strikingly little to say about the moral grounds and consequences of this second form of responsibility. In particular, there is very little discussion of the victim side of this equation: that people may have a moral right to be protected—perhaps even a right to protect themselves—against harmful actions, even when those actions are

disentangled, and—for the purposes of moving ahead on our present problem—should be disentangled. Assume, then, that conditions for moral blame depend on the agent's epistemic situation. Even so, the question of whether someone has been wronged as a result of my action, and whether I can accordingly be held morally liable for the resulting harm, does not depend on my epistemic situation. Significantly, this liability may include a duty to offer compensation, restitution, or in some other way to reverse the harm.

This distinction should not be confused with a distinction between "attributability" and "answerability" as contrasting perspectives on moral responsibility (cf. Watson 1996, Fischer and Tognazzini 2011). This terminology is used in a myriad different ways in the literature. Perhaps the best match for our purposes can be found in the work of Robin Zheng (2016, 2018), who proposes that actions are "attributable" to an agent only if they prescind from value judgments that in some relevant sense reflect that agent's moral personality. The point is then that one can be "answerable"—liable—even for consequences of one's actions that don't meet this attributability condition. Now, in an obvious sense, my account emphasizes the importance of liability to our moral affairs; moreover, I agree that it is vital to recognize that liability does not presuppose moral blame.[14] But I find no use for the contrasting idea of attributability here: I am happy to allow that the foreseeable consequences of epistemically justified prejudiced beliefs would be perfectly attributable to me—indeed, I have a hard time seeing why they would *not* be. But since epistemically justified prejudiced beliefs would be prime candidates for instances of non-culpable ignorance, I also think it is reasonable to withhold blame in these cases. This is in marked difference from philosophers who hold that attributability and moral blame go hand in hand (cf. Zheng 2018: 873).[15]

For a less theoretically burdened deployment of the distinction I have in mind, consider the distinction between "blame-responsibility" and "task-responsibility" developed in the literature on collective moral

committed in blameless ignorance. (For instance, Mason 2019 seems to hold that liability (in the absence of blame) can only be apportioned on consequentialist grounds, and therefore holds limited philosophical interest. By contrast, I hold that adopting the victim's perspective suggests a strong rights-based motivation for pursuing liability as a relevant dimension of moral responsibility, even in cases of blameless ignorance.)

[14] In this sense, my view differs (as does Zheng's) from that of Fischer and Tognazzini 2011. I'm not sure, however, whether the difference is substantive or merely terminological.

[15] Thanks to Evan Tiffany for discussion.

responsibility.[16] Blame-responsibility, as the name suggests, is the sort of responsibility that blemishes one's moral character. The crucial point in this literature is that one may still hold a form of moral responsibility—task-responsibility—even though one is not blameworthy in this sense. This distinction is essential to explaining why, for instance, even minor shareholders can be liable for damages caused by corporate actions. It may well be that only the executive officers bear moral blame for the actions. But even shareholders who had no say in framing the policy and who may not even have been in a position to know about it can still be held liable for the damages. It is not just legally well established, but also entirely morally appropriate, to empower people who have, say, been evacuated from their homes following a gas farm explosion, to extract compensation from blameless shareholders in the company that owns the farm. If people have a right to demand such compensation, it follows that this right cannot be contingent on finding that the shareholders were after all culpable for the act.[17] In effect,

[16] The terminology is due to Goodin 1995. I am following the account given in Stilz 2011. Even though I refer to the collective responsibility literature here, it is important to note that it is perfectly consistent with what I say that task-responsibility be understood in large part as a form of liability that attaches to individuals. Similarly, this notion of task-responsibility should not be confused with other notions from the collective-responsibility literature, such as Iris Marion Young's concept of "political responsibility" (cf. Young 2003, 2006). To be sure, like task-responsibility, political responsibility is detached from reactive attitudes such as blame or punishment. But the similarities end there. For one, political responsibility distributes much more widely than the responsibility that I am talking about: Young speaks of political responsibility as emerging from social connectivity alone, regardless of one's own actions within the social network. Relatedly, her account proclaims to be entirely forward-looking, rather than backward-looking: political responsibility is an irreducibly collective responsibility to effect positive change in the reigning conditions. Accordingly, your (individual) degree of responsibility is measured in terms of your power to contribute to such change. One upshot of this way of thinking is that, as Young herself notes, those who are systematically disadvantaged under these conditions can be said to bear a degree of responsibility for addressing their own plight. Just to be clear, I think Young's concept of political responsibility is an important addendum to our understanding of collective responsibility. But it's not what I have in mind here: rather, I have in mind a form of responsibility which, like more traditional notions of responsibility, attaches to specific persons (or institutions) precisely in light of what they have done (or failed to do). In that sense, it is individualist and backward-looking, even though it is (also) detached from considerations of blame and punishment.

[17] It is tempting to think that the explanatory burden here is assumed by a different moral principle, according to which minor shareholders are liable simply because they have unjustly benefitted from the commission of an injustice. While this may certainly be a collateral consideration in many cases, it need not apply in all cases. For instance, the injustice might well have occurred in the context of a larger scheme of action which has brought the company to the brink of bankruptcy, and from which shareholders accordingly stand to lose a lot of their investment. Even so, they might be held liable for the damages caused.

this amounts to an "evidence-relative standard" for blame-responsibility combined with a "fact-relative standard" for task-responsibility.[18]

10.3.1 Responsibility without *Mens Rea*: Lessons from Tort Law

This point calls to mind the diverging conceptions of responsibility expressed in criminal law and in tort law. Roughly speaking, criminal law is centered on the wrongdoer, and is structured around the ascription of *mens rea*—a guilty mind. This legal notion provides a clear analogy to the philosophical claim that moral culpability is conditioned on epistemic culpability. By contrast, tort law is centered on the rights of the victim, and stipulates that people may be held responsible for harms they have caused regardless of their epistemic situation.

As an illustration, we can look at how criminal law typically approaches harms imposed in self-defense.[19] Say one initiates defensive action against a person one believes to pose a serious and immediate threat to oneself: that action, or specifically, the harm that flows from that action, is paradigmatically justified only if the person is *in fact* posing such a threat. This raises the question of what happens if one has misjudged the situation, and the person was not, in fact, posing such a threat. In that case, one's self-defensive action might still be *excused*, but only if one's assessment of the threat was justified in light of the available evidence. The prevailing standard for invoking an excuse under criminal law, then, is to concede that one was wrong, but to maintain that one was nonetheless epistemically justified in believing one was in the right.[20]

But there is more to be said. For while one's ability to invoke an excuse may exempt one from *criminal prosecution*, it doesn't thereby exempt one from *all* kinds of legal liability. To the contrary, tort law stipulates that one may still be liable for compensating for the harms that one's actions

---

[18] While this terminology is well-established, my own understanding of it is highly indebted to Bolinger (MS).

[19] Cf. the Model Penal Code, 3.04, 3.09.

[20] Some of the relevant legal literature (e.g., Greenawalt 1984, 1986; Gardner 2007) is somewhat hampered by the hope of finding a unifying characteristic to distinguish a very broad range of excusing conditions—including intoxication and incapacitation—from the legal category of justification. By contrast, my discussion here is more narrowly focused on a particular kind of excuse, namely that which proceeds from a claim about blameless belief.

have caused.[21] These diverging notions of the grounds for liability testify to importantly diverging conceptions of responsibility for harm. Unlike criminal law, tort law fully permits that a liable party could be acting reasonably in light of the evidence available to him. These are, nonetheless, complementary rather than competing notions of responsibility. In brief, whereas criminal law is a tool for rebuking wrongdoers, tort law is a tool for vindicating the rights of victims. As one scholar has recently put it: "tort law identifies *relational, injurious* wrongs, and enables victims of such wrongs to demand responsive conduct from those who have injured them" (Goldberg 2015: 470). Accordingly, tort law is "in the business of empowering those who are wronged [...] rather than punishing those who commit crimes" (Goldberg 2015: 503).

That is to say, those who are harmed by our actions have a rightful claim, say, to equal consideration, which, when it is systematically undermined by prejudice, can amount to a claim of justice. In such a case, we owe it to the victim to reverse the harm or compensate for it in other ways. Alleging that one was epistemically blameless, or even justified, in holding one's beliefs in no way undermines this dimension of responsibility, even if it does plausibly exempt one from moral blame.[22]

10.4 Non-Culpable Wrongs?

This argument pivots on a distinctive notion of non-culpable wrongs. Some philosophers appear to find such a notion puzzling. By contrast, I think it is key to seeing our way to a viable platform for vindicating the rights of

---

[21] Cf. Botterell (2009: 176); Goudkamp (2013: 82–3). See also Goldberg 2015 for a broader overview of the status of excuses in tort law.

[22] For guidance in these matters, consider Justice O'Connor's dissenting opinion in *Nguyen v. INS*. Facing a complaint that an INS decision was discriminatory because it drew on an impermissible stereotype, the US Supreme Court ruled that because the alleged stereotype was based on a factual generalization, the Plaintiff could have no grounds for a claim of unlawful discrimination. In her dissent, O'Connor writes: "The majority articulates a misshapen notion of 'stereotype' and its significance in our equal protection jurisprudence. The majority asserts that a 'stereotype' is defined as a 'frame of mind resulting from irrational or uncritical analysis.' This Court has long recognized, however, that an impermissible stereotype may enjoy empirical support and thus be in a sense 'rational.' " In other words, the question of whether a stereotype is grounded in fact or otherwise rationally held does nothing to settle the question of whether someone who is judged in accordance with the stereotype has suffered discrimination, and therefore has grounds for seeking redress or compensation. (I owe this case to Erin Beeghly. See Beeghly forthcoming for fuller analysis.)

victims of prejudice and for considering prejudice as a problem that might warrant political intervention.

Recall that our question concerns the allocation of moral responsibility for harms suffered through prejudiced belief in cases where people are epistemically justified in holding those beliefs. As we have seen, not all harms are wrongs. But some philosophers claim that no harm can amount to a wrong unless it prescinds from a specifiable epistemic wrong. Miranda Fricker, as we have seen, takes epistemic culpability to be "prior to" moral culpability in the sense that "the question whether someone is morally blameworthy for an act or omission crucially depends on the epistemic question of whether there was non-culpable ignorance in play" (Fricker 2016: 35). But if we read this claim in light of commitments she explicitly takes on in her previous work, we would seem to be heading toward a rather more radical conclusion, according to which epistemic culpability determines not just whether someone is morally blameworthy for causing harm, but also whether the harm in question could even amount to a *wrong* in the first place.

Consider the following:

> A hearer may simply have a false belief about the speaker's level of expertise and/or motives, so that she gives him less credibility than she might otherwise have done. So long as her false belief is itself ethically and epistemically non-culpable (it does not, for example, result from an immoral hatefulness or from epistemic carelessness), there will be nothing culpable in her misjudgement of his credibility. It is simply an unlucky epistemic mistake of one or another familiar kind.   (Fricker 2007: 22)

About these cases, Fricker writes: "an ethically non-culpable mistake cannot undermine or otherwise wrong the speaker. It seems that the ethical poison of testimonial injustice must derive from some ethical poison in the judgement of the hearer" (2007: 22). She confirms this verdict later in the book, apropos a discussion of a person whose pathological shyness leads her interlocutors to interpret her as being shifty or insincere. This person may be significantly disadvantaged as a result, without her thereby having been wronged or suffered an injustice. Fricker writes:

> I am inclined, ultimately, to say that we should not consider this case to be an instance of testimonial injustice. For if the shy person is deemed to have

been wronged, it begins to seem that epistemically wronging someone through no fault of one's own is rather too easy to do. (Fricker 2007: 42)

The shy person is certainly disadvantaged, and in this sense harmed. But as Fricker argues in a later discussion (2007: 151), for something to constitute an injustice, it must not just be harmful but also wrongful. And the wrong in question must trace back to epistemic culpability on the part of the individual.

What should we make of this? There is no need here to dispute Fricker's verdicts on these particular cases. Instead, the point of concern is the implied generalization that accompanies these verdicts, namely that one cannot be wronged by epistemically innocent errors.

Presumably, Fricker holds this view precisely because she is overwhelmingly confident that prejudiced beliefs are, simply in virtue of being prejudiced, matters of individual epistemic culpability in the relevant sense, which therefore serve to trigger the conditions of wronging and thereby of moral blame. Obviously, it is the central claim of this book that this view cannot be supported.[23]

To claim that one has been wronged, and not merely harmed, say, by the discriminatory treatment of others is to claim that one has a right not to be treated in this way, and that justice requires that this wrong be reversed. This question matters deeply when we lift our gaze from person-to-person encounters and start thinking about the problem of prejudice as a more encompassing socio-political problem. After all, prejudiced beliefs are rarely the idiosyncratic contrivances of individual minds. Rather, they tend to be held by large groups of people, and to be reinforced through formal or informal social networks. By contrast, epistemic culpability is very much an individualist notion (as Fricker seems to confirm when she writes "Prejudices are judgements ... which display some (typically, epistemically

---

[23] In passing, we may ask why Fricker could not avoid this problem by simply insisting on her right to define prejudice so that it involves epistemic culpability. "Epistemically justified prejudice" would then simply constitute an oxymoron of sorts, perhaps better expressed as "false (but epistemically justified) negative stereotypes." The quick line of response to this strategy would be to point out that the problem of accounting for the harms caused by false, negatively charged social stereotypes (whatever their epistemic standing) doesn't simply go away by defining our terminology this way or that. Fricker's insistence that unless these stereotypes can be traced back to epistemic culpability, then the harm doesn't arise to the level of injustice, prevents us from forming good strategies for dealing with this problem. Quite simply: by defining prejudice in terms of the normative standing of the epistemic processes that give rise to it, we may end up having nothing to say about a large class of deeply problematic cases.

culpable) resistance to counter-evidence owing to some affective investment *on the part of the subject*" (Fricker 2007: 35, my emphasis).)[24]

Let's say we stuck with the assumption which connects culpability and wrongdoing, maybe in the following form: whenever there is widespread prejudice in an epistemic community, there must minimally be *some* epistemic agent who is culpable for it.[25] While I very much doubt this, we can grant the assumption for the sake of argument. When we look at the way that a particular belief is held by different members of a group, we may well find that only a subset of them are actually epistemically blameworthy for it. In that case, we would have to make crucial differentiations, holding that the targets of the prejudiced beliefs are wronged only by a subset of the holders of the belief, namely those that are epistemically blameworthy.

This is intractable and hard to form policies around insofar as the real harm of prejudice will often stem from aggregate effects (say, systematic exclusion from career opportunities), and cannot be traced directly to individual contributions. Moreover, it should be hard to swallow from the point of view of the victims, to whom it is scant comfort to learn that only some of the people who hold negative stereotypes against them are thereby epistemically irrational: the rest do so as a perfectly rational response to the regrettably biased socio-epistemic environment that they blamelessly happen to find themselves in. These reflections strongly suggest that any practical, action-oriented approach to remedying the impact of prejudice would do well to avoid adopting an account on which one has been wronged only if one can point to an epistemically culpable perpetrator.

Importantly, Fricker does seem sensitive to the moral considerations that animate this concern. For instance, she acknowledges (Fricker 2016) that it may be appropriate to expect people to feel a certain kind of *regret* even for the harms that they have blamelessly caused.[26] Let us grant, for the sake of

---

[24] Cf. Anderson 2012. Again, though, while it may seem tempting to level up and seek to address these issues in terms of some form of "shared" or "collective" epistemic responsibility, it is not clear that we stand to gain much by doing so. See section 7.4.1 for discussion.

[25] Fricker appears to suggest something along these lines in a more recent discussion where she now acknowledges that because many prejudiced beliefs will be supported by testimony from (presumptive) peers or authorities, particular subjects may be blameless, and indeed justified, in holding them (Fricker 2016: 40). In such cases, it might appear that we can still salvage a version of the thesis that links moral responsibility to epistemic culpability, by maintaining that the testimonial sources themselves would be epistemically culpable in holding the belief in question. But in light of the argument of this book, it is hard to see why this should be anything more than an article of faith.

[26] She is here inspired by Bernard Williams's notion of "agent-regret" (Williams 1993) which befalls, for instance, the lorry driver who blamelessly kills a child who runs into the road.

argument, the assumption that this state of regret tracks a genuine "owning" of moral responsibility.[27] Nonetheless, it doesn't tell the full story that needs to be told about harms arising from blameless prejudice. Fricker acknowledges, *en passant*, that the feeling of regret is also appropriately paired with a willingness to "make amends" and perhaps to offer compensation (Fricker 2016: 47–8). But this is, at best, an oddly indirect way of making the claim that really should be at stake, namely that victims of systematic prejudice have a *right* to demand such compensation. This is not a right that we can grant them unless we also grant that they have been made to suffer an objective wrong. And this is precisely what Fricker's position entails that we cannot do, except in cases where we are also able to identify agents culpable for wronging them. Rather than "agent-regret," then, what we need is a set of conceptual tools that takes seriously the notion of victims' rights in cases of harm arising from blameless ignorance. This is precisely what examples of task-responsibility and tort-law responsibility provide. By contrast, if these people haven't even been wronged, then questions of moral responsibility (in any form) will not even arise.

On my view, there is nothing mysterious about the notion of non-culpable wrongs. The question of whether some harm constitutes a wrong is just a question of what rights people have to be protected against such harms. It is a grave mistake to assume that our ability to identify some harm as a wrong depends on our ability to identify an epistemically blameworthy perpetrator. Your moral standing to protect your rights cannot, in general, depend on my epistemic situation. Given the highly non-ideal contexts in which most people are required to exercise their epistemic agency, there is just no reason to expect such close tracking between individual epistemic responsibility and the suffering of moral wrongs in the social realm.

This conclusion is also supported by reflection on preconditions for taking political action on prejudice. Suppose we are brought to recognize that a particular group is severely underrepresented in a certain vocation or field of study. We reasonably suspect that their qualifications are not given due recognition by the gatekeepers in the field in question, but we are unable to pinpoint particular agents at fault. Nonetheless, we fully expect that society at large, operating through its major social institutions, should take an interest in this matter. But why? If the harms they suffer do not amount to a wrong in the first place, it would remain unclear why society at large

---

[27] Though see Holly Smith (1983: 569–70) for an articulation of concerns about whether the notion of "agent-regret" really tracks moral reasons at all.

should be particularly concerned with mitigating those harms, for instance through the implementation of costly and controversial policy measures. While not uncontroversial, this point is well entrenched in liberal jurisprudence and political theory. The point proceeds from the recognition that such measures can in turn impose substantial burdens on blameless third parties. It then argues that the best, or only, way to justify such impositions is to maintain that the beneficiaries of the measures have certain rights that are currently under duress and that society's failure to protect these rights would constitute an injustice. These measures, then, are justified precisely as the best or only way to prevent or ameliorate the injustice in question. The reversal of the existing harm is a matter of vindicating justice, say in the form of fair opportunity, for systematically disadvantaged people: the justification for "deflecting" some of that harm onto other plausibly blameless subjects follows a familiar lesser-evil path. But without grounding in a claim about injustice, it is just not clear why these blameless third parties should be expected to accept the burden that is placed on them.[28]

10.5 Vindicating Victims' Rights

We have, then, converging conclusions from rather different lines of argument indicating that it is counterproductive to hold that the question of whether someone has been wronged (and not merely harmed) by another's prejudiced belief depends on whether the holder of the prejudice is epistemically culpable for it. The social and individual costs of prejudice are grave: seeking effective practical remedies, whether at the individual level or at the level of political action, requires us to adopt the language of right and wrong—justice and injustice—in addressing the matter long before we are in a position to consider the question of epistemic culpability.

We opened this chapter by considering the possibility that moral responsibility—at least in terms of the dimension connected with reactive attitudes such as blame or resentment—is significantly modulated by questions of epistemic responsibility. At the end of the day, is this a view we should take? It would take us too far afield to mount a full defense of this view here. Nonetheless, I will mention one respect in which it resonates with one of the book's underlying themes. Access to information is in many

---

[28] Debates in the 1970s concerning the justification of affirmative action, for instance, followed these tracks: see, e.g., Thomson 1973; Dworkin 1977a, 1977b.

respects a privilege. Conversely, being subjected to significant disinformation can constitute a form of victimization. As social epistemologists, we have come to reckon with the profoundly important role of socio-epistemic affordances in shaping one's overall intellectual character and outlook. Most of our beliefs are formed not in direct confrontation with a rich array of neutral evidence, but in response to what others believe, as filtered through educational institutions, peer networks, etc. In general, I think, we will want to make room for the idea that people who grow up in deeply prejudiced social settings, with severely limited rational access to contrary evidence, should in some relevant sense be counted as victims too. Holding these people to moral blame for the predictable consequences of their limited epistemic opportunities is to compound their plight.

But there is more to moral responsibility than this "agent-centered" dimension. And this further dimension of moral responsibility is not similarly constrained by the agent's epistemic situation. Tort law, as we have seen, offers a template for a "victim-centered" account of blameless wrongs. Some might worry that this kind of responsibility is not a genuine form of moral responsibility, precisely because it is so divorced from questions of moral blame.[29] I cannot see that much hangs on the question. The key, in my view, is to recognize that the ascription of such responsibility is crucial to the recognition of victims' rights: we cannot expect to move forward with public rectification unless we make the case that these people have been wronged, and will likely continue to be wronged for as long as the status quo persists. And that, surely, is a moral matter.

Is responsibility-without-blame a second-best option, a mere consolation prize? To the contrary, I believe that as we move toward victim-centered considerations, the responsibility-without-blame model can be seen as a potentially liberating and empowering idea. The responsibility-without-blame model makes clear that my standing to claim that I have been wronged is an objective matter. Accordingly, it should be no part of my evidential burden to demonstrate that you—my victimizer—were in a position to know better. But that is precisely what the opposite view would entail. Even less, I think, should a platform for remedial action burden victims of discrimination, tacitly or expressly, with having to make the case that their victimizers are bad people. This would be entailed by the view that one can be wronged by prejudice only in virtue of some "ethical poison in the judgement of" the prejudiced person, since "an ethically non-

---

[29] See, for instance, the discussion in Sher (2009: 12–16).

culpable mistake cannot undermine or otherwise wrong" anyone (Fricker 2007: 22). My approach thereby helps explain why commonly heard third-party interventions such as "I'm sure he didn't mean to do any harm" are entirely immaterial to the question of whether you have wronged me by your action, and whether you can be held morally responsible for reversing the damage. Quite simply, these are extraneous conceptual associations presenting further burdens and obstacles on which the bare claim of having been wronged should not depend.

10.6 Summary and Conclusion

In these final two chapters of the book, I have explicitly considered the moral consequences of the epistemology of prejudice. Most of the book's argument has proceeded on the assumption—culminating in the recognition of Gendler's dilemma in chapter 8—that assessments of epistemic normativity and assessments of moral normativity run on completely separate tracks. In chapter 9, I considered the possibility that this assumption might be false. In particular, I took up recent arguments to the effect that moral concerns can "encroach" on epistemic normativity in a way that could mitigate or perhaps even eliminate altogether the problems arising from Gendler's dilemma. Ultimately, however, I found that such arguments founder on the entanglement of moral and non-moral reasoning. Reflection on further examples in this chapter has led us to very nearly the opposite conclusion: in fact, it is epistemology that encroaches on morality, not the other way around.

The provisional upshot of this view is that we cannot be held to moral blame for wrongs that we are not in an epistemic position to identify as such. However, it is a mistake to think that the question of culpability has any bearing on the question of whether such harm would constitute a wrong in the first place. And precisely because they are wrongs, we are led to consider that even epistemically blameless agents can be saddled with responsibility for reversing or compensating for the harm. Though its philosophical significance is often overlooked, this idea of non-culpable wrongs, with distinctive concomitant responsibilities, is by no means new or ad hoc: it is quite familiar, for instance, from tort law. As I have argued, recognizing responsibilities arising from non-culpable wrongs is crucial to initiating political action on the consequences of prejudice, and also provides a less demanding platform on which victims of prejudice can seek to vindicate their rights.

References

Abramson, Kate. 2014. "Turning up the Lights on Gaslighting." *Philosophical Perspectives* 28(1): 1–30.

Alexander, Michelle. 2010. *The New Jim Crow: Mass Incarceration in the Age of Colorblindness*. New York, NY: The New Press.

Allport, Gordon. 1954. *The Nature of Prejudice*. 25th Anniversary edition. New York, NY: Basic Books, 1979.

Alston, William P. 1988. "The Deontological Conception of Epistemic Justification." Reprinted in *Epistemic Justification: Essays in the Theory of Knowledge*. Ithaca, NY: Cornell University Press.

American Law Institute, The. 1981. *The Model Penal Code*. Philadelphia, PA: The American Law Institute.

American Mathematical Society. 2020. "Letters to the Editor: Boycott Collaboration with Police." *Notices of the American Mathematical Society* 67(9): 1293.

Anderson, Elizabeth. 2000/2015. "Feminist Epistemology and Philosophy of Science." *Stanford Encyclopedia of Philosophy*. https://plato.stanford.edu/entries/feminism-epistemology/.

Anderson, Elizabeth. 2010. *The Imperative of Integration*. Princeton, NJ: Princeton University Press.

Anderson, Elizabeth. 2012. "Epistemic Justice as a Virtue of Social Institutions." *Social Epistemology* 26(2): 163–73.

Angwin, Julia, Jeff Larson, Surya Mattu, and Lauren Kirchner. 2016. "Machine Bias: Risk Assessments in Criminal Sentencing." *ProPublica* May 23, 2016. https://www.propublica.org/article/machine-bias-risk-assessments-in-criminal-sentencing.

Antony, Louise. 2016. "Bias: Friend or Foe? Reflections on Saulish Scepticism." In Michael Brownstein and Jennifer Saul, eds, *Implicit Bias and Philosophy*, Vol. 1. Oxford: Oxford University Press.

Appiah, Kwame Anthony. 1990. "Racisms." In David Goldberg, ed., *Anatomy of Racism*. Minneapolis, MN: University of Minnesota Press.

Aquinas, Thomas. *Summa Theologica*. Translation by the Fathers of the Dominican Province, in 3 volumes. New York, NY: Benziger Brothers, 1947.

Aristotle. *The History of Animals*. Translated by A.L. Peck. Cambridge, MA: Loeb Classical Library, 1965.

Arpaly, Nomy. 2003. *Unprincipled Virtue: An Inquiry into Moral Agency*. Oxford: Oxford University Press.

Ayres, Ian, and Joel Waldfogel. 1994. "A Market Test for Race Discrimination in Bail Setting." *Stanford Law Review* 46: 987–1047.

Ballantyne, Nathan. 2019. *Knowing our Limits*. Oxford: Oxford University Press.

Banaji, Mahzarin R. and Anthony G. Greenwald. 2013. *Blindspot: Hidden Biases of Good People*. New York, NY: Delacort Press.

Banks, R. Richard, Jennifer L. Eberhardt, and Lee Ross. 2006. "Discrimination and Implicit Bias in a Racially Unequal Society." *California Law Review* 94(4): 1169–90.

Barry-Jester, Anna Marie. 2016. "How MSG Got a Bad Rap: Flawed Science and Xenophobia." https://fivethirtyeight.com/features/how-msg-got-a-bad-rap-flawed-science-and-xenophobia/.

Barry-Jester, Anna Marie, Ben Casselman, and Dana Goldstein. 2015. "Should Prison Sentences Be Based on Crimes That Haven't Been Committed Yet?" https://fivethirtyeight.com/features/prison-reform-risk-assessment/.

Basu, Rima. 2019*a*. "What We Epistemically Owe to Each Other." *Philosophical Studies* 176(4): 915–31.

Basu, Rima. 2019*b*. "The Wrongs of Racist Beliefs." *Philosophical Studies* 176(9): 2497–515.

Basu, Rima and Mark Schroeder. 2019. "Doxastic Wronging." In Brian Kim and Matthew McGrath, eds, *Pragmatic Encroachment in Epistemology*. London: Routledge.

Battaly, Heather. 2018. "Can Close-Mindedness Be an Intellectual Virtue?" *Royal Institute of Philosophy Supplement* 84: 23–45.

BBC. 2009. "Saudis Open Hi-Tech Science Oasis." BBC September 23. http://news.bbc.co.uk/2/hi/middle_east/8270601.stm.

Beeghly, Erin. 2015. "What Is a Stereotype? What Is Stereotyping?" *Hypatia* 30(4): 675–91.

Beeghly, Erin. 2018. "Failing to Treat Persons as Individuals." *Ergo* 26(5): 687–711.

Beeghly, Erin. Forthcoming. "What's Wrong with Stereotypes? The Falsity Hypothesis." *Social Theory and Practice*.

Beeghly, Erin. *What's Wrong with Stereotyping?* MS. Book manuscript, under contract with Oxford University Press.

Beeghly, Erin, and Alex Madva, eds. 2020. *An Introduction to Implicit Bias: Knowledge, Justice, and the Social Mind*. New York, NY: Routledge.

Begby, Endre. 2013. "The Epistemology of Prejudice." *Thought* 2(2): 90–9.

Begby, Endre. 2017. "Perceptual Expansion under Cognitive Guidance: Lessons from Language Processing." *Mind & Language* 32(5): 564–78.

Begby, Endre. 2018*a*. "Straight Thinking in Warped Environments." *Analysis* 78(3): 489–500.

Begby, Endre. 2018*b*. "Doxastic Morality: A Moderately Skeptical Approach." *Philosophical Topics* 46(1): 155–72.

Begby, Endre. 2020*a*. "Evidential Preemption." *Philosophy and Phenomenological Research* Online First.

Begby, Endre. 2020*b*. "The Knowledge Norm of Assertion in Dialectical Context." *Ratio*, Special Issues on *Applied Philosophy of Language*, Early view.

Begby, Endre. 2020*c*. "The Problem of Peer Demotion, Revisited and Resolved." *Analytic Philosophy*, Early view.

Bentham, Jeremy. 1789. *An Introduction to the Principles of Morals and Legislation*. Edited by J.H. Burns and H.L.A. Hart. Oxford: Oxford University Press, 1970.

Berkeley, George. 1710. *A Treatise Concerning the Principles of Human Knowledge*. Edited by Jonathan Dancy. Oxford: Oxford University Press, 1998.

Berlin, Brent and Paul Kay. 1969. *Basic Color Terms: Their Universality and Evolution*. Berkeley, CA: University of California Press.

Bernier, Nathan. 2016. "What 1950s Texas Schoolbooks Can Tell Us about Today's Textbook Fight." https://www.houstonpublicmedia.org/articles/education/2016/11/17/177763/what-a-1950s-texas-textbook-can-teach-us-about-todays-textbook-fight/.

Bian, Lin and Andrei Cimpian. 2016. "Are Stereotypes Accurate? A Perspective from the Cognitive Science of Concepts." *Brain and Behavioral Sciences*, 40: e3.

Bicchieri, Christina and Peter McNally. 2018. "Shrieking Sirens: Schemata, Scripts, and Social Norms. How Change Occurs." *Social Philosophy and Policy* 35(1): 23–53.

Blanton, Hart and James Jaccard. 2008. "Unconscious Racism: A Concept in Pursuit of a Measure." *Annual Review of Sociology* 34: 277–97.

Blum, Lawrence. 2004. "Stereotypes and Stereotyping: A Moral Analysis." *Philosophical Papers* 33(3): 251–89.

Bolinger, Renee Jorgensen. 2020. "The Rational Impermissibility of Accepting (Some) Racial Generalizations." *Synthese* 197: 2415–31.

Bolinger, Renee Jorgensen. "Rights and Epistemic Risk: Beyond Subjective Permissibility." MS.

Booth, Anthony and Rik Peels. 2010. "Why Responsible Belief Is Blameless Belief." *Journal of Philosophy* 107(5): 257–65.

Botterell, Andrew. 2009. "A Primer on the Distinction between Justification and Excuse." *Philosophy Compass* 4(1): 172–96.

Boult, Cameron. Forthcoming. "There is a Distinctively Epistemic Kind of Blame." *Philosophy and Phenomenological Research*.

Bovens, Luc and Stephan Hartmann. 2003. *Bayesian Epistemology*. Oxford: Clarendon Press.

Brown, Jessica. 2018. "What Is Epistemic Blame?" *Noûs*, Early view.

Brown, Jessica and Herman Cappelen, eds. 2011. *Assertion: New Philosophical Essays*. Oxford: Oxford University Press.

Brown, Rupert. 2010. *Prejudice: Its Social Psychology*. 2nd edition. Malden, MA: Wiley-Blackwell.

Brownstein, Michael. 2018. *The Implicit Mind: Cognitive Architecture, the Self, and Ethics*. Oxford: Oxford University Press.

Brownstein, Michael, Alex Madva, and Bertram Gawronski. 2019. "What Do Implicit Measures Measure?" *WIREs Cognitive Science* 10(5):1–13.

Brownstein, Michael and Jennifer Saul, eds. 2016. *Implicit Bias and Philosophy*, Vol. 2. Oxford: Oxford University Press.

Buchak, Lara. 2010. "Instrumental Rationality, Epistemic Rationality, and Evidence-Gathering." *Philosophical Perspectives* 24(1): 85–120.

Carmichael, Stokely, and Charles V. Hamilton. 1967. *Black Power: The Politics of Liberation*. New York, NY: Random House.

Cassam, Quassim. 2016. "Vice Epistemology." *The Monist* 99(2): 159–80.

Castro, Clinton. 2019. "What's Wrong with Machine Bias?" *Ergo* 6(15): 405–26.

Chignell, Andrew. 2010/2018. "The Ethics of Belief." *Stanford Encyclopedia of Philosophy*. https://plato.stanford.edu/entries/ethics-belief/.

Chomsky, Noam. 1965. *Aspects of a Theory of Syntax*. Cambridge, MA: The MIT Press.

Christensen, David. 2007. "Epistemology of Disagreement: The Good News." *Philosophical Review* 116(2): 187–217.

Christensen, David. 2010. "Higher Order Evidence." *Philosophy and Phenomenological Research* 81(1): 185–215.

Clark, Herbert H. 1996. *Using Language*. Cambridge: Cambridge University Press.

Clark, Herbert H. and Catherine R. Marshall. 1981. "Definite Reference and Mutual Knowledge." In Aravind K. Joshi, Bonnie L. Webber, and Ivan A. Sag, eds, *Elements of Discourse Understanding*. Cambridge: Cambridge University Press.

Clark, Herbert H., and Edward F. Schaefer. 1992. "Dealing with Overhearers." In Herbert H. Clark, ed. *Arenas of Language Use*. Chicago, IL: The University of Chicago Press and CSLI Publications.

Clarke, Randolph. 2014. *Omissions: Agency, Metaphysics, and Responsibility*. Oxford: Oxford University Press.

Clifford, William K. 1877. "The Ethics of Belief." Reprinted in T. Madigan, ed., *The Ethics of Belief and Other Essays*. Amherst, MA: Prometheus Books, 1999.

Coady, C.A.J. 1973. "Testimony and Observation." *American Philosophical Quarterly* 10(2): 149–55.

Coady, C.A.J. 1992. *Testimony: A Philosophical Study*. Oxford: Clarendon Press.

Coady, David. 2012. *What to Believe Now: Applying Epistemology to Contemporary Issues*. Malden, MA: Wiley-Blackwell.

Cohen, L. Jonathan. 1989. "Belief and Acceptance." *Mind* 98(391): 367–89.

Cohen, L. Jonathan. 1992. *An Essay on Belief and Acceptance*. Oxford: Clarendon Press.

Cohen, Stewart. 1984. "Justification and Truth." *Philosophical Studies* 46(3): 279–95.

Collins, Stephanie and Holly Lawford-Smith. 2016. "The Transfer of Duties: From Individuals to States and Back Again." In Michael Brady and Miranda Fricker, eds, *The Epistemic Life of Groups*. Oxford: Oxford University Press.

Condillac, Etienne Bonnot de. 1746. *Essay on the Origin of Human Knowledge. Translated and edited by Hans Aarsleff*. Cambridge University Press, 2001.

Corbett-Davies, Sam, Emma Pierson, Avi Feller, and Sharad Goel. 2016. "A Computer Program Used for Bail and Sentencing Decisions Was Labeled Biased against Blacks: It's Actually Not That Clear." *Washington Post* October 17, 2016. https://www.washingtonpost.com/news/monkey-cage/wp/2016/10/17/can-an-algorithm-be-racist-our-analysis-is-more-cautious-than-propublicas/.

CRASSH. 2020. "Mask or No Mask? A Look at UK's Policy over Time." https://hscif.org/mask-or-no-mask-a-look-at-uks-policy-over-time/.

Creel, Kathleen A. 2020. "Transparency in Complex Computational Systems." *Philosophy of Science* 87(4): 568–89.

Crook, Robyn J., Roger T. Hanlon, and Edgar T. Walters. 2013. "Squid Have Nociceptors That Display Widespread Long-Term Sensitization and Spontaneous Activity after Bodily Injury." *The Journal of Neuroscience* 33(24): 10021–6.

Dallman, Justin. 2017. "When Obstinacy Is a Better (Cognitive) Policy." *Philosophers' Imprint* 17(24): 1–17.

Danks, David and Alex John London. 2017. "Algorithmic Bias in Autonomous Systems." In C. Sierra, ed., *Proceedings of the 26th International Joint Conference on Artificial Intelligence (IJCAI 2017)*: 4691–7.

Davidson, Lacey J. and Dan Kelly. 2018. "Minding the Gap: Bias, Soft Structures, and the Double Life of Social Norms." *Journal of Applied Philosophy* 37(2): 190–210.

Davis, Angela J. 1998. "Prosecution and Race: The Power and Privilege of Discretion." *Fordham Law Review* 67(1): 13–68.

Davis, Angela J. 2009. *Arbitrary Justice: The Power of the American Prosecutor.* Oxford: Oxford University Press.

Deary, Terry. 2010. *Horrible Histories: Ruthless Romans.* New York, NY: Scholastic Nonfiction.

del Pinal, Guillermo and Shannon Spaulding. 2018. "Conceptual Centrality and Implicit Bias." *Mind & Language* 33(1): 95–111.

DiPaolo, Joshua. 2019. "Second Best Epistemology: Fallibility and Normativity." *Philosophical Studies* 176(8): 2043–66.

documentcloud.org 2011. Sample COMPAS Risk Assessment. https://www. documentcloud.org/documents/2702103-Sample-Risk-Assessment-COMPAS-CORE.html.

Dorst, Kevin. 2019. "Why Rational People Polarize." *The Phenomenal World*, January 27, 2019. https://phenomenalworld.org/analysis/why-rational-people-polarize.

Dougherty, Trent. 2014. "'The Ethics of Belief' is Ethics (Period): Reassigning Responsibilism." In Jonathan Matheson and Rico Vitz, eds., *The Ethics of Belief.* Oxford: Oxford University Press.

Dovidio, John F., Miles Hewstone, Peter Glick, and Victoria M. Esses. 2010. "Prejudice, Stereotyping, and Discrimination: Theoretical and Empirical Overview." In John F. Dovidio, Miles Hewstone, Peter Glick, and Victoria M. Esses, eds, *The SAGE Handbook of Prejudice, Stereotyping and Discrimination.* Thousand Oaks, CA: SAGE Publications.

Dworkin, Ronald. 1977a. "Why Bakke Has No Case." *New York Review of Books* 24(18): 11–15.

Dworkin, Ronald. 1977b. "Reverse Discrimination." In his *Taking Rights Seriously.* London: Duckworth.

Easwaran, Kenny. 2015. "Dr. Truthlove; or, How I Learned to Stop Worrying and Love Bayesian Probabilities." *Noûs* 50(4): 1–38.

Ehrlich, H.J. 1973. *The Social Psychology of Prejudice.* New York, NY: Wiley.

Eidelson, Benjamin. 2013. "Treating People as Individuals." In Deborah Hellman and Sophia Moreau, eds, *Philosophical Foundations of Discrimination Law.* Oxford: Oxford University Press.

Elga, Adam. 2007. "Reflection and Disagreement." *Noûs* 41(3): 478–502.

Engelbrecht, Alta. 2006. "Textbooks in South Africa from Apartheid to Post-Apartheid: Ideological Change Revealed by Racial Stereotyping." In E. Roberts-Schweitzer, V. Greaney, and K. Duer, eds, *Promoting Social Cohesion through Education: Case Studies and Tools for Using Textbooks*. Washington, DC: World Bank Publications.

Enten, Harry. 2019. "A Gay President? The Majority of Americans Believe the Country Isn't Ready." https://www.cnn.com/2019/05/04/politics/poll-of-the-week-gay-president/index.html?no-st=1572367243.

Faktisk. 2017. "Innvandrere langt mer kriminelle, skrev Listhaug viste til ujusterte tall." https://www.faktisk.no/artikler/By/innvandrere-langt-mer-kriminelle-skrev-listhaug-og-viste-til-ujusterte-tall.

Fantl, Jeremy and Matthew McGrath. 2002. "Evidence, Pragmatics, and Justification." *Philosophical Review* 111(1): 67–94.

Fantl, Jeremy, and Matthew McGrath. 2009. *Knowledge in an Uncertain World*. Oxford: Oxford University Press.

Faucher, Luc. 2016. "Revisionism and Moral Responsibility for Implicit Attitudes." In Michael Brownstein and Jennifer Saul, eds, *Implicit Bias and Philosophy*, Vol. 2. Oxford: Oxford University Press.

Faulkner, Paul. 2007. "On Telling and Trusting." *Mind* 116(464): 875–902.

Feinberg, Joel. 1984. *Harm to Others*. Oxford: Oxford University Press.

Feinberg, Joel. 1988. *Harmless Wrongdoing*. Oxford: Oxford University Press.

Feldman, Richard. 2009. "Evidentialism, Higher-Order Evidence, and Disagreement." *Episteme* 6(3): 294–312.

Feldman, Richard and Earl Conee. 1985. "Evidentialism." *Philosophical Studies* 48(1): 15–34.

Fischer, John Martin and Neal A. Tognazzini. 2011. "The Physiognomy of Responsibility." *Philosophy and Phenomenological Research* 82(2): 381–417.

Fiske, Susan and Shelley Taylor. 1991. *Social Cognition*. 2nd edition. New York, NY: McGraw-Hill.

FitzPatrick, William J. 2008. "Moral Responsibility and Normative Ignorance: Answering a New Skeptical Challenge." *Ethics* 118(4): 589–613.

Fleisher, Will. 2018. "Rational Endorsement." *Philosophical Studies* 175(10): 2649–75.

Fodor, Jerry. 1983. *The Modularity of Mind: An Essay on Faculty Psychology*. Cambridge, MA: The MIT Press.

Frankish, Keith. 2016. "Playing Double: Implicit Bias, Dual Levels, and Self-Control." In M. Brownstein and J. Saul, eds, *Implicit Bias and Philosophy*, Vol. 1. Oxford: Oxford University Press.

Fricker, Elizabeth. 1994. "Against Gullibility." In B. K. Matilal and A. Chakrabarti, eds, *Knowing from Words*. Dordrecht: Kluwer Academic Publishers.

Fricker, Elizabeth. 2006. "Testimony and Epistemic Autonomy." In J. Lackey and E. Sosa, eds, *The Epistemology of Testimony*. Oxford: Oxford University Press.

Fricker, Miranda. 2007. *Epistemic Injustice: Power and the Ethics of Knowing*. Oxford: Oxford University Press.

Fricker, Miranda. 2016. "Fault and No-Fault Responsibility for Implicit Prejudice: A Space for Epistemic 'Agent-Regret'." In M.S. Brady and M. Fricker, eds, *The*

Epistemic Lives of Groups: Essays in the Epistemology of Collectives. Oxford: Oxford University Press.

Fritz, Jamie. 2017. "Pragmatic Encroachment and Moral Encroachment." *Pacific Philosophical Quarterly* 98(1): 643–61.

Gaertner, Samuel L., John F. Dovidio, and Melissa A. Houlette. 2010. "Social Categorization." In John F. Dovidio, Miles Hewstone, Peter Glick, and Victoria M. Esses, eds, *The SAGE Handbook of Prejudice, Stereotyping and Discrimination.* Thousand Oaks, CA: SAGE Publications.

Gardiner, Georgi. 2018. "Evidentialism and Moral Encroachment." In Kevin McCain, eds, *Believing in Accordance with the Evidence: New Essays on Evidentialism.* Dordrecht: Springer.

Gardiner, Georgi. 2019. "The Reasonable and the Relevant: Legal Standards of Proof." *Philosophy and Public Affairs*, Early view.

Gardner, John. 2007. "In Defence of Defences." In *Offences and Defences: Selected Essays in the Philosophy of Criminal Law.* Oxford: Oxford University Press.

Gates, Susan Wharton, Vanessa Gail Perry, and Peter M. Zorn. 2002. "Automated Underwriting in Mortgage Lending: Good News for the Underserved?" *Housing Policy Debate* 13(2): 369–91.

Gendler, Tamar S. 2011. "On the Epistemic Costs of Implicit Bias." *Philosophical Studies* 156(1): 33–63.

Gerken, Mikkel. 2011. "Warrant and Action." *Synthese* 178(3): 529–54.

Gigerenzer, Gert. 2008. "Why Heuristics Work." *Perspectives on Psychological Science* 3(1): 20–9.

Gigerenzer, Gert and Henry Brighton. 2009. "Homo Heuristicus: Why Biased Minds Make Better Inferences." *Topics in Cognitive Science* 1(1): 107–43.

Gilbert, D.T. and Hixon, J.G. 1991. "The Trouble of Thinking: Activation and Application of Stereotypic Beliefs." *Journal of Personality and Social Psychology* 60(4): 509–17.

Goldberg, John C.P. 2015. "Inexcusable Wrongs." *California Law Review* 103(3): 467–512.

Goldberg, Sanford. 2010. *Relying on Others: An Essay in Epistemology.* Oxford: Oxford University Press.

Goldberg, Sanford. 2015. *Assertion: On the Philosophical Significance of Assertoric Speech.* Oxford: Oxford University Press.

Goldberg, Sanford. 2017. "Should Have Known." *Synthese* 194(8): 2863–94.

Goldman, Alvin. 1979. "What Is Justified Belief?" In George Pappas, ed., *Justification and Knowledge.* Boston, MA: D. Reidel.

Goldman, Alvin. 2001. "Experts: Which Ones Should You Trust?" *Philosophy and Phenomenological Research* 63(1): 85–110.

Goodin, Robert E. 1995. *Utilitarianism as a Public Philosophy.* Cambridge: Cambridge University Press.

Gottfredson, Stephen D. and Laura J. Moriarty. 2006. "Statistical Risk Assessment: Old Problems and New Applications." *Crime & Delinquency* 52(1): 178–200.

Goudkamp, James. 2013. *Tort Law Defences.* Oxford: Hart Publishing.

Green, Mitchell. 2017. "Conversation and Common Ground." *Philosophical Studies* 174(6): 1587–604.

Greenawalt, Kent. 1984. "The Perplexing Borders of Justification and Excuse." *Columbia Law Review* 84(8): 1897–927.

Greenawalt, Kent. 1986. "Distinguishing Justifications from Excuses." *Law and Contemporary Problems* 49: 89–108.

Greenwald, Anthony G., Mahzarin R. Banaji, and Brian A. Nosek. 2015. "Statistically Small Effects of the Implicit Association Test Can Have Societally Large Effects." *Journal of Personality and Social Psychology* 108(4): 553–61.

Grice, H.P. 1989. *Studies in the Way of Words*. Cambridge, MA: Harvard University Press.

Guerrero, Alexander A. 2007. "Don't Know, Don't Kill: Moral Ignorance, Culpability, and Caution." *Philosophical Studies* 136(1): 59–97.

Hacking, Ian. 1999. *The Social Construction of What?* Cambridge, MA: Harvard University Press.

Hajek, Alan. 2007. "The Reference Class Problem Is your Problem Too." *Synthese* 156(3): 563–85.

Hall, Richard J. and Charles R. Johnson. 1998. "The Epistemic Duty to Seek More Evidence." *American Philosophical Quarterly* 35(2): 129–39.

Hamilton, D.L. and Sherman, J.W. 1994. "Stereotypes." In R.S. Wyer, Jr. and T.K. Srull, eds, *Handbook of Social Cognition: Basic Processes; Applications*. Hillsdale, NJ: Lawrence Erlbaum Associates.

Hammond, M.D. and A. Cimpian. 2017. "Investigating the Cognitive Structure of Stereotypes: Generic Beliefs about Groups Predict Social Judgments Better Than Statistical Beliefs." *Journal of Experimental Psychology: General* 146(5): 607–14.

Hanes, Richard C., Sharon M. Hanes, and Kelly Rudd. 2007. *Prejudice in the Modern World Reference Library*. Detroit, MI: Gale.

Hannon, Michael. 2019. "Are Political Disagreements Real Disagreements?" *Quillette*, August 20, 2019. https://quillette.com/2019/08/20/are-political-disagreements-real-disagreements/?fbclid=IwAR1D3HIGUnV_sDnBVT0yCem2Rcs0YNW9sefH3S-qfCvP6ivgVMHTzOthh2wI.

Hardwig, John. 1985. "Epistemic Dependence." *Journal of Philosophy* 82(7): 335–49.

Harman, Elizabeth. 2011. "Does Moral Ignorance Exculpate?" *Ratio* 24(4): 443–68.

Harman, Gilbert. 1973. *Thought*. Princeton, NJ: Princeton University Press.

Haskins, Caroline. 2019. "Academics Confirm Major Predictive Policing Algorithm is Fundamentally Flawed." *Vice* February 14. https://www.vice.com/en_us/article/xwbag4/academics-confirm-major-predictive-policing-algorithm-is-fundamentally-flawed.

Haslanger, Sally. 2007. "'But Mom, Crop-Tops Are Cute!' Social Knowledge, Social Structure and Ideology Critique." *Philosophical Issues* 17(1): 70–91.

Haslanger, Sally. 2011. "Ideology, Generics, and Common Ground." In C. Witt, ed., *Feminist Metaphysics: Explorations in the Ontology of Sex, Gender and the Self*. Dordrecht: Springer.

Haslanger, Sally. 2018. "What Is a Social Practice?" *Royal Institute of Philosophy* Supplement 82: 321–47.

Haslanger, Sally. 2019. "Cognition as Social Skill." *Australasian Philosophy Review* 3(1): 5–25.

Haslanger, Sally. 2021. "Practical Reason and Social Practices." In Ruth Chang and Kurt Sylvan, eds, *The Routledge Handbook of the Philosophy of Practical Reason.* New York, NY: Routledge.

Hawthorne, John and Jason Stanley. 2008. "Knowledge and Action." *Journal of Philosophy* 105(10): 571–90.

Heath, Chip and Amos Tversky. 1991. "Preference and Belief: Ambiguity and Competence in Choice under Uncertainty." *Journal of Risk and Uncertainty* 4(54): 5–28.

Henderson, Nia-Malika. 2019. "Whites (and Men) Only? Harris Goes There on the 'Electability' Argument." CNN. https://www.cnn.com/2019/05/06/politics/kamala-harris-joe-biden-electability-race/index.html.

Hesni, Samia. "How to Disrupt a Social Script." MS.

Hobbes, Thomas. 1651. *Leviathan.* Edited by Richard Tuck. Cambridge: Cambridge University Press, 1996.

Hoffman, Peter B. and James L. Beck. 1974. "Parole Decision Making: A Salient Factor Score." United States Board of Parole Research Unit: Report Two.

Hoffman, Peter B. and Sheldon Adelberg. 1980. "The Salient Factor Score: A Nontechnical Overview." *Federal Probation* 44: 44–53.

Hood, Christopher and David Heald, eds. 2006. *Transparency: The Key to Better Governance?* Oxford: Oxford University Press.

Hornsby, Jennifer and Rae Langton. 1998. "Free Speech and Illocution." *Legal Theory* 4(1): 21–37.

Horowitz, Sophie. 2014. "Epistemic Akrasia." *Noûs* 48(4): 718–44.

Horowitz, Sophie. 2019. "Predictably Misleading Evidence." In Mattias Skipper and Asbjørn Steglich-Petersen, eds, *Higher-Order Evidence: New Essays.* Oxford: Oxford University Press.

Hume, David. 1739–1740. *A Treatise of Human Nature.* Edited by David F. Norton and Mary J. Norton. Oxford: Oxford University Press, 2007.

Hume, David. 1748. *An Enquiry Concerning Human Understanding.* Edited by Tom L. Beauchamp. Oxford: Oxford University Press, 1999.

Hurley, Dan. 2018. "Can an Algorithm Tell When Kids Are in Danger?" *New York Times Magazine,* January 2.

Jackson, Elizabeth. 2019. "How Belief-Credence Dualism Explains away Pragmatic Encroachment." *The Philosophical Quarterly* 69(276): 511–33.

Jackson, Lynne M. 2011. *The Social Psychology of Prejudice: From Attitudes to Social Action.* Washington, DC: American Psychological Association.

James, James. 1896. "The Will to Believe." *The New World* 5: 327–47.

Jamieson, Kathleen Hall and Joseph N. Cappella. 2008. *Echo Chamber: Rush Limbaugh and the Conservative Media Establishment.* Oxford: Oxford University Press.

Jern, Alan, Kai-Min K. Chang, and Charles Kemp. 2014. "Belief Polarization Is Not Always Irrational." *Psychological Review* 121(2): 206–24.

Johnson, Gabbrielle M. 2020. "Algorithmic Bias: On the Implicit Biases of Social Technology." *Synthese* Online first.

Joyce, James M. 2010. "The Development of Subjective Bayesianism." In Dov M. Gabbay, Stephan Hartmann, and John Woods, eds, *Handbook of the History of Logic*, Vol. 10: Inductive Logic. Amsterdam: Elsevier.

Jussim, Lee, Thomas R. Cain, Jarret T. Crawford, Kent Harber, and Florette Cohen. 2009. "The Unbearable Accuracy of Stereotypes." In T. Nelson, ed., *Handbook of Prejudice, Stereotyping, and Discrimination*. Hillsdale, NJ: Erlbaum.

Jussim, Lee. 2012. *Social Belief and Social Reality: Why Accuracy Dominates Bias and Self-Fulfilling Prophecy*. Oxford: Oxford University Press.

Kahneman, Daniel. 2011. *Thinking, Fast and Slow*. New York, NY: Farrar, Straus and Giroux.

Kant, Immanuel. 1797. *The Metaphysics of Morals*. Edited and translated by Mary J. Gregor. 2nd edition. Cambridge: Cambridge University Press, 1997.

Keeley, Brian L. 1999. "Of Conspiracy Theories." *Journal of Philosophy* 96(3): 109–26.

Kelly, Daniel and Erica Roedder. 2008. "Racial Cognition and the Ethics of Implicit Bias." *Philosophy Compass* 3(3): 522–40.

Kelly, Daniel. Forthcoming. "Two Ways to Adopt a Norm: The (Moral?) Psychology of Internalization and Avowal." In Manuel Vargas and John Doris, eds, *The Oxford Handbook of Moral Psychology*. New York, NY: Oxford University Press.

Kelly, Thomas. 2006/2014. "Evidence." *Stanford Encyclopedia of Philosophy*. https://plato.stanford.edu/entries/evidence/.

Kelly, Thomas. 2008. "Disagreement, Dogmatism, and Belief Polarization." *Journal of Philosophy* 105(10): 611–33.

Kelly, Thomas. 2010. "Peer Disagreement and Higher Order Evidence." In Richard Feldman and Ted Warfield, eds, *Disagreement*, Oxford: Oxford University Press.

King, Alex. 2019. *What We Ought and What We Can*. New York, NY: Routledge.

Kleinberg, Jon, Sendhil Mullainathan, and Manish Raghavan. 2016. "Inherent Trade-Offs in the Fair Determination of Risk Scores." *Proceedings of the 8th Conference on Innovation in Theoretical Computer Science* 43: 1–23.

Kripke, Saul. 2011. "Two Paradoxes of Knowledge." In his *Philosophical Troubles: Collected Papers*, Vol. 1. Oxford: Oxford University Press.

Kunda, Ziva. 1999. "Parallel Processing of Stereotypes and Behaviors." In S. Chaiken and Y. Trope, eds, *Dual-Process Theories in Social Psychology*. New York, NY: Guilford Press.

Kurdi, Benedek and Mahzarin R. Banaji. 2017. "Reports of the Death of the Individual Difference Approach to Implicit Social Cognition May Be Greatly Exaggerated: A Commentary on Payne, Vuletich, and Lundberg." *Psychological Inquiry* 28(4): 281–7.

Lackey, Jennifer. 2006. "It Takes Two to Tango: Beyond Reductionism and Non-Reductionism in the Epistemology of Testimony." In J. Lackey and E. Sosa, eds, *The Epistemology of Testimony*. Oxford: Oxford University Press.

Lackey, Jennifer. 2007. "Norms of Assertion." *Noûs* 41(4): 594–626.

Lambrecht, Anja and Catherine Tucker. 2018. "Algorithmic Bias? An Empirical Study of Apparent Gender-Based Discrimination in the Display of STEM Career Ads." *Management Science* 65(7): 2966–81.

Landscape™. 2019. "Landscape™: Consistent High School and Neighborhood Information for Colleges." https://professionals.collegeboard.org/environmental-context-dashboard.

Langton, Rae. 1993. "Speech Acts and Unspeakable Acts." *Philosophy and Public Affairs* 22(4): 293–330.

Lasonen-Aarnio, Maria. 2014. "Higher-Order Evidence and the Limits of Defeat." *Philosophy and Phenomenological Research* 88(2): 314–45.

Lassiter, Charles and Nathan Ballantyne. 2017. "Implicit Racial Bias and Epistemic Pessimism." *Philosophical Psychology* 30(1–2): 79–101.

Leibniz, G.W. 1710. *Theodicy*. Edited by Austin Farrer and translated by E.M. Huggard. New Haven, CT: Yale University Press, 1952.

Leslie, Sarah-Jane. 2008. "Generics: Acquisition and Cognition." *Philosophical Review* 117(1): 1–47.

Leslie, Sarah-Jane. 2017. "The Original Sin of Cognition: Fear, Prejudice, and Generalization." *Journal of Philosophy* 114(8): 393–421.

Leslie, Sarah-Jane, and Adam Lerner. 2016. "Generic Generalizations." *Stanford Encyclopedia of Philosophy*. https://plato.stanford.edu/entries/generics/.

Levy, Neil. 2016. "Implicit Bias and Moral Responsibility: Probing the Data." *Philosophy and Phenomenological Research* 94(1): 3–26.

Levy, Neil. 2017. "Am I a Racist? Implicit Bias and the Ascription of Racism." *Philosophical Quarterly* 67(268): 534–51.

Lewis, David. 1969. *Convention: A Philosophical Study*. Cambridge, MA: Harvard University Press.

Lewis, David. 1979. "Scorekeeping in a Language Game." *Journal of Philosophical Logic* 8(1): 339–59.

Leydon-Hardy, Lauren. Forthcoming. "Predatory Grooming and Epistemic Infringement." In Jennifer Lackey, ed., *Applied Epistemology*, Oxford University Press.

Lieder, Falk and Thomas L. Griffiths. 2020. "Resource-Rational Analysis: Understanding Human Cognition as the Optimal Use of Limited Computational Resources." *Behavioral and Brain Sciences* 43: e1.

Lippert-Rasmussen, Kasper. 2013. *Born Free and Equal? A Philosophical Inquiry into the Nature of Discrimination*. Oxford: Oxford University Press.

Littlejohn, Clayton. 2012. *Justification and the Truth-Connection*. Cambridge: Cambridge University Press.

Littlejohn, Clayton. Forthcoming. "A Plea for Epistemic Excuses." In F. Dorsch and J. Dutant, eds, *The New Evil Demon*. Oxford: Oxford University Press.

Locke, John. 1689. *An Essay Concerning Human Understanding*. Edited by Pauline Phemister. Oxford: Oxford University Press, 2008.

Lum, Kristian and William Isaac. 2016. "To Predict and Serve?" *Significance* 13(5): 14–19.

Lycan, William G. 1977. "Evidence One Does Not Possess." *Australasian Journal of Philosophy* 55(2): 114–26.

Maguire, Barry and Jack Woods. 2020. "The Game of Belief." *The Philosophical Review* 129(2): 211–49.

Mallon, Ron. 2016. "Social Roles and Reification." In Julian Kiverstein, ed., *The Routledge Handbook of the Philosophy of the Social Mind*. New York, NY: Routledge.

Manne, Kate. 2017. *Down Girl: On the Logic of Misogyny*. Oxford: Oxford University Press.

Martin, Jonathan. 2019. "Many Democrats Love Warren: They Also Worry about Her." August 15. https://www.nytimes.com/2019/08/15/us/politics/elizabeth-warren-2020-ampaign.html.

Mason, Elinor. 2015. "Moral Ignorance and Blameworthiness." *Philosophical Studies* 172(11): 3037–57.

Mason, Elinor. 2019. "Between Strict Liability and Blameworthy Quality of Will." In David Shoemaker, ed., *Oxford Studies in Agency and Responsibility*, Vol. 6. Oxford: Oxford University Press.

McConahey, John B. 1986. "Modern Racism, Ambivalence, and the Modern Racism Scale." In John F. Dovidio and Samuel L. Gaertner, eds, *Prejudice, Discrimination, and Racism*. Cambridge, MA: Academic Press.

McHugh, Nancy A. and Lacey J. Davidson. 2020. "Epistemic Responsibility and Implicit Bias." In Alex Madva and Erin Beeghly, eds, *An Introduction to Implicit Bias*. New York, NY: Routledge.

McKinnon, Rachel. 2015. *The Norms of Assertion: Truth, Lies, and Warrant*. Basingstoke: Palgrave Macmillan.

Medina, José. 2013. *The Epistemology of Resistance: Gender and Racial Oppression, Epistemic Injustice, and Resistant Imaginations*. Oxford: Oxford University Press.

Mill, John Stuart. 1843. *System of Logic, Ratiocinative and Inductive*. London: John Parker.

Mill, John Stuart. 1859. *On Liberty*. London: John W. Parker and Son.

Mills, Charles W. 2005. "'Ideal Theory' as Ideology." *Hypatia* 20(3): 165–84.

Mills, Charles. 2007. "White Ignorance." In Shannon Sullivan and Nancy Tuana, eds, *Race and the Epistemologies of Ignorance*. Albany, NY: SUNY Press.

Mitchell, Gregory. 2017. "Measuring Situational Bias or Creating Situational Bias?" *Psychological Inquiry* 28(4): 292–6.

Monahan, John and Jennifer L. Skeem. 2014. "Risk Redux: The Resurgence of Risk Assessment in Criminal Sanctioning." *Federal Sentencing Reporter* 26(3): 158–66.

Monahan, John and Jennifer L. Skeem. 2016. "Risk Assessment in Criminal Sentencing." *Annual Review of Clinical Psychology* 12: 489–513.

Moody-Adams, Michele M. 1994. "Culture, Responsibility, and Affected Ignorance." *Ethics* 104(2): 291–309.

Moran, Richard. 2005. "Getting Told and Being Believed." *Philosophers' Imprint* 5(5): 1–29.

Mosby, Ian. 2009. "'That Won-Ton Soup Headache': The Chinese Restaurant Syndrome, MSG and the Making of American Food, 1968–1980." *Social History of Medicine* 22(1): 133–51.

Moss, Sarah. 2018*a*. "Moral Encroachment." *Proceedings of the Aristotelian Society* 118(2): 177–205.

Moss, Sarah. 2018*b*. *Probabilistic Knowledge*. Oxford: Oxford University Press.

Munton, Jessie. 2019*a*. "Perceptual Skill and Social Structure." *Philosophy and Phenomenological Research* 99(1): 131–61.

Munton, Jessie. 2019*b*. "Beyond Accuracy: Epistemic Flaws with Statistical Generalizations." *Philosophical Issues* 29(1): 228–40.

Mustard, David B. 2001. "Racial, Ethnic, and Gender Disparities in Sentencing: Evidence from the U.S. Federal Courts." *The Journal of Law & Economics* 44(1): 285–314.

Nesson, Charles. 1979. "Reasonable Doubt and Permissive Inferences." *Harvard Law Review* 92(6): 1187–225.

Nguyen, C. Thi. 2018. "Echo Chambers and Epistemic Bubbles." *Episteme*, First view.

Nielsen, Michael and Rush T. Stewart. Forthcoming. "Persistent Disagreement and Polarization in a Bayesian Setting." *British Journal for the Philosophy of Science*.

O'Connor, Cailin and James Owen Weatherall. 2019. *The Misinformation Age: How False Beliefs Spread*. New Haven, CT: Yale University Press.

O'Neil, Cathy. 2016. *Weapons of Math Destruction: How Big Data Increases Inequality and Threatens Democracy*. New York, NY: Crown Books.

O'Neill, Onora. 2002. *A Question of Trust?* Cambridge: Cambridge University Press.

Oswald, F.L., G. Mitchell, H. Blanton, J. Jaccard, and P.E. Tetlock. 2013. "Predicting Ethnic and Racial Discrimination: A Meta-Analysis of IAT Criterion Studies." *Journal of Personality and Social Psychology* 105: 171–92.

Oswald, F.L., G. Mitchell, H. Blanton, J. Jaccard, and P.E. Tetlock. 2015. "Predicting Ethnic and Racial Discrimination with the IAT: Small Effect Sizes of Unknown Societal Significance." *Journal of Personality and Social Psychology* 108: 562–71.

Pace, Michael. 2011. "The Epistemic Value of Moral Considerations: Justification, Moral Encroachment, and James' 'Will to Believe'." *Noûs* 45(2): 239–68.

Pasnau, Robert. 2014. "Epistemology Idealized." *Mind* 122(488): 987–1021.

Payne, B. Keith. 2006. "Weapon Bias: Split-Second Decisions and Unintended Stereotyping." *Current Directions in Psychological Science* 15(6): 287–91.

Payne, B. Keith, Laura Niemi, and John M. Doris. 2018. "How to Think about 'Implicit Bias'." *Scientific American*. https://www.scientificamerican.com/article/how-to-think-about-implicit-bias/.

Payne, B. Keith, Heidi A. Vuletich, and Kristjen B. Lundberg. 2017*a*. The Bias of Crowds: How Implicit Bias Bridges Personal and Systemic Prejudice. *Psychological Inquiry* 28(4): 233–48.

Payne, B. Keith, Heidi A. Vuletich, and Kristjen B. Lundberg. 2017*b*. Flipping the Script on Implicit Bias Research with the Bias of Crowds. *Psychological Inquiry* 28(4): 206–311.

Peels, Rik. 2016. *Responsible Belief: A Theory in Ethics and Epistemology*. Oxford: Oxford University Press.

Puddifoot, Katherine. 2017*a*. "Stereotyping: The Multifactorial View." *Philosophical Topics* 45(1): 137–56.

Puddifoot, Katherine. 2017*b*. "Dissolving the Epistemic / Ethical Dilemma over Implicit Bias." *Philosophical Explorations* 20(1): 73–93.

Puddifoot, Katherine. 2019. "Stereotyping Patients." *Journal of Social Philosophy* 50(1): 69–90.

Quong, Jonathan. 2015. "Rights against Harm." *Proceedings of the Aristotelian Society* (89): 249–66.

Rae, James R. and Anthony S. Greenwald. 2017. "Persons or Situations? Individual Differences Explain Variance in Aggregated Implicit Race Attitudes." *Psychological Inquiry* 28(4): 297–300.

Rawls, John. 1971. *A Theory of Justice*. Cambridge, MA: Harvard University Press.

Rawls, John. 1982. "Social Unity and Primary Goods." In Amartya Sen and Bernard Williams, eds, *Utilitarianism and Beyond*. Cambridge: Cambridge University Press.

Reichberg, Gregory M., Henrik Syse, and Endre Begby, eds. 2006. *The Ethics of War and Peace: Classic and Contemporary Readings*. Malden, MA: Blackwell Publishing.

Reid, Thomas. 1764. An Inquiry into the Human Mind on the Principles of Common Sense. In William Hamilton, ed., *The Works of Thomas Reid*, Vol. 1. Edinburgh: MacLachlan and Stewart, 1872.

Reid, Thomas. 1785. Essays on the Intellectual Powers of Man. In William Hamilton, ed., *The Works of Thomas Reid*, Vol. 1. Edinburgh: MacLachlan and Stewart, 1872.

Ritchie, Katherine. 2019. "Should We Use Racial and Gender Generics?" *Thought* 8(1): 33–41.

Rhodes, Marjorie, Sarah-Jane Leslie, and Christina M. Tworek. 2012. "Cultural Transmission of Social Essentialism." *Proceedings of the National Academy of the Sciences* 109(34): 13526–31.

Rini, Regina. 2017. "Fake News and Partisan Epistemology." *Kennedy Institute of Ethics Journal* 27(S2): 43–64.

Roberts, Julian V. and Andrew A. Reid. 2017. "Aboriginal Incarceration in Canada since 1978: Every Picture Tells the Same Story." *Canadian Journal of Criminology and Criminal Justice* 59(3): 313–45.

Rosen, Gideon. 2003. "Culpability and Ignorance." *Proceedings of the Aristotelian Society* 104: 61–84.

Rosen, Gideon. 2004. "Skepticism about Moral Responsibility." *Philosophical Perspectives* 18(1): 295–313.

Saul, Jennifer. 2013. "Scepticism and Implicit Bias." *Disputatio* 5(37): 243–63.

Schank, Roger and Richard Abelson. 1977. *Scripts, Plans, Goals and Understanding: An Inquiry into Human Knowledge Structures*. Hillsdale, NJ: R.P.L. Erlbaum.

Schiffer, Stephen. 1972. *Meaning*. Oxford: Oxford University Press.

Schimmach, Ulrich. 2019. "The Implicit Association Test: A Method in Search of a Construct." *Perspectives on Psychological Science*, Online first.

Schoenfield, Miriam. 2012. "Chilling out on Epistemic Rationality." *Philosophical Studies* 158(2): 197–219.

Schroeder, Mark. 2018. "When Beliefs Wrong." *Philosophical Topics* 46(1): 115–27.

Sher, George. 2009. *Who Knew? Responsibility without Awareness*. Oxford: Oxford University Press.

Siegel, Susanna. 2017. *The Rationality of Perception*. Oxford: Oxford University Press.

Siegel, Susanna. 2018. "The Rationality of Perception: Replies to Begby, Ghijsen, and Samoilova." *Analysis* 78(3): 523–6.

Silva, Paul. 2018. "A Bayesian Explanation of the Irrationality of Sexist and Racist Beliefs Involving Generic Content." *Synthese*, Online first.

Silva, Paul and Luis R.G. Oliveira. Forthcoming. "Propositional Justification and Doxastic Justification." In M. Lasonen-Aarnio and C. Littlejohn, eds, *The Routledge Handbook of the Philosophy of Evidence*. London: Routledge.

Simion, Mona, Christoph Kelp, and Harmen Ghijsen. 2016. "Norms of Belief." *Philosophical Topics* 26(1): 374–92.

Simons, D.J. and C.F. Chabris. 1999. "Gorillas in our Midst: Sustained Inattentional Blindness for Dynamic Events." *Perception* 28(9): 1059–74.

Singer, Daniel J., Aaron Bramson, Patrick Grim, Bennett Holman, Jiin Jung, Karen Kovaka, Anika Ranginani, and William J. Berger. 2019. "Rational Social and Political Polarization." *Philosophical Studies* 176(9): 2243–67.

Slobogin, Christopher. 2018. "Principles of Risk Assessment: Sentencing and Policing." *Ohio State Journal of Criminal Law* 15(2): 583–96.

Smith, Holly. 1983. "Culpable Ignorance." *Philosophical Review* 92(4): 543–71.

Srinivasan, Amia. 2020. "Radical Externalism." *The Philosophical Review* 129(3): 395–431.

Staffel, Julia. 2019a. *Unsettled Thoughts: A Theory of Degrees of Rationality*. Oxford: Oxford University Press.

Staffel, Julia. 2019b. "How Do Beliefs Simply Reasoning?" *Noûs* 53(4): 937–62.

Stahler, G.J., J. Mennis, S. Belenko, W.N. Welsh, M.L. Hiller, and G. Zajac. 2013. "Predicting Recidivism for Released State Prison Offenders: Examining the Influence of Individual and Neighborhood Characteristics and Spatial Contagion on the Likelihood of Reincarceration." *Criminal Justice and Behavior* 40(6): 690–711.

Stangor, Charles. 2009. "The Study of Stereotyping, Prejudice, and Discrimination within Social Psychology: A Quick History of Theory and Research." In T.D. Nelson, ed., *Handbook of Prejudice, Stereotyping, and Discrimination*. New York, NY: Psychology Press.

Stalnaker, Robert. 1978. "Assertion." Reprinted in *Context and Content: Essays on Intentionality in Speech and Thought*. Oxford: Oxford University Press, 1999.

Stalnaker, Robert. 2002. "Common Ground." *Linguistics and Philosophy* 25(5–6): 701–21.

Steup, Matthias. 1999. "A Defense of Internalism." In L. Pojman, ed., *The Theory of Knowledge: Classical and Contemporary Readings*. 2nd edition. Belmont, CA: Wadsworth Publishing.

Stilz, Anna. 2011. "Collective Responsibility and the State." *Journal of Political Philosophy* 19(2): 190–208.

Strawson, P.F. 1962. "Freedom and Resentment." In Gary Watson, ed., *Proceedings of the British Academy 48*. Oxford: Oxford University Press.

Sunstein, Cass. 2002. "The Law of Group Polarization." *The Journal of Political Philosophy* 10(2):175–95.

Sutton, Mike. 2010. "Spinach, Iron and Popeye: Ironic Lessons from Biochemistry and History on the Importance of Healthy Eating, Healthy Scepticism and Adequate Citation." *The Internet Journal of Criminology.* http://www.intern etjournalofcriminology.com/Sutton_Spinach_Iron_and_Popeye_March_2010.pdf.

Tetlock, Philip, Orie V. Kristel, S. Beth Elson, Melanie C. Green, and Jennifer S. Lerner. 2000. "The Psychology of the Unthinkable: Taboo Trade-Offs, Forbidden Base Rates, and Heretical Counterfactuals." *Journal of Personality and Social Psychology* 78(5): 853–70.

Thomson, Judith Jarvis. 1973. "Preferential Hiring." Reprinted in *Rights, Restitution, and Risk: Essays in Moral Theory.* Cambridge, MA: Harvard University Press, 1986.

Titelbaum, Michael G. Forthcoming. *Fundamentals of Bayesian Epistemology.* Under contract with Oxford University Press.

Toole, Briana. 2019. "From Standpoint Epistemology to Epistemic Oppression." *Hypatia* 34(4): 598–618.

Turner, John C., Michael A. Hogg, Penelope J. Oakes, Stephen D. Reicher, and Margaret S. Wetherell. 1987. *Rediscovering the Social Group: A Self-Categorization Theory.* Oxford: Blackwell.

United States Department of Justice. 2014. "Attorney General Eric Holder Speaks at the National Association of Criminal Defense Lawyers 57th Annual Meeting and 13th State Criminal Justice Network Conference." https://www.justice.gov/ opa/speech/attorney-general-eric-holder-speaks-national-association-criminal-defense-lawyers-57th.

University of Washington. 1998. "Roots of Unconscious Prejudice Affect 90 to 95 Percent of People, Psychologists Demonstrate at Press Conference." *University of Washington News,* September 29. https://www.washington.edu/news/1998/09/ 29/roots-of-unconscious-prejudice-affect-90-to-95-percent-of-people-psychologists-demonstrate-at-press-conference/.

US Supreme Court. 2001. *Nguyen v. INS* 533 U.S. 53 (2001). *Justia.* https://supreme. justia.com/cases/federal/us/533/53/.

van Fraassen, Bas. 1980. *The Scientific Image.* Oxford: Clarendon Press.

Vitoria, Francisco de. 1532. *Relectio de Indis.* In Anthony Pagden and Jeremy Lawrance, eds, *Francisco de Vitoria: Political Writings.* Cambridge: Cambridge University Press, 1992.

Washington, Natalia and Daniel Kelly. 2016. "Who's Responsible for This? Moral Responsibility, Externalism, and Knowledge about Implicit Bias." In Michael Brownstein and Jennifer Saul, eds, *Implicit Bias and Philosophy,* Vol. 2. Oxford: Oxford University Press.

Watson, Gary. 1996. "Two Faces of Responsibility." *Philosophical Topics* 24(2): 227–48.

Weatherson, Brian. 2008. "Deontology and Descartes' Demon." *Journal of Philosophy* 105(9): 540–69.

Wedgwood, Ralph. 2002. "Internalism Explained." *Philosophy and Phenomenological Research* 65(2): 349–69.

Weiner, Matt. 2007. "Norms of Assertion." *Philosophy Compass* 2(2): 187–95.

Weisberg, Jonathan. 2020. "Belief in Psyontology." *Philosophers' Imprint* 20(11): 1–27.

Welsh, Andrew and James R.P. Ogloff. 2008. "Progressive Reforms or Maintaining the Status Quo? An Empirical Evaluation of the Judicial Consideration of Aboriginal Status in Sentencing Decisions." *Canadian Journal of Criminology and Criminal Justice* 50(4): 491–517.

White, Roger. 2005. "Epistemic Permissiveness." *Philosophical Perspectives* 19(1): 445–59.

Williams, Bernard. 1985. *Ethics and the Limits of Philosophy*. London: Fontana.

Williams, Bernard. 1993. "Moral Luck." In Daniel Statman, ed., *Moral Luck*. Albany, NY: State University of New York Press.

Williamson, Timothy. 1997. "Knowledge as Evidence." *Mind* 106(424): 717–41.

Williamson, Timothy. 2000. *Knowledge and its Limits*. Oxford: Oxford University Press.

Williamson, Timothy. 2011. "Improbable Knowing." In Trent Dougherty, ed., *Evidentialism and its Discontents*. Oxford: Oxford University Press.

Williamson, Timothy. Forthcoming. "Justifications, Excuses, and Skeptical Scenarios." In F. Dorsch and J. Dutant, eds, *The New Evil Demon*. Oxford: Oxford University Press.

Wimsatt, William C. 2007. *Re-Engineering Philosophy for Limited Beings: Piecemeal Approximations to Reality*. Cambridge, MA: Harvard University Press.

Winawer, Jonathan, Nathan Witthoft, Michael C. Frank, Lisa Wu, Alex R. Wade, and Lera Boroditsky. 2007. "Russian Blues Reveal Effects of Language on Color Discrimination." *Proceedings of the National Academy of the Sciences* 104(19): 7780–5.

Witt, Charlotte. 2011. *The Metaphysics of Gender*. Oxford: Oxford University Press.

Worsnip, Alex. 2019. "The Obligation to Diversify one's Sources: Against Epistemic Partisanship in the Consumption of News Media." In C. Fox and J. Saunders, eds, *Media Ethics, Free Speech, and the Requirements of Democracy*. New York, NY: Routledge.

Wright, Crispin. 2004. "Warrant for Nothing (and Foundations for Free)?" *Aristotelian Society Supplementary Volume* 78(1):167–212.

Young, Iris Marion. 2003. "From Guilt to Solidarity: Sweatshops and Political Responsibility." *Dissent* Spring 2003: 39–44.

Young, Iris Marion. 2006. "Responsibility and Global Justice: A Social Connection Model." *Social Philosophy and Policy* 23(1): 102–30.

Zagzebski, Linda T. 1996. *Virtues of the Mind: An Inquiry into the Nature of Virtue and the Ethical Foundations of Knowledge*. Cambridge: Cambridge University Press.

Zerilli, John, Alistair Knott, James Maclaurin, and Colin Gavaghan. 2018. "Transparency in Algorithmic and Human Decision-Making: Is There a Double Standard?" *Philosophy & Technology*, Online first.

Zheng, Robin. 2016. "Attributability, Accountability, and Implicit Bias." In Michael Brownstein and Jennifer Saul, eds, *Implicit Bias and Philosophy*, Vol. 2. Oxford: Oxford University Press.

Zheng, Robin. 2018. "What Is My Role in Changing the System? A New Model of Responsibility for Structural Injustice." *Ethical Theory and Moral Practice* 21(4): 869–85.

Zimmerman, Michael J. 1997. "Moral Responsibility and Ignorance." *Ethics* 107(3): 410–26.

Zimmerman, Michael J. 2008. *Living with Uncertainty: The Moral Significance of Ignorance.* Cambridge: Cambridge University Press.

Zynda, Lyle. 1996. "Coherence as an Ideal of Rationality." *Synthese* 109(2): 175–216.

Index

For the benefit of digital users, table entries that span two pages (e.g., 52–53) may, on occasion, appear on only one of those pages.

Printed and bound by CPI Group (UK) Ltd, Croydon, CR0 4YY